# Always
## a part of me

# Always
## a part of me

### Surviving Childbearing Loss

Amanda Collinge

Sue Daniel

Heather Grace Jones

ABC
BOOKS

Published by ABC Books for the
AUSTRALIAN BROADCASTING CORPORATION
GPO Box 9994 Sydney NSW 2001

*First published April 2002*

National Library of Australia
Cataloguing-in-Publication entry
Collinge, Amanda.
    Always a part of me: surviving childbearing loss.

    ISBN 0 7333 1000 1.

    1. Infants (Newborn) – Death – Psychological aspects. 2.
    Infertility – Psychological aspects. 3. Bereavement –
    Psychological aspects. 4. Miscarriage – Psychological
    aspects. I. Daniel, Sue. II. Jones, Heather Grace. III.
    Australian Broadcasting Corporation. IV. Title. V. Title:
    Life matters (Radio program).

155.937

*Designed by Midland Typesetters*
*Cover design by Kerry Klinner*
*Set in 10/14 pt Jessica Light by Midland Typesetters*
*Colour reproduction by Colorwize, Adelaide*
*Printed and bound in Australia by Griffin Press, Adelaide*

5 4 3 2 1

For all the babies, conceived and conceived of,
not of this world, but imprinted on our souls.

# CONTENTS

# ACKNOWLEDGMENTS

This book would never have been delivered without the support of our partners, Ian Walker and Frank Rodi. Special thanks to Madeline Hourihan.

Thanks also to Lyn, Barry and Kay Walker, Marianna Rodi, Erina Reddan, Rowena Ivers, Mandy Brett, Ray Moynihan, Vivien Altman, Brian Peate and our editors Matthew Kelly, Susan Morris-Yates and Jacqueline Kent for their assistance and encouragement. Above all we would like to pay tribute to our contributors for their bravery and generosity.

Artwork on page 62 is reproduced by kind permission of Maria Miranda; the artwork on page 128 by Deborah Kelly and Tina Fiveash is part of the 'Hey Hetero' series produced with the assistance of the Sydney Gay and Lesbian Mardi Gras.

# PREFACE

## Professor Robert Jansen

When, in the early 1980s, I was about to establish my infertility practice in Macquarie Street, Sydney, I met a woman who gave me an insight into the privilege of being a gynaecologist.

It was a Saturday morning and I was looking for a suitable location for my new office. The realtor who was showing me various properties had had a night of it, and probably a morning too, or so it appeared from her runny mascara and scratched nail polish. She seemed to shudder at the notion that I was a gynaecologist, and said, 'How can you bear to always see women at their worst?'

I knew straightaway that she had missed the mark. It was only on that Saturday that I was seeing a woman at her less-than-best. In the years since, I've rarely seen anyone comparably untidy seeking my advice in my office.

I don't expect any special standard of appearance. Where I am even surer that I am being singularly honoured, though, is the openness with which women, and their partners, take me to the depths of their relationship with each other, their ambitions, their fears...indeed, their very being. After the hour or so I spend with them on first meeting, I seem to know more about them than I do about most of my friends and acquaintances. And the overwhelming feeling I have, as my colleagues in similar medical practices have, is that we have seen, and see, people at their best, sometimes plain and sometimes dressed-up, often vulnerable, usually anxious, generally accepting what help we can aspire to give, making us part of their world with respect to their thwarted expectations for having a child, and revealing themselves so personally and honestly.

'Children are poor men's riches', according to the medieval

proverb. Today, we could say, 'Children are lucky people's riches'. And when nature lets us down in this regard, the treatment that underpins our aspirations, increasingly, is IVF. We're fortunate that in Australia today in vitro fertilisation (IVF) is probably more affordable than in almost any other country. But IVF, too, has its special downside.

Acknowledging as we professionals should do of the suffering brought on by unwanted childlessness, we also live with, and ideally try to anticipate, that brought on by hopes we help raise with treatment, only to see them dashed once again when treatment fails. Of course IVF is not the answer to everyone's childlessness; and distressingly often, still, pregnancy does not follow this costly treatment. Ideally, though, going through the trials and tribulations of such a treatment program still strengthens relationships and improves the future.

I hope I have shown people who have consulted me my capacity for empathising with them. Although of course people vary in how much they want such *Eingefühl* ('feeling one with', as the Germans put it)—not everyone wants such a mental intrusion—it is still a privilege to join others' worlds in a way that can be compassionately meaningful, moving to deeper empathy if a person's distress or despair invites it. Yet the constraints of time more than natural boundaries of privacy still limit the extent to which most couples will bare their aspirations to a thoughtful professional. And at the end of the day the professional can only move so far into a client's or patient's personal journey.

So, for one reason or another, *Always a Part of Me* takes me and my fellow doctors and nurses further into the realm of personal responses to childlessness, into a mostly private but searing world of frustration and thwarted ambition and further than we, with a duty for detachment and perspective as well as for compassion and context, can regularly gain access to. And that is another privilege.

# FOREWORD

## Geraldine Doogue

One of the truly biggest changes in this exceptionally volatile generation is that people will talk publicly about what were previously deemed private matters. So accustomed have we become to it in the last ten to fifteen years particularly, we fail to realise what a monumental shift this represents. Once people talk, things change. Once they articulate feelings that were strictly constrained either within themselves or their home, they set up an altered state of communal experience. This book, *Always a Part of Me*, is a moving example of the power of people to break taboos by simply describing how they felt when the everyday aspiration of having a baby was not fulfilled.

This happens so often in real life, but somehow doesn't seem to make it into popular discussion. I remember a couple of my mother's friends in Perth not being able to have children. It seemed a tragedy to me, as a child, particularly for one woman who, to my childish mind, would have made a marvellous mum. But no one ever thought it was appropriate to ask this woman anything at all about this absence of children. Mum, who knew her well, didn't seem to know whether she definitely could not conceive or whether there'd ever been a miscarriage or whether her childlessness was voluntary—hardly believed possible in the 1950s, but we shouldn't rule it out! It just wouldn't have been right to ask, and the presumption was that she certainly wouldn't say much, would never embarrass people with unnecessary emotion, would 'move on'. Her husband wasn't even considered in the equation—well, not so that I heard.

When I had trouble conceiving my second child, I used to

think sometimes about this woman and wonder what her story had really involved. The subtle constraints against her blurting anything out were considerable. Thankfully, we have learned that this might amount to a form of repression but more than that, that it's not necessary. By shutting up and closing down we deprive ourselves of a collective experience, as well as asking individuals to cocoon themselves from others at times of great need.

People have different responses to the level of disclosure they will read in these various accounts. But I doubt very much whether readers will not see authentic human experience at an intense level. Sometimes I wondered why people were quite so upset; sometimes I wondered why they weren't exploding with agony. Sometimes I pondered whether we early twenty-first century beings are disproportionately unwilling to recognise that Nature does not guarantee perfect children, makes choices about the quality of child and is a ruthless matriarch.

Undoubtedly, though, the contributions made me question further the whole meaning of children in modern communities. These testaments demonstrate something vividly—individual dreams of creating a family are incomparably powerful. They creep up on people and tap away throughout all other activity. Nothing else quite compares with this pull on people's emotions and hopes.

Consequently, the losses of infertility are much harder to bear than generally recognised. So many dreams are wrapped up in the desire for a child, so many aspirations for optimal self-development. *Always a Part of Me* names some of this along with the more obvious acute grief of stillbirth, infant death or miscarriage. I believe that many who have been through this experience will find much solace from reading some of these accounts. As someone who has interviewed many about their most intimate moments, I recognised that these have a candour that was at times rather shocking but always enriching. They add considerably to our understanding of life, death, the universe and everything. I wish my mother's friend had lived long enough to have access to them.

# INTRODUCTION

We'd known each other for years, working at ABC Radio early in our careers, and more or less stayed in contact. But it was the power of shared experience that really brought us together years later. Sue had lost a baby at birth, Heather Grace had been trying unsuccessfully to conceive for five years, and Amanda was recovering from an IVF miscarriage. Different journeys in some ways, but ultimately they had landed us in the same boat: wanting to mother but unable to. Hungering for the babies we had lost or never found. Watching as all our friends conceived, bought prams, paraded their delightful bundles round town and whinged about sleepless nights. Our grief was somehow unseemly, our stories guaranteed conversation-stoppers. It was a relief to be in each other's company, to be understood and accepted, and quite soon the idea for this book was born.

We were appalled at the paucity of literature addressing childbearing losses. Sure we'd each come across how-to-cope manuals and books that focused on specific aspects of repro-duction, but there was nothing that spoke to us. So we set about collecting stories from men and women who have survived stillbirth, neo-natal death, miscarriage and infertility. And what we had initially sensed is evident in the resulting anthology. The desire to create family may be thwarted in different ways, but the emotional terrain is the same. Despite their individual circumstances, each contributor to this book has had to grapple with the same shattered dreams of parent-ing, the same isolation.

We wanted to undo ideas about a hierarchy of grief, in which some losses are acceptable to mourn and others are not. And to create a resource that would enable people to at least begin to understand the process of losing not only a child, but the dream of that child. To give some comfort and perhaps hope to those who have survived reproductive losses and enlighten friends and family. We wanted to explore recovery from tragedy and consider new ways of creating family.

What struck us in compiling this book were the difficulties facing our contributors. Some people who started out wanting to contribute changed their minds at the last minute, others asked that we change their identities. Once again we were reminded that the repercussions of public disclosure are unacceptably high. Open discussion of stillbirth, neo-natal death, infertility and miscarriage is still taboo, so tragic outcomes are far more common than we think, and catch us ill-prepared. They are everyday experiences, yet ours remains a culture lacking the language to adequately confront the enormity of these losses.

We live in so-called liberated times. The media is saturated with sex, but the climate is anything but understanding of issues around childbearing loss. Our bodies are increasingly medicalised and the fertility business is big money. In 2000 the prime minister tried to ban fertility treatment for unmarried couples and lesbians. The following year the Catholic Church pursued his cause in the High Court, arguing that IVF for single women is a transgression of God's law. Central to the legal battle was the case of Leesa Meldrum, whose story appears in the following pages. It's as if the basic right to reproduce should be available only for married heterosexual couples, and the right to grieve reserved for them as well. While some of the contributors to this book are married, many are not. What's important is that they all simply wanted a child.

There are stories from those who opted for medical intervention, some succeeding, some not. Different cultural perspectives are canvassed, as are opting for adoption and choosing not to parent. Our contributors write from varying stages of grief. Some are still drowning, others have reached resolution, but ultimately their stories are linked by the sheer force of their hope, tenacity and imagination.

As the book grew, so did our bellies. One by one each of us fell pregnant, and finally successfully delivered three precious babies. Sue now has a toddler, Finn, to keep her on her toes, Gracie a six-month-old cupcake and an even bigger problem with housework, and Amanda is slave to the beautiful Lucia.

Finally, this anthology is a tribute to all the babies who lived and died, those who lived in the womb only and those only ever dreamed of. We would like to thank our contributors, many of whom revisited the worst times of their lives to tell their stories.

*Amanda Collinge*
*Sue Daniel*
*Heather Grace Jones*

# THE BABY MEMORIAL

## Petria Wallace

*Thirty thousand stillborn babies are buried at the West Terrace cemetery in Adelaide. If you walk down the tree-lined paths, past the rows of grand headstones to the very back corner of the cemetery, you'll find the bare ground of unmarked graves. Trains regularly rattle past and the surrounding landscape is industrial. As you tread through the short grass, there is nothing to indicate the identity of the babies concealed beneath your feet.*

*For years women have been making a futile pilgrimage to this place, trying to find out what happened to their babies.*

*Up until the late 1970s, it was hospital policy to take charge of a baby's burial. A mother's request to see her child was brushed aside 'for her own good'. No one bothered to tell the family what had happened to their baby. Generations of women were left crippled by the anguish of unresolved grief.*

*Some women slowly went mad. Their marriages collapsed. Others went on to have more children, nursing their grief in silence. All of them were haunted by nightmares of what might have happened to their dead child. They feared the baby had been thrown into the hospital incinerator. Or they believed the child had been wrapped in a sugar sack and flung into a pauper's grave with a stranger's corpse.*

*This is the story of how these women found their lost babies.*

### Judy Potter

Darren was born on 13 May 1974 and he died on 14 May. He was almost 31 weeks, about 30 weeks and five days when he was born. He was my very first child.

I really didn't get a good time in hospital. The nurses were kind but the medical staff were very condescending. I asked what happened to my baby and no one told me anything. I could have been an orange that they were giving injections to. I was an inanimate object. They didn't listen to me. Every time I asked what happened to Darren I was met with a solid wall of silence.

My husband had a piece of paper shoved in front of him to say, 'Sign this and we'll take care of everything'. That was just the way they dealt with people back then. They thought they were protecting you by not telling you anything. As we know now, that was wrong—in fact it has caused untold heartache.

I think the cruellest thing was not knowing what happened to Darren. My husband didn't know. We were just told to go away and forget it, go on a holiday, forget about it, have another baby. And the nurses were saying, 'We'll see you up here in a year in labour ward. Don't worry about it'. It was like it never happened but it did—you know—it did happen. It was my baby.

### Mrs G

I'm writing in reference to my baby son who was stillborn on 20 March 1948. I never saw my baby. They took him away and none of us ever saw him or were told what happened to him. I remember being terribly upset when one of the assistants at the hospital told me they fed all those sorts of things to the dogs. At the back of the hospital they had a yard wired where there were huge guard dogs and for all these years I've grieved because I still don't know what the truth was. There seems to be some hope now that my baby is in the West Terrace Cemetery with a lot of other babies. He was my third son out of five children. I hope you can help me.

*For most women, a visit or phone call to West Terrace cemetery ended in frustration. Depending on which staff member you struck, you might be told there was no record of baby burials or that it was too difficult to find the information. It was rare to find someone prepared to open up the burial books and look.*

*Then in 1994 David McGowan took over as manager. He was a*

*bureaucrat who liked a challenge—the more difficult the better. And he understood the pain of losing a child. David's son had died soon after birth.*

*His appointment was a lucky break for the women searching for their babies.*

### David McGowan—West Terrace Cemetery manager

I had just started to manage the cemetery. I noticed a trickle of inquiries—two or three a week—of mothers coming in asking if there was any record of the babies buried here. And I said, 'Well, I don't know—let's go and look'. And I started to find them. The story given to me by some of those women was that they had in fact been there before but the office staff had said they couldn't find them. They were there—the thing was you had to know what you were looking for. For example you'd say, 'When did the baby die?' and, say, the baby died on the first of January: under ordinary circumstances you'd expect the baby to be buried within three or four days. But because I knew the way the hospital system worked, I started to look a month or two months later. And that's how I found them. It took me about a week to find the first baby.

I didn't expect what happened next.

I got a call from Caroline Harry, the head social worker at what was then called the Queen Victoria Hospital. She said she had a client in her office whose baby had died some twenty years before. And there was this dreadful unresolved grief which was making this woman quite ill. And because nobody knew where the baby had been buried or what happened to it, it was felt that just making the effort of looking might offer some catharsis for her grief. So I undertook to see what I could find and about half an hour later I found the baby. Caroline rang me back and said, 'Are there any others?' And I said, 'Yes, we've been looking for a couple of weeks now. And, yes, we can find them. We can actually find the grave, we know what day it was, and how many babies were in the same grave.'

She put the word out and the trickle almost instantly became a flood. Instead of getting two or three calls a week, we were getting two or three calls an hour. It became a full-time job for Penny Brennan my administrator.

Remember, this information was not on a database—it involved a painstaking search of paper records. We used to meet every afternoon and say, 'What have we got?' And I decided that if the baby was not in our cemetery, we would search for it in other cemeteries. For example, there was one baby whose mother was particularly upset and we were very anxious to get a quick resolution for her, and we could find nothing. We used to search the records for up to four months after the babies' deaths. Nothing. So I backtracked and said the other way of finding these records are the mortuary records. So we rang the hospital and bribed the fellow with some beer to go down to the dungeons and get old mortuary records. And sure enough we found it. What had happened—in one of those dreadful human mistakes—was that the child's body had been put into the mortuary fridge and forgotten. So the baby had been buried at West Terrace cemetery but it was six months after its death. And that is why we hadn't been able to find it.

Early in the piece the questions started to come up—how were the babies buried? I made a decision that I would find out what did happen by going back to the old gravediggers. And if the mothers asked I would tell them the truth—good or bad. Like the belief that they were buried by putting them in a sack and dropping them into somebody else's grave when there was a funeral on. There were lots and lots of stories like that. Even if that had been true, I was going to tell them. Because I believe it is easier to deal with what you know for certain than what you don't know. So I tracked down the retired gravediggers and they told me.

Around the time of World War I when birthing was taken out of the homes and put in the hospital it became the hospital's responsibility to deal with the problems arising out of the delivery of a stillborn baby. It was the hospital that would go to the mother and say, 'We'll look after it, dear.' And it wasn't seen as a sensitive human problem but as a disposal problem.

The hospitals would have a contract with an undertaker. They would collect the body and bring it to the cemetery. And while the names were recorded in the burial registers, there was no mark on the grave and the information was not given to the mothers.

The gravediggers used to collect the babies in a wheelbarrow to take them down to the graveside. They put sand at the bottom of the grave. And they would take them down the ladder one by one, and arrange them in a circle. And at the end of that they refused to fill in the grave until they had found a clergyman to pray over them. They'd find someone who'd just finished a funeral to come down and do the babies.

When the gravedigger told me this I was so excited I hugged him, because I had found not only the truth, but a palatable truth. It wasn't going to cause the families any more grief. And as I said to many of the mothers, 'It wasn't the funeral you would have held. But it is better this happened than all the things you feared.'

*David McGowan gave Penny Brennan the job of searching for the babies. She became part detective, part social worker for the 5000 women who contacted the cemetery.*

### Penny Brennan, cemetery administrator

We have mothers in their forties, fifties, sixties, seventies and even eighties and nineties coming here, so some of the mothers' births go back a long way. It has always been there at the back of their minds. They've never been able to forget. And I think in finally being able to take a step to do something about this—to actually find out where their baby is—has helped them find peace after all these years.

It all became real to them then. There had been a conspiracy of silence in a way. Nobody talked about it because they didn't want to upset the mother. It became a very unreal thing to them. In fact many of the mothers said they wondered if it had happened at all—they thought they'd dreamed it. And it wasn't until they could actually see the grave that they could come to terms with their baby's death.

I spoke to one woman who had never told her husband how she felt about the loss of her baby. She bottled it all up. When she read an article about what was happening at West Terrace cemetery, she cried and told her husband for the first time about her anguish. He was completely overwhelmed that he'd never known. He used to ring me as well and tell me how she was going.

Once this woman found her baby's grave and had grief counselling, she said all the grief had gone and she had been left with a feeling of happiness. It was like her life had opened up again.

*In 1996 the West Terrace cemetery built a memorial to the 30 000 stillborn babies buried in its grounds. Judy Potter put all her energies into lobbying politicians to make the dream of a memorial a reality.*

*Three Adelaide artists designed the memorial to create a peaceful space for the parents to sit and remember their babies. A semicircular stone wall and seat looks out onto the graves. Each baby's name is engraved onto a leaf set into a terracotta tile. These are laid out in circles radiating out from the wall. Over time they will patinate to resemble a carpet of autumn leaves.*

*On 10 March 1996, 3000 people turned up to a dedication ceremony for the baby memorial. It was the funeral their babies had never had. This letter to David McGowan is from one of the mothers who travelled to Adelaide for the service.*

Two years ago when I found my baby's grave at West Terrace after twenty-eight years of fearing to look, I thought I'd completed my healing process. I'm a social worker by profession and I thought I knew a fair bit about emotional healing. I arranged for my baby's plaque and considered everything complete. I saw no reason to travel right across the continent to Adelaide simply for the dedication service, but my mother—in her seventies—was older and wiser and she insisted on paying my airfare, and she was right.

For me it was a gathering up of loose ends, a final conclusion to spent anguish. Two things particularly stay in my mind from that day. One was Sally Cooper's glorious music, which created an atmosphere of contemplation despite the heat, crowds and cameras. The other was your own courageous decision to tell us honestly and exactly what happened to our babies. It was appropriate. I had not realised until that moment what an enormous unanswered question I'd carried around with me for so long. Even two years ago I hadn't the courage to ask it. For thirty years I'd been pushing out of my mind an appalling image of slit trenches, plastic bags and galvanised iron. Truly, the unknown is more awful than the known. Thank you for replacing that image for me, thank you for the details, thank you for the truth. Thank you above all for the respect that West Terrace displayed at a time when society was not respecting us or our babies.

*Postscript—David McGowan received an Order of Australia for his work at the cemetery. He has returned to work as an engineer at the Women and Children's Hospital in Adelaide. Penny Brennan is still helping mothers find their babies. And Judy Potter believes she has finally accepted her son's death. Other cemeteries across Australia are building baby memorials and helping families to find the location of their babies' graves.*

# NINE CARESSES FOR AN ACHING WOMB

Penny O'Donnell

## Introduction

*Our daughter Ruby was stillborn on 28 June 1998. We never found out why she died. Until it happened, I didn't realise how many pregnancies end in tragedy. Nor did I realise how many people around us had suffered, often in silence, the loss of their children. To lose someone you love is always traumatic. Mourning an infant who has never drawn breath, who has never been an independent person, is particularly devastating. My body repaired itself quickly after Ruby died. It took a lot longer for my anguish and anxiety to give way to hope and trust in the future. My husband Salvador and I were deeply touched during this time by the love and support of our families, our friends, the health professionals who looked after us, our neighbours and colleagues. Not everyone was gentle or sensitive. One acquaintance suggested I get a bird or a dog as a replacement. It didn't matter as long as they didn't try to pretend that our baby never existed. That reaction was the hardest, most hurtful and cruel. Fortunately it was rare. More often there were words that made a difference, meals left on our doorstep, flowers, visits, thoughtful attempts to talk about and celebrate the memory of our little girl. Such gestures were balm for my aching womb. A caress is the gesture of someone who cares. Here are nine caresses for you.*

## 1. Baby

Smoke bellows from the chimney. The smoke is white. So are the uniforms of the women from the funeral parlour. My sister

8

tells me they wear white because it's better than looking at men in black. White ladies, white car, white coffin, white roses, white smoke. I look again at the chimney. I look at my dad who is also looking at the chimney. Grandparents are not meant to bury their grandchildren. Parents are not meant to bury their kids.

Ruby's coffin is small. Ruby is my baby. I am at the crematorium watching the chimney and realising that my baby is about to go up in smoke. My body shudders. I find myself in the toilet, dry retching and gasping for air. My mother comes in. She tells me I don't have to do this. But I want to say goodbye. I want to be here. I want to watch my baby's slow trip to the flames.

We wait for our turn. There is no priest, no ceremony, and no crowd. Just us, sitting quietly staring at a small box with flowers on top. It looks so far away. The woman from the funeral parlour asks me if I want to get closer. What a great idea!

I rest my cheek on the lid and talk to her now in these last precious moments. I tell her the names of all the people who love her. I describe each one in turn. It must be madness but I feel happy there, talking to my girl. I have so much to tell her.

The woman from the funeral parlour signals that our time is ending. This is it then, the final moment that I've been dreading. The mother has to leave her child. My dad stands and starts reading. 'The Lord is my shepherd; I shall not want...' His voice falters then gets louder and louder, invoking the full strength and beauty of those old words. 'Yea, though I walk through the valley of the shadow of death, I will fear no evil: for thou art with me.' I know I have to get up, turn my back on her and go.

I look for the curtains. The last time I was at the crematorium the curtains closed so you couldn't see the coffin going into the fire. I ask the woman from the funeral parlour if the curtains will close. She says she can arrange it if that's what I want. If that's what I want? I swallow the scream that wells up in my throat: I want my baby.

## 2. Embrace

She died in utero at thirty-four weeks. She stopped moving one day and I went to the hospital to check on her. Avon, the midwife, tried to find her heartbeat. Greg, the doctor, told me she was dead. Then they held me tightly between them. They held me very, very tightly. It takes courage to face death. Avon and Greg are courageous people. They stayed holding me through the shock, the shaking and the moaning.

You couldn't tell from the outside that there was anything wrong with me, or with her. I still looked pregnant. My body was inflated. My hands still wandered to my belly, ready to calm those wriggling feet with rhythmic strokes. I was still an expectant mum.

I had to tell my husband Salvador. He was at work. I rang him. I told him the baby was dead. He told me he would be there soon.

She had to come out. There was no way around it. I had to deliver her. They offered to fast-track the procedure by inducing the labour. The midwives, the doctor, the social worker, they all explained everything to us, in detail. There was so much information. There was even a booklet called *When a Baby Dies*.

Salvador and I had to make decisions. They were all ugly ones: when to start? The drip or the gel? Autopsy or no autopsy? Burial or cremation? Salvador said we could go home for the night and make the decisions the next day. It was such a relief. I just wanted to hide. We drove home, ate dinner, watched TV. My mum flew up from Melbourne, my sister and brother-in-law came over from the other side of the city and there were lots of phone calls.

In the morning the baby was still there in my belly. I did not want the fast track. I wanted things to happen slowly so there was time to get used to them. I kept thinking that maybe it would help if I read the information that was in the booklet that was in my bag over there by the wall. I did not read the booklet. I did not want her to come out.

It was a midwife called Sarah who told us about maceration.

Maceration is the blistering and peeling of skin, soft dead skin soaked in amniotic fluid. Sarah talked to us about how the baby might look after she was born. I had opted for the gel but my cervix was tough. Nothing happened all day. That was the Saturday. Sarah said the baby might be bruised from the birth. Bruised and macerated. I asked Sarah questions: Where will the baby go after she's born? Who would take her there? Could I see her afterwards? What if she couldn't come out? What if I couldn't let her go? Sarah was steady and strong. She told me that the sooner the baby came out the better.

I began to walk up and down the room. Salvador walked with me. My mum kept watch. Back and forth we went, and I tried to convince myself that it was time. But the baby was stuck, wedged in by an elbow and no amount of gel—or manual manipulation—could shift her. As the hours passed and Saturday became Sunday it was apparent that things could get even worse. We learned new words: 'ruptured uterus', 'hysterectomy' and 'the vertical cut'. The most likely option now was a caesarean section. The doctor said he'd prefer to do a horizontal cut but he would have to do a vertical cut if she was really stuck. He told me that future pregnancies and deliveries might be more difficult with a vertical cut. We listened carefully to this new information. It sounded like a script from a TV drama, not something that was happening to me.

They took her out at 6.42 pm on Sunday evening, 28 June 1998. Salvador and my mum were there to take her little body from the midwife, wash her, dress her and hold her until I could get there.

I combed my hair before I took her in my arms. Her hair was thick and black. I unfolded the baby blanket. I held one tiny hand in mine. Then I undid the baby suit and took out one leg. A pink sock was keeping her toes warm. The foot looked so fragile, limp. Blood began leaking from one nostril. I wiped her face with a tissue.

The midwife came to take her away at midnight.

We were all exhausted. Mum slept on a couch in the TV room. Salvador slept on the cot bed by my side. He held my hand all night. He put a pillow there between us for our hands to rest on together. I lay awake. I kept thinking they had done a hysterectomy on me while I was unconscious on the operating table. I was sure I would die if I went to sleep.

### 3. Feel

The Stillbirth and Neonatal Death Society (SANDS) has a twenty-four-hour help line. Joanne was the parent supporter who counselled me in those first few hours after we heard the news. As she listened to my story she started breathing heavily into the phone, clearly upset. The thing I most remember about her is that immediate empathy. She knew what we were going through, she'd been there herself.

Joanne was practical. I made a list from her suggestions:
- Ask for a separate room (the sound of crying babies can be upsetting).
- Think twice about an autopsy (the majority come back inconclusive).
- Think about the way you want to give birth (follow your plan, take the drugs they offer, don't suffer unnecessary pain).
- Think about who you want present (partner, family).
- Take time to be with the baby (take her clothes, any presents or toys you want to give her, she will start to deteriorate after five or six hours).
- Think about seeing and holding her again after she is taken to the morgue (the social worker can arrange this).
- Think about mementos (take the camera, ask for handprints).
- Think about ceremonies, flowers, candles, the funeral.

Joanne said to call her anytime about anything. In fact, she phoned me while I was in the hospital. Her support was profoundly comforting.

### 4. Favour

We asked to see the hospital priest. Salvador was brought up as a Catholic, his entire family lives in El Salvador, Central

America, and his mother said she would like us to get the baby blessed. Father Greg was unusual. He wore sandals, jeans and a sweatshirt promoting the hospital's children's foundation. He talked about God as 'him or her' and was open to the idea of ordaining women as priests.

Father Greg didn't waste words. He wanted to know who we blamed for Ruby's death. The question was shocking. Salvador and I looked at each other. I can't remember what we mumbled, but we tried to make it clear we didn't blame anyone. Father Greg wasn't easily convinced. 'Then why did this happen to nice people like you? Why didn't God stop it happening? Is God making you suffer? Well, then, why did it happen?' It was an unusual approach to bereavement counselling, more like sitting an exam than quiet counsel.

Father Greg didn't bless dead babies for distant grandmothers. However, on the day we left the hospital he named and blessed Ruby for us, sat with us next to her lifeless body, performed a healing ritual, read a poem written by another bereaved mother and invited us to come to his church anytime we needed to talk. He left us better than he found us.

We held a second ceremony, a civil funeral service, later that same day. Neither Salvador nor I have specific religious beliefs, but we wanted a ritual that included those closest to us to formally say goodbye to our daughter. My mum and dad were there along with one brother, two sisters and a brother-in-law. Salvador's friend Wil drove up from Canberra to join us. Lorna was the civil celebrant who conducted our service. My sister Sarah assisted her.

Sarah knows about rituals and she organised everything, only insisting that we choose the words that should be spoken. That was a very painful task. I couldn't think of anything meaningful to say, let alone a poem or a song. Sarah guided us through the steps of reconstructing Ruby's story: when she died, how she died, who was there. The narrative included her place in our families, the hopes we had for her and memories we would keep.

It was a short, beautiful service. We sat together in the little room near the hospital morgue set aside for bereaved parents. The light of dozens of tiny white candles placed around vases of white freesias, tulips and roses filled the space. Ruby's corpse sat in a carrycot on a small table at the front; her face shielded from view by a cloth.

*Ruby, may you reach your journey's true destination. You are free.*
*As long as the wind whispers in the trees,*
*as long as flowers grow and birds call, we will remember you.*
*Our love goes with you, until we meet again.*

### 5. Stroke

It was hard for me to speak after Ruby died. I did not want to be alone but I did not want to be talking. It felt as if I would give away too much if I said anything at all about what had happened.

I asked my friend Lili about the silence. She told me not to worry about it, that the words would come in their own time. It was very good advice. I asked Lili to help me think about the baby. She reminded me that Ruby has a spirit as well as a body and that her spirit will stay with me. Her words, like arrows, went straight to the heart. In place of limp fingers I could imagine all sorts of spirit-like things: birds, the wind, trees, rocks, and the waves crashing onto the cliffs at Coogee. Lili also gave me a way of dealing with the raw wound on the bottom side of my flabby stomach. She said the body is a map of our experiences. I look at the scar in the mirror and see the boundary staked out by my little girl.

### 6. Touch

I kept a diary for a while after Ruby died. I didn't write every day, just in those moments when the grief felt like craziness, when feeling crazy was too depressing or when I needed to remind myself that what had happened was very sad and that was why I felt very sad.

*Sunday 12 July 1998*
*It's three-hundred-and-thirty-six hours since Ruby died. I'm stuck. One thought won't go away: perhaps I killed her without realising. I must have killed her. No one else did. The doctors cannot find a cause of death. The autopsy was inconclusive. Perhaps I was too distracted, too busy with other things, not focused enough on the fragility of the new life growing inside me. Perhaps I could have done something to save her. Perhaps I worked too hard and didn't rest enough. Perhaps I should have walked more and done less yoga, or done more yoga and less swimming, more swimming, walking and yoga…*

This demented game of 'perhaps' would go on and on even though I knew it was useless. The grief counselling cassette said that guilt is often the way of expressing love that has nowhere to go.

*Sunday 26 July 1998*
*Mick called from the hospital. Three weeks, six days and eighteen hours have now passed since Ruby died. Mick sounds tired and jubilant. His son, Vincent Patrick, has just been born. Young Vince weighs three kilos and looks like his dad. Jo, his mum, laboured twenty-eight hours, without drugs, to bring him into the world. Mick says he and Jo want us to visit them in hospital. I can't stop crying but I think we should go anyway.*
*    Later…*
*    Jo was moving around stiffly when we got there. The baby boy stretched out his arms, flushed and cried out. Salvador held him, held the little body that moved, the little baby with red blood coursing through his veins. Why did our baby die?*

Mick and Jo are old and dear friends and our babies were due within weeks of each other. Before Ruby died, Jo and I would meet on Saturday mornings in Bondi Junction to attend yoga classes for pregnant women. We would sit next to each other on the mats, stretch out our cumbersome bodies and— thinking all the while about the baby—breathe deeply into the belly.

*Sunday 16 August 1998*
*Ruby died seven weeks ago now. I can't find anything about stillbirth on*
*the Internet. I've tried online medical journals, feminist health sites and*
*chatrooms for grieving parents. There are plenty of poems for dead*
*babies, but nothing much in the way of research data. Yesterday I spoke*
*to Dr Greg. His voice was warm. He said Avon and he had talked a few*
*times about what had happened to us. It almost hurt to hear the*
*gentleness of his voice. Dr Greg knows all the details, more details than*
*me. He read that fatal ultrasound, he took her out, and he prescribed*
*the morphine. I told him it had made me feel too foggy, drugged out. He*
*laughed and told me that wasn't such a bad thing sometimes.*

Salvador didn't share my quest for answers. He dealt with
Ruby's death in his own way. Sometimes that was hard for me.
Other times it was a relief to hear a different perspective.
Salvador said we should not suffer any more. He said some
people are just not meant to have children. They do all they
can but it doesn't work. Others don't particularly care and they
have children without thinking. He reminded me that we did
everything we could to have our child.

## 7. Kiss

A woman is not classified as 'infertile' until she has actively
tried for twelve months to become pregnant. There are
dozens of fertility management self-help books to encourage
the right kind of activity. Some focus on testing cervical mucus
for sperm-friendly stretchiness and wetness. Others demonstrate how to read your own body-at-rest temperature so you
can plot your progesterone levels and pinpoint the day you
ovulate. There are books on diet, herbs, exercise and gender
selection. There are even texts that show you how to chart your
lunar cycle to establish when the energy of the moon will
help you breed.

Of course all these methods also require sex. The books
recommend that relaxed sex is best. Sex should not be a chore.
Sex should not equate to baby making. You should not keep
the charts by the bed, countdown to the 'peak' moment, or

always raise your legs in the air for one hour afterwards in order to encourage the sperm's journey. Sex should be a good stress release, not a constant reminder of failure.

We didn't need sex to remind us of failure. We tried for two years, suffered two miscarriages and then lost our daughter in an unexplainable stillbirth. We were classified as 'unlucky' but not infertile. We tried again, and again. We tried to relax, to be optimistic, to enjoy ourselves. It was such hard work. Especially when Day 28 came around again. When you have a regular menstrual cycle like mine then you know precisely when to be hopeful and when to despair. Waiting took up the rest of the time. There were 281 more days of waiting.

Then, by some miracle, we got lucky. The moon and the mucus and the hormones and herbs combined to produce results. Or was it that we relaxed? In any case, I got pregnant again.

## 8. Nuzzle

James Salvador will be one year old soon. He weighs just over 11 kilos, has seven teeth and spends most of the day pulling himself up to a standing position and cruising around the furniture. He has great legs, especially the thighs. They are smooth and succulent like fresh pork chops.

Our boy is healthy and happy but he never sleeps enough. As a result we, his parents, are constantly tired and a bit grumpy. Jim doesn't seem to notice. In the morning, when we bring him into our bed, he gets so excited that he grabs Salvador's hair, tugs at it violently and either bites into his shoulder or slobbers all over his cheek. Jim's vitality is as awesome as it is endearing. It is no wonder he refuses to waste time lying prone in a cot.

## 9. Pamper

People frequently ask me if James Salvador is my first child. No, I say, we lost our first child. There's nothing like the mention of a dead baby to stop a conversation.

Photos of a dead infant are more confronting. I never show mine. They are too bleak. Ruby's face is all mottled, her eyes are raw wounds and her lips bright red. I am cradling her body with one hand, and clutching my mother's hand with the other. Those photos stay in the baby book in the cupboard next to the urn that holds Ruby's ashes.

Yes, I keep my daughter's remains in the cupboard in our bedroom. I don't know what else to do with them. I couldn't face burying her in a cemetery in the middle of winter, much less scattering her ashes to the four winds. So the only alternative was to bring her home.

The urn is no bigger than a fist. It is silver-coloured with a gold flash on each side. My sister Jane helped me choose it. We picked it out from a catalogue at the crematorium and then waited while they located the right box of ashes and made the transfer. I opened it when I got home, curious. Inside there is half a cup of powdery bones and a metal staple, perhaps from the coffin.

I also have beautiful things to remind me of Ruby. Her handprints—black on white cardboard—hang in a frame on our bedroom wall. Beside them is a sketch of our baby lying in peaceful repose. A former midwife called Sue, who lives in the high country around Mt Kosciuszko, did the drawing from one of those terrible photos I just mentioned. I never met Sue because we did business by mail, but I'm sure she has a kindly eye and a generous heart.

There is also a box of letters and cards with messages of sympathy and condolence. They came, often along with flowers—hyacinths, roses, lilies, waratahs, sweet peas, cyclamen, poppies and tulips—from family and friends, from people I hadn't seen for years, who somehow heard of our loss; even from people I barely knew, like the teacher from the yoga school. Together, in my mind, they formed Ruby's memorial garden, a splendid place of colour and connection, of fragrance and fecundity, of grace and grief.

Another keepsake is a quilt. A midwife called Vanessa gave it to me, just before I went into the operating theatre. It came from a bag of quilts that had been made by other bereaved mothers. My mum picked it out. Most of the quilts had hearts or squares in gentle hues, but Mum passed over the pastels and suggested instead the one quilt made of interesting geometric patterns and striking colours—red and black, purple, gold and blue. Every time I look at that quilt I'm glad she was bold.

When I look at my mum I often think of Ruby. My mum is the most important reminder I have of my little dead baby. For me, stillbirth was not only about losing a child. It changed my understanding of motherhood. Not only did my mother come to help me as soon as she heard the news, she accompanied Salvador and me as we dealt with the trauma, the details, the impact of the tragedy. In doing so, she helped me see mothering not only as a relationship of love and interdependence, but also of great tenacity. Children do such unexpected things. My first child died. Dying did not figure at all in my pregnant imaginings just as I'm sure that flying to Sydney to see her forty-year-old daughter through a stillbirth did not figure in my mum's plans for that week. And yet she did it.

And by doing it, she enabled me to do a very difficult thing. Two days after the caesarean section, I woke up in a panic. I couldn't remember what Ruby looked like. Everything that had happened was hazy. The panic got worse after Louise, the social worker, brought me Ruby's handprints and a small plastic bag with her hair clippings. I looked at them in horror. When did she get them? Why was someone else touching my baby?

The day got busy after that. The doctor came to check on me, there were funeral arrangements and a visitor or two. The panic came back in the afternoon as I thought again about seeing Ruby. I started coughing, it was hard to breathe. At that point my sister Jane arrived with Mum. Jane said straight away that I should go and spend time with the baby. Mum said she'd go with me.

The social worker took us to a room marked private. Ruby was there, lying in a blue spotted carrycot, waiting. Mum warned me she would be cold to touch. I lifted her out. Her skin was pink, her hair black like her father's, black eyebrows and eyelashes as well. She had my nose, mouth and chin. She looked like both of us. She looked like any other sleeping baby. Nothing leaked. I held her in my arms. She was so beautiful. I cradled her little body and walked with her, whispering words of endearment.

We stayed for half an hour. It was enough. The panic had abated to be replaced by a deep sense of tranquillity. Even as I write these words now, years later, I can recall the intensity of that experience of holding my beloved daughter's corpse, of tracing the contours of her face with my finger. In that moment, I felt mother-love and I knew with absolute certainty that it was something I would always remember.

# LIFE AFTER LAYLA

## Michael Shaw and Vanessa Gorman

*Michael*

I think I need to say to begin that my story feels as if it doesn't belong with the others in this book. My story is not really about the longing for a child followed by the grief of losing her. More it is an exploration of an intense passage in my life that began at the onset of pregnancy.

Vanessa and I had long argued about the merits of having a child. Both of us fairly immovable in our opposite camps. She kept hoping that 'one day I would change' and that some miraculous child instinct would wake up in me and dissolve the growing gulf that appeared between us. I kept hoping that one day she would say to me that she just wanted me and could drop the idea of having a child. The choice ranged from hard to impossible for the two of us. On the one hand part of me believed the propaganda that maybe it really would 'make a man of me'. On the other, in my heart of hearts, it was always 'not now', at best it was 'not yet'.

But saying 'no' invited a wave of judgments. Who was I to question the natural order? Just another man with the Peter Pan syndrome, caught in perpetual adolescence. My escapist tendencies were painfully highlighted but I still felt that parental life was not what I was pulled to explore. I still believe it isn't a journey to be taken lightly. The other aspect of the whole argument was as a reflection of part of our connection. I'd always felt that there was a part of me that needed an extended period of time alone. We met when I was just a couple of months out of a marriage and our foundation was built around a feeling, never fully resolved in me, that I wasn't ready. As Vanessa's biological clock ticked over, the possibility of time out for me seemed impossible. We were both stuck, then Vanessa got pregnant. We saw how it happened very differently. She felt she had my agreement and I felt tricked. Somewhere in the nature of how people love each other, especially when they're disagreeing and refusing to properly hear each other, makes me believe that we were both right. Not that I thought that at the time. But however it happened, Vanessa was definitely pregnant!

It was a wild journey. I wanted nothing but a happy pregnancy for her but I couldn't get away from the fact that it was making my life a misery. Not that she was; in truth, she was incredibly understanding of me. It was more the thought of what lay up ahead. It wasn't only that I was certain that I didn't want a child, it was also that I felt intensely self-critical for feeling that way. I kept seeing an image of Jimmy Stewart in some movie finding out his wife was pregnant and getting so happy and excited he accidentally smashed a lot of glasses. I had the awful realisation I was not the man I thought I would be as a boy. I was caught between wanting for myself those early images of how I imagined I would turn out, and the desire for a deep acceptance of myself as the adult I actually was.

As it turned out, this journey was to be anything but an expected one and soon all my fears and reactions were to be irrelevant. During labour I was staggered by how much pain Vanessa could cope with. I was armed, it seemed, with a lot of misinformation: mainly, that as a man what I most needed to do was not engage with the woman's pain. I think it probably freaks some men out but I wish I had been helped to be in there with her, in her pain, not excluded from it. After an event like this, it's impossible to not have all these niggles. And underneath them the thought that it could have turned out differently, 'If only I'd...' kept coming back to me.

Anyway, I did my best to be there but be 'unengaged'. A stance I absolutely regret. At the same time I was trying to 'really be there'. Impossible. It wasn't until Layla appeared that my water broke and I fully arrived. Layla came courtesy of an emergency caesarean with Vanessa exhausted, drugged and already on some level, psychically aware of what was about to happen. My baby arrived in a pool of meconium gasping for breath with a painful frown and blue cheeks. Nurses rushing around, lungs being sucked, she was shown briefly to us and then put on a trolley and rattled away at speed. It was a troubled birth but I thought it would all be all right. Vanessa started to tell me that she was dying. I didn't understand so I told her that people didn't die from caesareans and that she was OK, just exhausted. I wasn't to know she was speaking directly for our daughter.

I left Vanessa in the operating theatre and went into the emergency ward to meet my nemesis, my Layla. She lay, helpless and close to death, trying to breathe in a humidicrib with a team of doctors all around her, and it wasn't until this point that I fully realised the seriousness of the situation. Despite all of the warnings from the nurses, it left me shocked. Everything I'd believed about my life started to fall apart. Those old myths 'of course nothing could really go wrong' or 'stuff like this just doesn't happen to me' disintegrated. Part of me felt I'd made all this happen, I curled up in tears but soon, very soon all I wanted to do was be with her.

I was amazed at how much love there was in my body for her. Suddenly I was kneeling beside her trying to pour my love into her. I thought my love could keep her alive somehow. As if this had been the missing part of the picture and to give it now would fix everything. Even though I'd been for the previous year in various states of frozenness, when I met the very thing I was dreading, my heart threw open its doors and willed her to live. I held her hand, or rather she held my finger and I told her over and over that she was wanted. I knelt beside her in amongst all the hospital equipment and the photo flashes and the strange noises and in an uncharacteristically unselfconscious way proclaimed my love. Maybe 'God' had planned this all so that I could really choose her and all would be well.

Layla was flown from Lismore to Brisbane by helicopter. A friend and I drove up behind her. I wanted to go in the helicopter with her but it wasn't allowed. The last news I heard in Lismore was of a possible recovery. I left feeling that order had been restored. Away from her I moved out of the love-state I had been in. I resumed my state of naive confidence. I don't understand why. We had pizza on the way.

After we arrived in Brisbane we were kept in a waiting room for quite a while. I saw four men in deep emergency rushing Layla and her machine into the hospital. I remember thinking how serious it looked but at least I knew that really it would be OK. After about another half hour, they wouldn't let me in to where she was being worked on in Brisbane; something I still feel angry about. The doctor came out and told me she was almost gone. I was dumbstruck but also embarrassed that I didn't know somehow. I don't think my face showed anything in response.

They asked me if I would like to hold her which meant taking her off life support and effectively ending her life. I could see by looking at her that her struggle was almost done and I wanted so much to hold her once before she left. She hadn't been held at all in her life, not once in the traumatic painful time she'd had to live. I accepted and finally got to hold my child. I wanted everyone to go away and give me this moment. It's not a moment to be with strangers. I closed everyone out except her and sometime in the following few seconds she died. I couldn't feel exactly when but I could tell she was gone. It was to my body what physics must feel like to five-year-olds, a quiet non-comprehension. When I look back the whole memory has a dreamlike quality that's very hard to describe, but I know I held her for a half an hour or so.

Too soon there were practicalities that needed sorting and I needed my mind back. Truthfully I couldn't figure out what the hell to do. They asked me if I wanted to wash her. They told me to go and sleep, that they would organise the release forms in the morning. I sensed the danger of the hospital taking over from human contact and I started longing to be with Vanessa, Layla's mother. I just wanted to get out of there.

My friend Geoff helped me handle the difficult and some-times absurd red tape. The night nurse armoured with some hospital rank insisted, 'You need to take her back in a plastic bag'. That has to be one of the more ridiculous things I've ever heard. What's the rule? No dead babies to leave this hospital unless they're in a carrybag? Anyway the bag assumed another level of significance as we got back on the road to Lismore and headed toward Vanessa.

After Layla died I gradually lost contact with her again, just as I had when I left her the first time in Lismore. Now I was holding in my arms a carrybag with something I couldn't comprehend inside. In the overloaded place I was in I felt because I'd been so resistant to her all along I had no right now to grieve. No right to claim my connection as father. I was holding Vanessa's most cherished object, who was also the symbol of my own shortcomings. Numbed out, I carried her in the bag the whole trip. If I could send a psychic apology into a place that she might exist, I would say, 'I'm sorry. I'm sorry I left you in the carrybag. I wish I had spent my last hours with you alone holding you and looking at you.'

When I arrived back at the hospital I picked up her little body wrapped in cloth, took her out of the bag and carried her in towards her mother. It was about five in the morning and I hesitated for a moment at the door to Vanessa's room. Would she think I killed her? Would she hate me for delivering her such a broken package? Would she see that I had already lost my connection to our child and hate me? When I saw her I felt deeply relieved. Not just because she didn't hate me but also because I needed her then, a loving familiar face in the chaos of what had just happened.

In some ways my essential journey with Layla ended there. A year later I'm still finding and looking for the connection between our souls partly because once I passed her body over to her mother I entered the process of helping Vanessa cope with a landslide of grief. My own feelings have been harder and slower to open.

My feelings have been so different to Vanessa's, as indeed, any father's experience is different to a mother's in birth, though the differences are exacerbated in this case. I still wonder if I felt enough. If I felt sad enough. Regardless, I felt honoured to be with Vanessa and felt a deep need to help her through and to be a safe harbour for her. It's a difficult thing to explain but I did feel very opened by the following months. The degree to which love was extended to us. How deeply needed I was. How raw everything became and of course coping with the sometimes fleeting memories of my time with Layla.

Six months later the obvious question arose about another child. Although I wanted to give Vanessa one to help her, it wasn't enough of a reason for me. Even after everything, the role of parent was still not appealing. I said, 'No'. It ended our relationship. It's early days yet and it's a very uneasy ending. We are both having a lot of trouble letting each other go. I'd like to be able to write the next chapter of this story and know it worked out for her and for me, but such is the nature of the unknown, as Layla is testament to. This is the chasm that these events have left and life has never had more difficult choices for either of us.

I know one thing, though. I'm privileged to have shared the journey through life and death with Layla. A journey that I will never really understand or feel resolved about. Regardless of how life works out, I feel a larger, albeit bruised, man.

### Vanessa

I have a little saying on my fridge, half joking, half serious: 'It may be that your sole purpose in life is to serve as a warning to others.'

Some days I feel like a casualty of the feminist revolution. I had followed my mother to the barricades. Her battle cry was not about finding a husband and raising a family, but about getting into university and climbing the career ladder. I wish now that she had taken me aside at thirty and said, 'Enough of the high flying. If you want a family you better stop mucking about.'

I had always desperately wanted a family but I waited too long. Somewhere between the generation of my father and my partner, men had a silent revolution and realised they had a choice: to procreate or not. It was no longer a given. My partner Michael came down on the reluctant side and because I loved him I let the argument about a baby go on for too many years.

I could blame him, I could blame feminism, most days I blame myself. But in truth I am just a casualty of that dark force known as the cruel hand of fate. Most days I find myself in a wretched place of grief.

It is now two days before my fortieth birthday. I no longer have a partner and I no longer have a child. This time last year, it seemed I had all I ever longed for.

When I turned thirty-eight, the last of my sand had felt as if it was slipping through my hourglass. I knew I was entering the danger zone to even conceive. Arguing with Michael about my desire for a baby, I sometimes felt like a desperate animal pleading for my very survival. When I got pregnant that year I felt like I had just slipped in under the wire. The wand showed two pink stripes and the weight of the world lifted from my shoulders.

Michael didn't react well to the news he was to be a parent. He felt he was being taken on a journey he hadn't fully agreed to. He started talking about leaving the relationship some time after the baby was born. And on one level that plunged me into bouts of insecurity but on the level that really counts, a great wave of happiness, hormones and massive relief swept through me and I surged forth into pregnancy, blossoming open more and more through the forty-one weeks until my heart was as ripe as my body, waiting for my little girl to enter the world.

I thought I had slipped under the wire, but it caught around my throat and strangled us. Strangled me with grief and my baby daughter Layla of her very breath. After a long and distressing labour ending in an emergency caesarean, Layla died eight hours after birth from complications of meconium asphyxiation. She had pooed in the womb and took a breath of black tarlike liquid deep into her tiny lungs. The word 'nightmare' seems too tame to describe the journey of my world falling apart. Existence was playing my own private horror movie.

I have bayed at the moon this year. I have banged the steering wheel and screamed in the shower. I have sobbed in the carpark at Woolies and into the shoulder of Michael more times than I could remember. I have wished other babies dead so that someone might share my grief. I have cringed with shame at the dark side of my soul and ridden the wild beast of grief till it exhausts me.

And all the anger and the fear and the pain and the tears have only one simple but primal lament. *I want her back. I want her back.*

Losing a baby, *losing Layla,* was losing a part of myself. I lost a part of my own body. No other loss is as hormonally gut-wrenching.

And yet, most horror movies also have moments of great, dark beauty. To face the monster of our worst nightmares is to be broken open to a glimpse of a deeper part of ourselves. Moments of brutal truth that strip us bare. These are some glimpses of the primal journey of losing my baby daughter.

*First night*
Our first night home from the hospital was Layla's only night in the house we've renovated to receive her. We had been granted the unusual gift of taking her body home for twenty-four hours before her cremation.

It is the stillest night I can remember. Not a puff of wind, no frogs, no crickets. Utter silence. She lay between us in the bed and when I was sure Michael was asleep I took her onto my side and cradled her tightly under my chin. Her body, rock solid cold that morning, has thawed throughout the day, especially after the warm bath before her ceremony.

I slept and woke after 2 am. She is still there but so still. Silent as the night. I began to sing the lullaby we sang that afternoon at her ceremony.

*You kissed my blood and your blood kissed me...*

Michael stirred and came up on one elbow. His attention suddenly brought me to tears but the movement in and out of tears was not so great and we began to sing together.

*Brighter than the brightest star, you are, by far...*

We forgot some of the words but sung defiantly on in mutters. We sung into the dark, on and on, shattering the silence. Sometime after that we drifted off again.

I woke before dawn, lost in a dream I couldn't hold onto. She was still eerily silent, cradled against my chest. I began to stroke her hair and then moved down caressing her face. I loosened the bunny rug and tracked a path down to her neck and shoulders, my breath catching at the softness of the skin beneath her neck. I began a long caress from the shoulders up to her cheek, around her scalp, curling her hair as I go went then down across her eyes, over her nose, her mouth, down to her chest and back towards the shoulder. I stroked obsessively, a desperate braille reading. Her body was due to be burnt before lunch.

When my sister Alex arrived we checked her bunny rug for bloodstains. In intensive care they'd worked on her hard for eight hours before handing her to my partner Michael to die. She'd been leaking blood from her mouth and nose for a couple of days now, made worse the warmer she got. Alex and I had been tending to it with great discretion, like we would a daughter's first menstruation.

'She's leaked a little blood from her mouth overnight,' she whispered, unwrapping her outer rug and placing it on the bed so the bloodstain was hidden from view. We wrapped her in the white muslin with red hearts and joked that the blood-stains will blend in. Alex tucked a tissue in as a bib.

'Keep that there for the drive to the crematorium,' she said conspiratorially, 'and try to keep her head back when you hold her.'

All neatly wrapped now, I cradled her tenderly under my chin, just like she was sleeping. A single teardrop of blood fell from her nose, almost as if she was trying to tell me she understood my heart was breaking.

Standing at the door to the chapel I knew it was almost time to let her go. My heart was thumping, swollen with unassail-able despair. I was unable to turn back, unable to walk forward. Her tiny white coffin waited in front of the red velvet curtain.

Michael held onto me as I lowered her into the white satin

lining of that obscene bassinet. My chest seemed to be exploding from within. It was five days since her death and I was dimly aware that my heart was finally, literally shattering. We placed the lid over the last glimpse of her precious face and sang her through to the other side.

*Last rites*
The breasts are often the first things to shout *Hey, there's somebody else in here!* They swell and harden during pregnancy. Mine grew month by month; my 12Bs turning into magnificent 14Cs. My nipples grew, too, and darkened. I could feel my breasts readying themselves, evolving towards their biological destiny.

A lover can do no more erotic thing to me than put my nipple in their mouth. And it was like this I waited for my daughter. Like a lover. Longing to feel her mouth on me and my love flowing into her body. Aching to hold her warm skin to mine.

After her death, on the second day I had her body, I tentatively peered inside her mouth. The tubes they had put down her throat had bloodied her saliva which had turned now to a thick brown mucus. Horrified I quickly closed it, pushing her stiff jaw upward. My breasts throbbed, unaware.

My milk started to come and people brought me in cold cabbage leaves to put down my tightly bound bra and sage tea and homeopathic remedies. The milk stopped. But then one morning, three days after we had cremated her body I woke to find the front of my cotton night dress drenched. At first I couldn't work out where all this moisture had come from. I genuinely didn't know. And when it dawned on me I felt a kind of alarmed and embarrassed shame. I called the district nurse who suggested in polite words that I should 'milk' myself of the build-up.

I stood at the bathroom mirror and squeezed each breast toward the nipple, marvelling somewhere at the sight of sticky fluid emerging from my flesh. My body split between triumph and despair. Breasts, eyes, heart; all weeping. Mourning my daughter like a grieving widow.

*Sex and grief*

Michael and I began a sexual relationship again, soon after Layla's birth and death. Which is surprising because it had been a while since we had had sex. In the last half of my pregnancy I began to embody those old English words of fulsome and mettlesome. I felt all woman. Basically I was so horny I was eyeing off the doorknobs.

Unfortunately, Michael was hermetically sealed against contact, closed down in trepidation and despondency about our impending arrival. It was not until Layla was struggling for breath that his heart opened in love for her. And after she died, his heart opened even more as the wave of love from friends and family washed over us. And as his heart opened, his sexuality seemed to rekindle.

As I lay wounded in bed from the caesarean, tended to by my mother and sister, he began to stay up late and surf porn sites over the internet. Our internet bookmarks were a study in hilarious juxtaposition. Nasty and rude sex acts dot com sat uneasily above the Stillbirth and Neonatal Death Society dot org dot au.

He would come to bed and hold me while I cried and I would feel his erection grow rock hard against my thigh. And I would lie there, barely able to twist, four layers of my abdomen sewn together just above the shaved strip of pubic hair, my heart broken in two for the loss of Layla and I would feel my passion for him start to also rise. It was part passion and part desperate need to feel someone close. And we would whisper earnest truths about our love, reassuring each other of survival in our storm-lashed dingy.

And because it was too soon after birth for him to penetrate me he slid a pillow beneath me and spread my legs and kissed me so gently, like he was licking dewdrops off the edge of a palm frond.

A confusing thrill shot through my veins and and I shook my head in lust and disgust that I could enter into an act like this so soon after her death. But I lay there and let the wave rise, surrendering to my grief and desire.

And as the wave rose, an image of the green and silver of the operating room flashed through my head, and the stiffness of

Layla's body when she came back from the cool room that second day.

It was like the scar above my pubic bone was the dividing line separating some disembodied pleasure zone from the tortures of my mind and heart. After this many years his tongue was skilled and so the orgasm rose and Michael let out a low rumble, responding to my confused passion. Involuntarily I squirmed, worrying I might tear the stitches and render myself infertile forever more. Still the pleasure grew and I moaned and thought *what kind of slut would allow herself this pleasure when her baby daughter is only recently dead* and still Michael's tongue worked on me until the wave overtook thought.

Ecstatic shivers of joy washed over me, somehow unleashing the sobs that rose from the fissures of every cell, wracking my body and rending the air with wild noises. Sobs of pain borne on the wings of bodily delight, infused with the quiet glow of utter shame.

### The primal grief of losing Layla

Michael and I have separated now. Having another baby is not the direction that is pulling him for now. And a year after her death, I have accepted without feeling shock anymore that Layla is not coming back.

I rage at the world. I despair that maybe I have left further childbearing too late. I feel fear I will never love another like I have loved Michael. I wonder why my daughter had to die. I want the world to go away. I want them all to come close and offer their sympathy.

I hate with ferocity and shock myself with dark thoughts fantasising about disasters that may befall others. I dream each night of saving drowning and distressed children. I cry tears of pain and frustration. But underneath it all is just my grief. Underneath it all, again and again rises that primal chant *I want her back. I want her back.*

But I have been dealt an unlikely gift. A consolation prize if you like. By surrendering to my grief, by letting it arise when and where it lashes me, I have come to understand more of the rise and fall of life itself.

# SUNNY SAILOR BOY

## Sue Daniel

Long legs. Big hands and feet. Soft folds of skin. Tufts of black hair. A little baby at rest after a long birth.

These are the things I see when I look back at our baby photos.

It was his first birthday when I finally sat down and filled the photo album; black and white and colour; the pregnancy, me smiling and healthy; his birth, full of trauma in a grey-blue hospital; and his farewell, where he lies surrounded by frangipani flowers.

He's there in our room when I wake up...sepia tones of blankets surrounding his little face, which could be in repose.

His red lips stand out in another image, where my fingernails still show the blood of his birth.

In another he's cradled in my husband's arms and the warm water of the bath, where I'd laboured only hours before.

I speak to him silently when I look at these photos, telling him I will always love him, never forget him.

My diary comforted me in the sleepless hours after his death.

### Monday 23 March 1998

*We lost our baby boy Luka when he was born yesterday morning at 11.14 am. It was the most painful birth you can imagine.*

*I was put on a drip to induce my labour. Once it went in the contractions started to blend together and I cried and cried because when our midwife Sheryl finally examined me my cervix was only six centimetres dilated. So they gave me an epidural to give me a break.*

*The baby started to come down very quickly then, so they let me try naturally again—and I did try very hard—I screamed so loud it was like listening to another person. I got very close to doing it but my sore back was unbearably painful. So they topped up the epidural and I was like a pincushion, totally covered in wires and tubes.*

*The registrar on duty used a vonteuse, a suction cap to pull the baby's head out. I helped push (without pain) and visualised him coming out (without stitches or tears to my vagina) and he did, straight onto my tummy.*

*But he wasn't awake and they took him away immediately to the warming table. It was an emergency because he couldn't breathe.*

*I didn't know—but Ian did.*

*I kept saying to Ian, 'Believe in him, darling.' Luka was so strong and healthy inside me I couldn't believe he could just go like that.*

We named him after an Irish singer we love, Luka Bloom. His music was playing as I was losing my son.

That day I found it hard to cry. We had to call our parents and friends. My mother was alone in the house while Dad went to the shop, but I could hardly say, 'I'll call you back'. Somehow it was worse having to tell them the news—I wanted to protect them from it but it also made it real.

Ian and I just went onto autopilot from the shock.

Our midwives Shea and Sheryl helped us through that numbness. They seemed to know how the simple acts of bathing, dressing and holding him would help us begin letting go while also celebrating his life.

One of my favourite photos is of the three of us in the bath. The texture of the image shows his beautiful skin, just like his father's.

But there's another photo that's so hopeless it's almost unbearable to look at. I'm on the bed with Luka in my lap, looking out the window, while Ian sits next to me with his head in his hands.

It hurts me to see that moment, especially because Luka simply looks like he's asleep, but I'm not holding him in my arms. We're three lonely souls on our own journeys. I felt he was still with us that day. The next day his spirit was gone.

When people arrived it felt strange. We all held him again

and I remember feeling proud of him—my baby! I knew him in a way no one else could. Where was the strong personality I'd known in my belly?

They took me out of the hospital in a wheelchair, and I'll never forget the sorrow and confusion on people's faces as I went by.

We decided to take Luka with us for the night, and I'm so glad we did.

*As I write he's in a cradle in our room, and in the morning Shea and Sheryl will take him back to the hospital for a post-mortem. We all need to know what happened for our peace of mind, future babies and to help resolve the grief. He's incredibly beautiful—just like his father—with my feet and legs and blue blue eyes. The colour of the ocean—but only on some wild days. My heart is breaking—it's not real but it happened.*

*We all take so much for granted in life, and I'll value it so much more now and hope we can have another little one to share it all with.*

*I don't want to wait long, but I'll never get over this, not fully.*

Only the next day I went walking with a friend, and saw women carrying their babies in pouches, slung casually across their bodies.

It was unbelievably painful. All the dreams I cherished, the images I had of myself would have to be reassessed, as they had been when I got pregnant.

I so much wanted to be a mother. A child to share the joy of life, play with my friends and their babies, know the love of my family, dance and sing and swim with, and read to in the evenings.

Luka's death came as even more of a shock because I'd had such a good pregnancy. I wasn't nauseous, I felt energetic and excited most of the time, and people said pregnancy suited me. The only premonition I had was saying to one of my midwives during the labour, 'He doesn't want to come out'.

The labour was very hard. I had three days of contractions which came mostly at night and petered out during the day.

I was exhausted by the time we went to the hospital to try and get things going properly.

Our birth classes had prepared us for the possibility of intervention, warning not to get too attached to the idea of natural birth. But what they didn't prepare us for was this horror.

I remember the sense of unfairness. To have had such an awful birth with no reward at the end. No beautiful baby to soften the pain.

### Wednesday 25 March 1998

*Early a.m. sometime.*

*Trying to take each day as it comes.*

*Physically sore and becoming more emotionally vulnerable by the hour.*

*Every time I go to the toilet there's new blood—how much blood can a person lose? It frightens me.*

*I see Luka's face in my mind constantly.*

*He's beautiful, sleeping and serious like a little buddha.*

*Sheryl and Shea are like a lifeline for me at the moment with so much to talk about regarding the birth and how we're feeling. Shea told me there's no 'right' way of coping, except to do what you feel.*

*Hope is a word I've turned to a lot in the last couple of days, and strangely enough I do have a lot of it.*

That week we held a naming ceremony and cremation for Luka. Every day more flowers and cards arrived, and they continued in a steady stream for what seemed like weeks after our baby's death.

It made us feel very supported and loved, and made me realise the importance of connecting with people after such a terrible event. The acknowledgment of his life and death was vital to us.

Strangely enough, I felt happy sometimes, and felt guilty for it. But I think I knew that Luka had been happy inside me, he had a wonderful time for his short life, and he knew he was loved.

He felt the rhythms of the ocean as I swam, he heard great

music and went to parties, he was nourished by good food, and he listened to his daddy's voice, singing with excitement about his arrival.

Friends told me Luka would want me to be happy, and I believe that.

### Saturday 28 March 1998

*Dreams of holding Luka's hand. I had the same one twice during the pregnancy. I vividly remember the feeling of reaching down to hold his hand, as if he was reaching out to me from inside the womb.*

*Black depression descended on me twice today. I'm exhausted, which doesn't help, and having trouble catching up.*

*Mum and Dad bought us a grevillea—soft pink—because it resembled the flowers in Luka's bouquet at the cremation. I wanted another memory of him planted here, as well as the gum Ian's brother Neil gave us.*

*We planted it as part of his naming ceremony—and put the placenta under it. A red-blood nourishing thing to help the earth hold his memory.*

### Sunday 3 May 1998

*I went for a check-up with my GP last week, and burst into tears as soon as I walked into the room. She was fighting back tears herself. I cry a lot about the whole uncertain nature of what we've been through.*

*Why Luka died we may never know, but if he caught an infection . . . it's torture not knowing how. She said what happened to us was incredibly rare but we need to know that from the specialists.*

*I hope we can hear that, but I'll never trust in the word 'safe' again. I couldn't keep him safe even though I did everything in my power.*

### Tuesday 5 May 1998

*Every day I relive parts of what happened. Questioning everything; was there anything we did or didn't do? There are no answers and it's so unfair.*

### Wednesday 13 May 1998

*I've been worrying that if my waters leaked during pre-labour and I didn't know, an infection might have been able to get in. What sort of bug could have caused a lung infection, and how did it get in?*

*All I did was lie around the house, have baths and go for walks. Could having sex have caused it?*

*I'm sobbing now as I write this. Terrible pain doesn't seem to lessen, even as we approach eight weeks after Luka's death. It's good to cry; it makes me know I'm alive and something terrible has changed my life forever.*

### Monday 18 May 1998

*We had the post-mortem meeting on Thursday. Luka died from lack of oxygen, it turns out, nothing to do with an infection at all.*

*It was a relief for both of us. Because I couldn't understand how that could have happened.*

*So strangely the inexplicable becomes easier to deal with. They don't know why it happens but it occurs in about one in a thousand births.*

Some people didn't understand that Ian and I could accept the outcome; that we would never know why Luka couldn't breathe. Neither of us felt the need to lay blame. We never saw any indication that Luka was in trouble, despite having a monitor attached to my belly the whole time.

People didn't realise how painful it was when they said things like, 'Why did they let you stay at home in labour for all that time?' As if that had somehow contributed to our baby's death.

My only doubt was whether Luka would have lived if we hadn't induced the birth. But I know I wasn't strong enough to go on, and I'll never know if things would have got under way naturally.

We went searching for an obstetrician to support us through a second pregnancy. One said it would be 'high risk', and I would need to be attached to a monitor constantly through the birth.

But we couldn't agree. Having a monitor had not prevented Luka's death. I wanted to try for a natural birth again.

We still had a long way to go before getting pregnant again.

After the results of the post-mortem I read and searched for meaning in everything. Other people's experiences of death were very comforting.

For the first time in a long time I thought about my little sister Lucy. She died when I was five, my parents' last child. The images that remain are of a tiny baby wrapped up in my grandmother's arms, and my parents' intense grief on the day she died. We never really talked about it and I realised it had left me with a deep fear of death.

I was brought up an atheist, so religion held no comfort for me, and it really upset me when people told me Luka was in a better place, or that he died for a reason. What a load of crap.

What I knew unshakably was that Luka was with me all the time.

### Tuesday 30 June 1998

*We're trying for another baby.*

*I feel excited, sad, a bit confused. My thoughts and memories of Luka are present, but the gaps in between are getting bigger. Getting pregnant again will be a tribute to him, and it's important for us to try again, even though we're afraid.*

### Friday 28 August 1998

*Another blow. Yesterday I started to miscarry, and my obstetrician said the baby had never really formed. We feel very unlucky, and I guess even more scared about trying again.*

We took that miscarriage as a sign that we weren't ready, physically or emotionally, for another baby.

He or she would have been due around Luka's birthday, which felt wrong.

It's true that anniversaries and special occasions are the

hardest times. For a long time we took Luka's photo with us everywhere so he was there with us.

On his first birthday we went to a place on the coast where we'd spent a lot of time during the pregnancy. On Sunday morning, the day of his birth/death, I went out onto the verandah feeling very fragile.

A dog came to say hello and brought his very old and slobbery ball for me to throw, and all of a sudden I felt better. It was as if my little boy was right there, reassuring me. It sounds weird but it was a connection with his soul.

On New Year's Eve 1998, missing Luka terribly, we dragged ourselves to a big party in the lush north of New South Wales. Midnight came and we danced with Ian's sister Kay, tears rolling down our faces, and felt another milestone pass.

I turned to counselling, meditation, yoga and swimming. I talked and talked to friends, trying to be open about my feelings. Ian and I felt different things at different times, which was a strain.

Ian had to work very hard, too soon after Luka's death, and it forced him to contain his feelings in a way I didn't have to. I worked part-time and felt strongly that my priorities had changed.

As we approached the second pregnancy, I started to feel Ian's fear, and it seemed as if his grief was still terribly intense.

I felt like I needed his utmost strength and clarity beside me, so I asked him to do a course on grief. It made a huge difference.

I was afraid during my next pregnancy in a way I could never have imagined.

The legacy of Luka was still with me.

I had to work hard to realise that this was a different baby and a different birth which would have a different outcome.

### Saturday 9 October 1999

*Every day on the toilet I look for blood—a repeat of last year's mis-carriage. At work there was the fine pink, so faint I wasn't sure. The prettiest pale pink, I almost thought it was the skin of my fingers through the damp toilet paper. My heart started to pound violently and the heat went straight to my face.*

*What to do? I rang my friend Mary, who was so calm. I rang my obstetrician and the facts he quoted made me feel better. 'Ten per cent of women bleed through pregnancy and still have healthy babies, and after two good ultrasounds there's only a one per cent chance of problems'.*

*I'm going into a sense of limbo now. Between the time of morning sickness and the first kicks there aren't any physical signs I can clutch onto for reassurance.*

*Last week after the ultrasound I cried tears of pure joy to know that he or she is so real. I rub my tummy and say hello every day. Yet it's the nature of life to be uncertain, and I can't be sure of anything.*

*My chest is often clutched tightly closed with grief, so I have to consciously relax. It's a fine line between happiness and such deep sadness, and the latter often still wins.*

### Saturday 23 October 1999

*I've felt terribly lonely in the last two weeks—a sense that no one can understand, and when I do tell them how I feel, there's a blankness.*

*I just told Ian I feel like a leper, a reminder of terrible things in the world. Being around a large group of people just makes me feel more alone.*

*One of my midwives really wanted to listen to the heartbeat and feel my tummy, and I just completely freaked out. I was terribly fright-ened—what if the baby's dead? I couldn't do it.*

So much fear, even though I knew it was just that, there was no tangible reason for it.

I guess some people find it easier to just keep busy, but I couldn't, so instead I kept meditating and tried to express my fears to my dearest friends and family.

We found ways to connect with Luka and let our anxieties go, and welcome our new baby. Our birth class teacher suggested we have a ritual for him and the new baby, by lighting candles and talking about them.

Out of the blue one day when I was six months pregnant we

were asked to be support people to two close friends having their first baby. It was a real turning point for both of us because we realised we were more prepared and stronger than we thought.

I gave birth to our son Finn on 9 April 2000. It couldn't have been a more different experience, less than five hours of labour, in the birth centre, with no intervention.

This time hardly any photos were taken because we didn't have time. I also didn't have time to be afraid of what might happen.

Finn looked the spitting image of his brother when he came out, which was a shock. As time's gone by he's become very different, although in the half light, breastfeeding, he still reminds me of Luka.

He cried long and loud from the minute he burst into the world, a sign of his incredible life force.

### Sunday 16 April 2000

*We've survived and mostly revelled in the first week of Finn's life!*

*I've noticed some amazing things.*

*Luka's grevillea bush has been flowering like mad.*

*Our downstairs neighbour brought us two gardenia flowers from the plant we were given after Luka died. They bloomed on the day Finn was born. She said it was as if Luka was speaking to his little brother: 'One for you and one for me'.*

*Kookaburras have been visiting in the mornings. I've heard them here before but only rarely.*

*Finn's been smiling the last couple of days too—not sure if the smiles are directed at us but they sure are beautiful.*

Not long after Finn's birth we bought tickets to see Luka Bloom in Sydney, but we were new parents and far too ambitious. What we didn't know was that our midwives had asked him to dedicate a song to our son. Some time into the gig he whispered into the microphone. 'This is for Finn'. And sang 'Sunny Sailor Boy'.

The next night my friend Erina hand delivered a thank-you

note with a photo from us to Luka Bloom. So the story came full circle and I feel at peace with my baby's death.

Finn is almost a year old, and what a year it's been.

Writing now is hard because I wonder when he reads this story how he'll feel. He didn't replace Luka, he is himself. Somehow I think he is a strong personality and it will be OK, but I'm reluctant to say how hard it's been.

I developed post-natal depression, and our loss very likely contributed to that.

With that came terrible anxiety about his welfare, and black feelings I couldn't control. Feelings of inadequacy as a mother, and the need to make things perfect for him.

It's as if having a second child should make things all right, but of course it's not so simple.

The sadness about Luka hasn't gone, but it's so much softer now.

I feel a lot better, with the support of my husband, my friends and family, and Finn is just the most beautiful, funny, gentle and alive son I could ever wish for.

Sundays have always been hard. We often light a candle and listen to songs that seem to have been written for us. But the music brings cleansing tears.

Luka knows we love him and miss him, and we'd give anything to have him here in our arms.

I have the deep blue of the sea to remind me of his eyes forever.

*Sue Daniel, Ian Walker and Luka*

# ONE IN TEN THOUSAND

### Ian Walker

In the casino of life I have become a great and terrible loser, a member of one of the planet's crappiest clubs. No one chooses to join and the cost of membership is sky-high. The parent who has lost a child is a true leper. Bereft, a curse to friends and loved ones, especially other parents...a constant reminder of all that is shitful and possible in the great gamble of life.

I have no faith in numbers. A ten-thousand-to-one chance took away my first-born son in the first minutes of his life. The doctors told us there would only be a million to one chance of it happening again. Instead, a one-in-seven mishap cheated us of our next baby only ten weeks after conception.

My partner Susie mentions bad omens she witnesses on the bus on her way to work. A car crash, a body covered in a sheet, a crowd of gawpers. Then more strong images visit her on the train: a premonition of a friend's miscarriage, a spatter of blood in the toilet bowl.

The phone rings. Shattered peace. A tightness in her voice. 'I'm bleeding!' I know the words are code for 'Death'. Another death. My head is spinning. I am drowning in the same stinking vomit of fear and panic as I did only three months ago. Too soon for more pain.

I rage at the computer keyboard writing these words as my wife waits to pass the bloodclot that amounts to our hopes and dreams. She will endure the pain of expulsion, but nothing will rush to fill the hole in her heart, a heart so worn and bloodied with grief over the death of our son, Luka.

Getting pregnant quickly again would be a good idea, we thought. A new birth date to re-focus our attention, give us back our future. A sibling for Luka is to be born close to his first birthday and the anniversary of his death. We tentatively try to embrace the idea. A silent promise to Luka the new baby will in no way be a replacement, a substitute, a 'subby bubby'. You, dearest boy, will always be our first-born child.

But death cheats us this time even before life takes hold. I learn the medical term and bandy it around, introducing it to people like it's a new friend. So precise, so impersonal. A 'blighted ovum', not even a foetus. A scientific way of saying 'not a real person'. We are supposed to take comfort in this. The proud parents of one dead baby and a blighted ovum!

Again my legs have been kicked out from under me. I never believed in curses, maybe now I do. How piteous are the cries of, 'Why me?' Why not me? Why anyone? Who's idea of a joke is this? Not my idea of God.

The day of Luka's death still clutches at my heart. I cannot shake its clarity, its slow-motion horror playing out over and over again in my head. I can see the baby's head crowning. It's a sweet moment of relief after a gruelling three days of non-eventful pre-labour. A long torturous night where Susie weeps and screams frustration and pain with each relentless wave of drip-induced contraction.

Daylight is a reminder of the many hours that have passed since we were transferred from the birth centre to the labour ward. None of the potions, pumps or magic bath oils of the 'white witches' (our beloved midwives Shea and Sheryl) had worked. Baby wouldn't come. Nature let us down. Time for the world of medical science to step in and take charge.

The move deflates our confidence. Our midwives don't seem welcome there. Sharp lines of demarcation, petty rivalries and hospital politics infuse the space and bubble underneath as a cheap subplot to the main drama. The room seems neatly designed for doctors to poke and prod and take readings from the machines that go 'ping'.

Fluoro lighting blows any chance of a spiritual ambience. Susie's leg cramps in the pathetically tiny bath. Floor-to-ceiling built-in cupboards hide an array of equipment which only spells horror in my mind. There is nowhere to stand without being in the way. Just the kind of reminder a first-time father needs as he's taking stock of just how useless an appendage he really is during childbirth.

Waiting for the next epidural to kick in, I take a breather outside. It's a brilliant bright Sunday and I shake my fist at the sun. Its radiance seems to mock my desperation. I pray to the stars and the moon, the ocean, the earth to please help us in our hour of need. Don't let us down. Please don't let us down.

I come close to passing out with the fatigue and the stress. But how can I not be there to see my baby come out? As the blackness closes in, I lift myself off the floor with my last bit of strength.

Susie gives a final push, baby is out and lifted up onto her tummy. 'It's a boy!' I cry, happier than I could ever imagine. But the feeling lasts only seconds. A flicker of darkness on our midwife's face says something's not right. Baby won't breathe. A flurry of activity. Frantic suction and cardiac massage on the tiny limp body. He's turning blue in front of my face. My world is shattering.

Susie tries to encourage me to stay with him, hold his hand, let him know I'm there. But I know it's no use. We've lost him. She's sitting on the bed surrounded by tubes and bloodied towels, in a post-partum bliss state unable to move. How to tell her it's not okay? Our baby is dead. It can't be true. Not like this. Not to us.

No one wants to know why Luka died more than we do. How can a near-perfect pregnancy end with a dead baby? In the weeks afterwards, the tortured questioning almost paralyses us. A lung infection is the first suspect. Everyone has a theory...some are shared with us, some are whispered behind our backs, in neighbours' houses, in hospital corridors. All of them are unhelpful. Most find someone to blame.

The final autopsy mentions 'intra-uterine hypoxia' plus a list of other long words in brackets, which adds up to a lack of oxygen causing haemorrhaging. The doctors can't tell us whether this happened gradually over a period of weeks, or days or just during the labour.

An unexplainable neonatal death is a one-in-ten-thousand

event, the doctors tell us. Like a mantra, they talk percentages as if the numbers themselves had healing or protective powers. But I know they are the product of a world that wants answers to everything. Certainty. A technological fix. It's our goddamn birthright as white educated middle-class good-hearted Australians.

Others find comfort in the cross. Amongst the dozens and dozens of thoughtful and loving cards and letters we receive from people after Luka's death (some who we'd never met) is one which fells me. It asks us to take solace in the fact that Luka is 'in a better place'. I'd still like to hear them tell me what place they could be thinking of, somewhere better than in the loving arms of his parents?

I wish I could say compassion washed over me after such a loss, that it visited me with a light touch on the shoulder and made me connect with the pain and suffering of the whole world. Fuck acceptance, impermanence. Enlightenment, I thought. Fuck Buddha, fuck Christ, and fuck a God who would put such a high price on my spiritual education. What could I possibly learn from this that would be worth that much?

Without a God to save me, I cast around for demons to blame for my cursed state. I picked on John Howard. That part was easy. He was the symbol of everything that was wrong with the world. A small-minded, mean-spirited man who wanted to drag my country back to the picket-fenced, whitebread certainty of the 1950s. The debate over the stolen generation babbled on over the airwaves in that parallel universe others knew as 'the real world'. I now knew better than most what it felt like to have a child stolen from you. 'Say "sorry" to those people, you weak prick,' I found myself screaming at the prime minister's visage on television. 'Plenty of people said sorry to me.'

Why would I want to bring a child into a world run by such fools, bound-up in fear of difference, fear of change, drowning in numbers, ruled by economists? My anger is obviously getting the better of me and has to be directed somewhere more useful.

The sessions with my grief counsellor help. I am liberated

by our wild and free-ranging conversations on the nature of being, of parenting, of loving, of hurting, of death and afterlife. He reassures me it is sadness, not depression, I am stuck in the middle of. The more sadness that enters our lives, he tells me, the bigger capacity for joy also. It was a 'shift in thinking', a 'refocus' I found extremely comforting. It's something I now know to be true.

The other thing he asks of me, though, is much more difficult. What I crave so desperately is the lost relationship with my son. I need to find ways of getting to know him, of keeping him alive in my thoughts. I am terrified of forgetting. I need 'Luka time', he advises me, time I would normally have spent perhaps walking on the beach, holding his hand, showing him the world, talking to him, playing in the sand.

At times this felt like playing along with a too-cruel hoax upon myself. Was it crazy to try to get to know a dead baby, pretend to watch him grow, show him all the things we would have done together? Sundays work best. Sunday will always be sacred, Luka's day. We play the cassette tape of 'Songs For Luka' we made after his death. It begins with REM's Michael Stipe singing 'Everybody hurts, everybody cries, everybody hurts sometimes'.

Grief is chaotic moments of extreme highs and lows. Some wear it like a badge, some wield it like an axe, some keep it in a tightly sealed jar in the deep freeze. I read something Anna Maria Dell'oso wrote about 'the high plains of grief' where 'the bereft' gather, people whose grief seems too immense. I know it well. It's the feeling of having slipped into a parallel universe, still spinning in the same direction as everyone else, but the atmosphere is different. It's a lonely place where the air is thin and you learn to breathe in shallow sips. There are times when things seem quite normal, only nothing is quite the same. There is no turning back, although I've wished it many times in the last three years.

The knife-edge in my gut has gone now. No one can live in that raw state forever. But in its place is a dull ache, a deeper and unchainable vessel that stills lurches at the dock of my being, smashing its defences with erratic timing.

Ours is still one of the saddest stories I have ever heard. To be actually in it is confusing, overwhelming at times, surreal at others, even comforting. Nothing as bad could ever happen again.

This new credo seems to work for a while, at least until our next pregnancy when fear creeps back and takes up residence in our house like an unwanted backpacker. Our innocence has been lost forever. Despite what anyone says, the only thing we really know is that no one can promise what the outcome will be.

Most days I feel the burden of living with the saddest story. Friends reassure us we are strong, brave, courageous. It sounds like they're talking about somebody else. Most times I feel I'm treading water, just keeping my head from going under. I wave at the people on the shore who wave back when maybe I'm really trying to tell them I'm drowning.

I cry less often now but when the tears come sometimes it feels like they might never stop. I've started singing again. It helps mend the soul. Our new son Finn turns one in a few weeks. I've bought myself a new guitar and have been putting the final touches to a song about his birth. He's a captive audience and most easy to please. My ego is metering at dangerously high levels. Perhaps my rock star days aren't over after all.

Being a new parent is the best and hardest thing I've ever done. It has made me a better person, taught me more than I could imagine. And, for me, there is some comfort in the chaos. I am learning to celebrate the uncertainty of life, to run ahead of it so it doesn't run me down. When it does, I scream at it with all my heart and sing a song in sweet surrender. I'm a lucky man, after all.

# MY BEAUTIFUL GIRL

## Rachel

I had my first daughter when I was nineteen. At that stage I'd never wanted children at all—who does at nineteen? At the same time, I never wanted Jasmine to be an only child; I hoped that one day I'd have more kids and she'd have brothers or sisters. But after I had Jasmine I thought, 'OK, I've got a beautiful baby, I love her'—and then I got on with my life. I'm a very independent person, I always wanted a career or to do well at whatever I was doing. It wasn't until I accidentally fell pregnant the second time, had an ectopic pregnancy and lost it, that I realised how happy I was to be pregnant again. And from then on I thought, 'I want to have another child', and my husband was the same.

I was OK losing that pregnancy because I'd known that there was something wrong from the beginning. I didn't have any of the pregnancy symptoms I'd had before when I was pregnant with Jasmine, I didn't feel sick—I just didn't feel pregnant; and then the day I was told I had an ectopic pregnancy, I had to have an operation to have part of my tube removed. It was a shock going into the surgery but I honestly felt it was too early to feel a great loss. I hadn't really bonded with the idea of being pregnant and when I lost it, I think my husband was more distressed than I was. I didn't have enough time to be upset because I was in pain. I accepted that the ectopic was something that happened to me and it wasn't my fault.

I had to wait three months until after the operation before I could try to have another baby, and after another few months I was starting to get really, really anxious. Each time I got my period I would get upset and I started thinking, 'God, I'm not going to get pregnant, maybe the ectopic's wrecked my chances.' That's when I started really feeling the desperation to have another baby. So I went and saw a midwife.

We switched days and four weeks later I found out I was pregnant and I just couldn't believe it. It was great; I almost instantly had morning sickness, I actually felt pregnant, and I was optimistic. But I also didn't want to be too excited about it. After an ectopic you have to wait eight or nine weeks to make sure it's not another one, so we had to get through that, and then we had to get past the first three months because of the chances of miscarrying in that time. But we got through the ectopic stage—OK it was in the uterus, not in the tube; that was great. A few weeks later we got past the twelve weeks and we started to relax, but we didn't tell anyone except close family until I was about sixteen weeks. By then my morning sickness had settled and I was getting bigger, and I felt the baby kicking quite early. We thought this was it, and we couldn't get over how happy we were.

We knew from sixteen weeks that we were having a girl, which we were over the moon about because we really wanted two girls; it was important to me for Jasmine to have a sister because I hadn't had that. We'd given her a name and even though nobody else knew the name and nobody else knew that she was a girl, we both knew. With us, she was a person; she had an identity.

I couldn't believe that something so good was actually happening to us. We were all prepared. Our whole lives changed because of it. From being really sociable people, and social drinkers as well, as soon as we got pregnant we were happy to stop having so much of a social life. We were more concerned with the family, what were we going to do with the house and stuff like that. So when I was about thirty-eight weeks pregnant we were actually finalising things and getting a few things done around the house, getting things ready before I had the baby.

Up until then I'd gone to Alukura, the local Indigenous women's health centre, and because I'd worked there I felt very comfortable there. In the last four weeks I started going to the hospital and I felt really exposed because I was seeing people who didn't know me. I think I felt that maybe something was going to go wrong. Even though I'd been feeling that everything was so good, in hindsight there was this underlying feeling that things weren't really going to be all right.

Part of this was because of my dreams. I never saw my baby's face in any of my dreams. When I was pregnant before, I'd seen details of how Jasmine looked, but when I was pregnant with Chloe I didn't see those things. Consciously it meant nothing to me, but I think subconsciously something was telling me, *It's not going to be all right*. I think being Aboriginal that this is important. We believe that there are signs that tell us things and for me, my dreams were a sign. Plus, my husband's twin brother was coming down and because of this twin thing, there are these unexplained things that happen. I said to my husband, 'Maybe we're going to have the baby early.' We hadn't seen him throughout the whole pregnancy and I felt as if he was coming down for a reason. In the end he was here to give my husband support. My husband doesn't have any family here and he was only supposed to be coming overnight, but in the end he was with my husband when the hospital rang to say that there was no heartbeat.

But before that I was at home sitting at the computer and all of a sudden I felt so sick. I went into this panic. I just knew something was wrong—I hadn't felt the baby move and I panicked. It's like when there's been an accident and your mind is racing. I felt numb. I sat there and told myself, 'Don't panic, don't panic, it's all right, she's just sleeping', because Chloe was an extremely active baby. She would kick and kick and I remembered the last time I'd actually felt her kicking had been the previous afternoon and I thought, 'Shit, surely she couldn't have, surely I couldn't have not known that she hasn't kicked'. So I went into my room and I lay down and prodded my stomach where I always felt her little arms were, and I pushed down on what I think was her arm, pushed down on it and I felt it slowly come back up. I knew then there was something wrong because when I'd done that any other time, she would kick back—I would feel a response.

So I rang Alukura, and it was funny because the receptionist was one of my best friends, and she was pregnant at the same time. We were really happy that we were both pregnant together, and when I rang up, the first thing she said to me was, 'What's wrong? Is something wrong?' I don't know if it was my voice or what it was, but she knew that something was wrong and then I spoke to the midwife and told her I hadn't felt the baby move for a while, and she said, 'Don't panic, it might be all right.'

I'd read somewhere that sometimes when babies get bigger and have less room they don't move so much and if that happens, just go in and hear the heartbeat and everything is fine. But when I got to Alukura, for ten minutes they couldn't find anything. I knew then. That's when I went into shock. I completely shut down and the midwife said, 'Don't panic. Let's go to the hospital' and she said they would probably find the heartbeat when we got there. So we went up there and she put the ECG on, and she couldn't find anything and for about ten minutes she kept trying. Then she got a doctor and they said, 'Look, we need to send you down for an ultrasound.'

When they said I needed the ultrasound I knew it was to confirm that she wasn't alive anymore, and the first thing I thought was, 'How am I going to tell Jasmine and my mum and everybody?' I felt like I'd let everybody down. I felt, God, she's not alive anymore, how am I going to tell them, how are they going to act? And they'll probably think that it's my fault. I didn't even look at the ultrasound screen, I couldn't because, having seen her alive and kicking and then nothing, I just couldn't look. The first thing I said to my husband was, 'How do I tell Jasmine?' How do I tell a seven-year-old kid that her baby sister is not alive anymore?' She isn't going to be a big sister—I mean, she will be a sister but her sister is not going to be alive. She's not going to take her sister home. The things we said we were going to do when I brought her home, how our lives were going to change—we weren't going to do that. We'd even spoken about what it would be like when Chloe was older, and I just had no idea how I was going to explain it to Jasmine. In the end, luckily, it was my mum who picked Jasmine up and told her.

Anyway, then I had to go through being induced. They gave us the option of going home and thinking about it, or picking up some stuff and coming straight back to the hospital. I just couldn't stay home, knowing that I was pregnant—and looked pregnant to everybody else—and my baby wasn't even alive. I just wanted to go and get my things and get going. So we came home and got our things and we told my mum, and that was difficult.

I spent Friday afternoon being induced and not having her till two days later, on Sunday at six-thirty in the morning. It was very, very slow because I hadn't had a vaginal birth before; with my first daughter I'd had a caesarean. The birth was actually a really positive thing, because even though I was in shock, and she wasn't alive, I got to carry out the birth the way I wanted, the way that I'd planned. I don't know how, but I was assertive enough to say, 'This is what I want to do'. And I did it; and when I had her, not having experienced it before, I couldn't believe how mentally I was just on another level and when I was giving birth to her, I didn't think she was dead. Afterwards my husband was there, his mother, my mother and we also had Jasmine. We really wanted Jasmine to be there because we wanted to be completely open with her about what had happened and I think doing that made it a lot easier on her. She was able to accept and see. For a little seven-year-old girl, she handled it so well.

We all held Chloe, but at that stage I was so exhausted I was really holding her because I thought, 'This is what I should do.' I held her and spent some time looking at her, but I was so tired, all I wanted to do was sleep. Then we asked them to take Chloe away and I went to sleep.

I was absolutely tired. I hadn't slept for three days. I was in total shock; I don't think I even started the grieving process then. It wasn't until I'd slept all of Sunday and woken up on Sunday afternoon that I thought, 'I had a baby and that's all I want.' And not having her was the hardest thing, because it isn't a mental thing, it's an instinct. I never realised how strong, how strong the maternal instinct is. What tells your body, or what tells you, you want your baby. You've gone through birth, you want your baby—and it just wasn't possible.

First you realise she's not alive and then you start thinking about everybody else, and I never really thought about myself. At that stage I put up this self-protective barrier where I told myself I had to be strong: OK, it's happened, accept it, you've got no choice. Do what you have to do. You just have to get along with your life again. That's how I've dealt with it when anything difficult has happened in my life and I was so wrong. I found out later, the more barriers I put up the harder it was for me to come to terms with what happened and really let it go. I never realised how I was going to feel in the future, how I was going to feel in six weeks' time, six months', in a year's time—I had no idea how goddamn hard it was going to be.

My biggest thing was the guilt; there was so much that contributed to me feeling guilty. One was the way that things were handled at the hospital. My guilt was compounded because I felt I wasn't told enough. I didn't realise that I could dress her, put her in the things I'd already bought her; I just didn't know. I think that there was so much more that could have been done to make things easier and the guilt that, as a mother and as a wife, I'd let my husband down and I'd let Jasmine down was enormous. Not that anyone blamed me— the support I had was unbelievable.

I felt all the medical procedures were explained properly to me. I understood what was happening to me, the way they explained it to me was great. But I think they were able to do that because they understand the procedures—I don't think they really got what I was going through emotionally. They didn't seem to understand that this was someone who had already bonded with their baby. They were very caring, but in terms of explaining how you might react to it and letting you know there are things that you can do that in the end will make your grieving process easier, they were terrible. Chloe's death was made harder because those things weren't explained properly. Death is so final. When you realise she's dead, you have to make decisions when you are in shock. There are really important decisions you have to make and they have to be the right ones at that time, because if they are not the right ones, later on you can't change it. When I woke up, and I realised, Shit, it's happened, it's not a nightmare; all this has really occurred—that's when I realised, That's my baby and I've lost her. And I told my husband that I wanted to see her, I wanted to hold her. But by the time I did, she was frozen.

That was a difficult thing, seeing her like that. I was really frightened. I took a bit of time, I looked at her and that's when the grieving process set in.

That was fourteen months ago. We still don't know exactly why she died. When she was born she had the cord wrapped around her neck twice and it was very, very tight. The midwife really struggled to get it off. The autopsy wasn't a hundred per cent confirmed but they said that the spots that she had on her lungs were consistent with asphyxiation, so it was likely that she'd been strangled by the cord. The midwife said she was positive it had been the cord.

But when I found out that she wasn't alive I automatically thought, 'What have I done?' I had a glass of wine when I was pregnant; and for a while I had a blocked nose and I thought maybe it was the nasal spray, or maybe it was swimming in the pool and bouncing her up and down. I just thought I was to blame. I thought I had done something to contribute to her death even when they said to me, 'You know with the majority of cases they don't have a cause of death, babies just seem to die.' I couldn't believe that, I couldn't understand that, I couldn't understand, Why a baby? How could a baby die before it's even born? What a cruel thing to do to somebody, how can you let somebody get pregnant, let them carry it for this long and then all of a sudden say, 'You're not going to be a mum and dad any more'?

For Indigenous women the rate of infant deaths, stillbirths and neo-natal deaths and miscarriage is very, very high, but a lot of factors come into that, like with Aboriginal health in general. It's a common thing in the community that Aboriginal women, especially here in Alice Springs, experience the loss of a baby. But when it happens within your own family it's different. Our family is quite small compared to other Aboriginal families and there are strong expectations about having children. We were the only ones who had just one child for so long. It was like, 'Come on, you have to have another child.' I really felt the expectations—all my mum's Aboriginal family have got loads of kids, some of them have got sixteen grandchildren, and my mum has only one. It's unheard of. I wanted my mother to be a grandmother again, I wanted my daughter to have a brother or sister, my husband to be a father. In losing Chloe I felt like I'd let everybody down.

We've had really good support, though. When I left the hospital that night and came home and the house was covered in flowers, we were overwhelmed. That was good, that really helped. It made me realise that people really acknowledged that it was a loss, that we loved her and we lost her.

But at the start I shut everybody out except immediate family. I didn't want to see anybody. Being Aboriginal I've got a fairly big family. I've got a lot of cousins and aunties and all of that, who were very supportive, but I just couldn't, I just couldn't see them. Seeing them crying and them being sorry, and the hugs and all that was really, I think, acknowledging that this had happened—and I hadn't yet. I hadn't really come to terms with it, and being home and doing practical things like the service and all of that was accepting that it had happened, and I don't think I was really ready for it. My first instinct was to say, 'OK, it's happened; just leave me alone, I'll work it out.' The biggest thing for me was not having any control. We didn't know how to get on with life. I was on my maternity leave—do I have to go back to work? Do I still get paid? What happens with Jasmine? What do I do with all these questions going around my head?

I've found the way that Aboriginal people deal with grief is so much more expressive than non-Indigenous people. I'd walk down the street and run into a non-Indigenous person I've known most of my life or worked with for so long, and I would tell them and they would have no idea what to say. But I could run into somebody who was a work colleague and not very close, an Aboriginal person, and they would hug me and kiss me, and it made me feel much better. I knew that they were showing that they cared and that they were really genuinely sorry.

I had four months off after I lost Chloe and even six months later I would see people and they would say, 'How are you going, what did you have, a boy or a girl?' and to tell them was a really hard thing. But I wanted to talk about her and acknowledge that she was our daughter. Acknowledge that she existed.

I think there are things that we did that made things a lot easier. Cremating her was a really good thing for us. She's at home where she's supposed to be, she's with her mum and her dad and her sister. We wanted to have her with us no matter where we lived. Both our parents are religiously minded so having a service was really important to them. Initially I was totally opposed to the idea, but once we had the service I felt we'd said goodbye and we'd been really respectful to her. It took a long time to organise though; it was six weeks until after the autopsy.

I knew I was never going to replace her, but immediately afterwards I just wanted to have another baby. Three months later I got pregnant, and it just was the worst thing I could've done. I ended up sick and miscarrying at twelve weeks. It was too early, I was still too raw. But it really didn't affect me the way I thought it would; even though it was another loss it felt minor compared to losing Chloe. I was upset, but I think it really made me realise I had to be ready emotionally before I have another baby.

Once I accepted that, I made an agreement with myself that grieving is a process. I knew I was going to be so sad, I didn't know how long for, and I also knew that while I wasn't going to get over Chloe's death, I'd learn to live with it. I also accepted that I've got to get on with it. I've still got a life, I've still got a daughter, I've still got a husband. But fourteen months later, it's still hard.

There are things I do that make it easier. I've got her little quilt that I love, and her footprints, and I've got photos of our daughter and every time I look at them I cry. I used to look at them every day, I'd end up sneaking off to look at the photos.

At least I can never ever forget what she looks like.

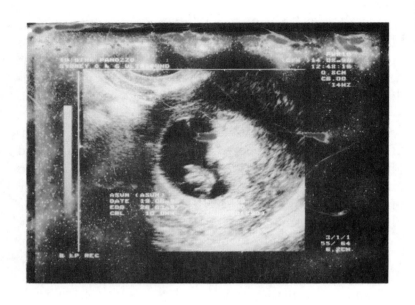

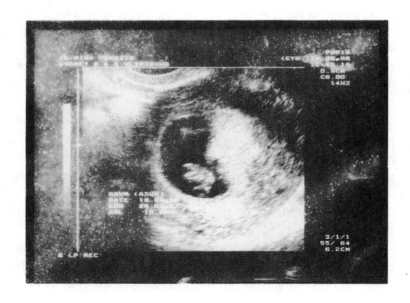

# CRY BABY

Dina Panozzo

### Shock

My boom boom baby
There she is
Boom boom boom.

My heart stops...
No. Her heart stops!

I stop dead,
she's dead!

My lovely boom-boom girl.
Heart beating in my throat.
Boom boom boom.

Heart torn out. Broken heart.
Like yours baby boom-boom.

Baby don't cry,
Mamma's coming too.

Flesh of my flesh 'Betrayed by my flesh, the biggest betrayal of all'

Flesh of my flesh
Seven years of wishes
Seven years of trying
Four babies dying
Dina – Dina crying

### What's up, Doc?

Well, doctor, I feel well enough, everything is working, it's just...I've got this ache, this feeling of betrayal somehow. You can have them well into your forties, they said. That's what women do these days. Not the full story, was it? Everyone's doing it later, they said. Betrayed! Stupid, stupid, stupid me. I believed it. But it's the *exception* to the rule, isn't it? Not the rule! I'm not the exception, am I? My third baby died as well.

Well doctor, I'm *Italian par la morte di dio.* I can't be childless! Did you know that Italy's population growth is zero? Zero...nothing, *niente*, yes, we have no tomatoes today! Minus zero, is that possible doctor? And it's Pope country too.

I've got a cat called Monkey. A jumpy kinda kitty. A little creature. Bought her secretly from the world after I'd lost my second baby. Mothered her instead. In bed with us, little kitty, I'd hold her above our heads and say 'yes...yes...little baby, *bella creatura mia.* Do you love your mummy and daddy?' She'd go 'meow' and 'purrp...purrp' with her arms outstretched, pupils wide, legs hanging, soft little leather paws. Looking hard into her eyes for some deeper recognition, I was.

Squeezing her a little tighter. I wanted more.

'That's it. That's all she does, Dina. It's a cat.' Meow.

Pathetic, ah?

### Dead Loss—Pisa

Four babies lost. Last one in Venice. Why Italy? I was born here. I love Italy. Venice Film Festival. I'm playing movie star. Standing ovation for twenty minutes! Desperate drive back to my village with my sister to find mad cousin Elio. Reminds me of Papa. His wild horse. Forcing us to ride him. Eating baby goat freshly killed that morning. My poor sister Bella a vegetarian! She sings Papa's opera. It soothes the savage breast. Grappa bubbling. Blood dripping. Drive to Florence hospital. Ultrasound. No heartbeat!

*(A very long pause)*

Phillip and I fall apart. I hate Italy now. Get outta here. The Devil at Medici Travel Agency takes my money and forgets to fix French visa.

Must get to Paris. Have to fight for visa at consulate—no time. Making up any stories they want just so I can get out. 'I lost my baby.'

'That's a normal tragedy.'

'Sorry, it has to be more dangerous because we are breaking the rules.'

Make up hellish and wild stories in half an hour. 'My sister's in grave danger.'

'What danger?'

'Well, there are men there. Yes. Bad men ... Threatening her.'

Like this! I squeeze my fingers around Phillip's neck—oops! Impressed with my acting, they give in. Deadline. End of day. Pick up tickets from Medicis. Pick up by 7 pm in Pisa? But we're in Florence! Two-hour drive and only one hour to get there.

Freak storm hits Florence. Superstrada accident on news. Highway closed! Take the long road. Drive like demons. Even death. Get to Pisa. Locked on circle route. Spiralling. We can see the airport and the Leaning Tower. Can't get off the circle! The Tower leaning further each time round. Get there. Rain. Run madly. Last chance to escape the horror of Italy. Got to get on that plane. Run. Run. Fall to knees in the rain. Look to heavens. Give up. Give up Dina. Crying. No. No. Run, run!

Reach the counter of Pisa private airport. Smiling Italians. Relaxed. All OK. Don't shut till everyone boards. 9 pm! Aahh, salvation in Pisa. *Un miracolo!* A miracle escape.


### Fuck fertility

Like a dark secret close to my chest, I play it again, that paranoid card. Flunk! On the table. I go and see The Last Ditch Specialist Professor M—Fertility Specialist Extraordinaire. Top of the crop he is, the best south of the equator they say. A god really. We're in his Macquarie Street office, high up, and I'm looking for the last word on all of this fertility stuff. How small is the window left for me, at forty-three with four babies lost? What's left?

I'm looking for something new, I tell him. I want new information, give me a word, something new to hang on. There must be a word on all this. Give me a reason. Give me some hope. Give me life!

This'll be great. I know it'll be great, I say to Phillip. No more, 'You're getting old, you left your run a little late...did you try Chinese herbs? Naish's Pregnancy Diet? Cut the carrots, swallow the folate, rub the yam, plant the passionfruit. Do the tests, all the tests, sperm, blood, tubes, ovaries, womb, oestrogen, progestogen, family histories. *Really* want it, pray to God, dream the baby, be with pregnant women, rub their babies. Act pregnant, act old, very old, act retired, shuffle, cut the stress, cut the whine, cut the yearning, go to bed, cut the bed. IVF stats in my face...at thirty-eight a 15 per cent chance, thirty-nine 10 per cent, forty 7 per cent, forty-one half of that, forty-two well, fuck, you're too old.

*Gravida vechiavadis* to you too! 'Science' he says...and he should know I thought...yes, yes, that's it, give me something. At $300 a pop I deserve a sign. Phillip's paid $160 just to sit in and watch, for fuck's sake!

He draws on a big white quarto-sized piece of paper, upside down. That's pretty smart for a start, I thought, draws circles for us. Cells. And lots of little dots circling the cell circles. He announces these are 'mitochondria'. *Yes!* That's it, that's the new word, that's what we obviously need to understand I thought. *Mitochondria.* Ah ha! Dignity at last, a real scientific word. The facts at last. Chemistry here. Opening up new possibilities. 'Yes, yes, tell us more,' I say excitedly. He demonstrates with his Mont Blanc pen, giving it a top-notch feel, that these little spotted circles are energy, zooming round and round the cells, protecting and nurturing the eggs. The mitochondria is what gives the eggs their verve. Zipping along through your life, until they start to slow down, losing their bounce, their spark, dropping the bundle so to speak. A bit like my pupils at that point, small and dead. No spark left, just a dull idea, a dull dead ache. No pop.

I lean across the desk and say, 'So, prof, what you're saying is I'm getting old? Is that it? Is that what you're saying?' All this for 300 bucks! It all stopped dead. In some way I wanted it all to stop. Dead. But instead I said, 'So this is where my story ends, huh?'

We're all silent. 'There is, of course, one last option.' My pupils widen. Pop... 'A donor egg.'

Phillip jerks his knee into my leg... 'Let's not go there.'

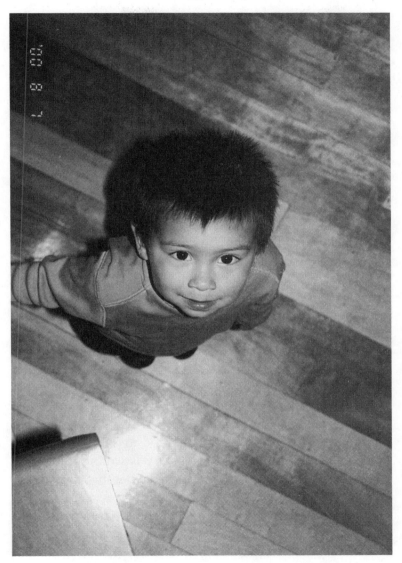

Our son Luis. Born 9 May 1998 in Guatamala, arrived Sydney, Australia 25 June 2000.

# MADDIE

## Sahara Herald Shepherd

The pregnancy was one of the most difficult things I've ever been through. It so shattered my illusions of pregnancy. I'd thought that it was going to be this maternal ideal of growth and beauty and at one with the baby. I just vomited every day during the whole pregnancy. I became really demoralised by it, because when I went to the doctor and midwife they were like, 'Oh, it'll end at twelve weeks'. Twelve weeks went by and then it was, 'Oh it'll end at thirteen, it'll end at fourteen. Oh, no one ever vomits past sixteen weeks.' I tried various alternative medicines, from Chinese herbs to acupuncture, to naturo-pathic. Nothing helped and it became very frustrating for me, because it was like, 'Oh, have you tried ginger tea?' and it was just like, if one more person mentions ginger tea ... I've got ginger tea coming out of my arse.

People were kind of dismissive of it until they actually saw me vomit and saw how violent it was. I would have vomit coming out of my nose. And I knocked myself out twice on the porcelain of the toilet because it was so rough. I started feeling, not negative towards the baby, but negative towards the pregnancy in general. But none of the doctors seemed to be worried because I was gaining weight and the baby seemed to be healthy and all the ultrasounds and everything were fine, and no one seemed to give it a second thought.

In hindsight, you think of things that happened. I was down in Bondi and I was walking down to the bakery, and this guy walked past me dressed up like a hippy hobo, and he looked quite mad. Anyway, I got out of the car and was walking past him, and he clapped and pointed at my stomach, and said, 'You're dead', and kept walking. I flipped out, I was really upset.

68

I brooded on that for a couple of days, and I never told Brad, and I still haven't.

Then this series of events happened right at the end, where I began to feel more and more distressed. We went to the hospital to check out the birthing centre. My mum was there, Brad, and my private midwife that we'd hired, because I'd been feeling so miserable we got someone specifically to look after me. I burst into tears, and I said, 'How far along do I have to be before they might induce me?' She kind of looked at me oddly, and asked why. I said, 'I just don't want it to go on any longer'. She said, 'Well they're not going to induce you early unless there's some indication'. I didn't have a feeling that there was something wrong, but I wanted the baby to be out of me.

A friend bought me a book. I read the jacket and it said there was an interview in there with a friend of mine, Sue. The last time I'd seen her, I'd driven past as she was walking down the street, and she was pregnant. I thought, oh wonderful, I want to read Sue's story. So on the Sunday night I got into bed and read it. And I wasn't aware that her baby had died. I was so heartbroken, I wanted to ring her right then. I had a big pile of books next to my bed, and it was the first time I'd ever actually opened the sections in the back on what happens if your baby dies. It's this really inane information that's completely useless. Anyway, I went to bed that night and I had a very sad heart, but I woke up the next day, and I felt really good. I thought, maybe I've come to the end. I went out to lunch with Ken. He said, 'You seem to be much happier today'. I said, 'It's the best I've felt the whole pregnancy'.

I went home and I was on the phone with my girlfriend Zai, who'd just had her baby two weeks before. She said she'd been reading that quite often when a baby dies in utero the doctor might ask the mother when was the last time they felt the baby move. I was silent for a moment, and she went, 'What's wrong?' I was like, 'I can't remember Maddie moving today.' So I got off the phone and I said something to Brad, and he said, 'Oh no, everything's fine. If you're worried, give the midwife a ring in the morning'. So I went and had a bath. She loved it when I was in the water; it felt as though she was having a swim too.

And there was nothing. By this time I was starting to get quite distressed, so we rang our midwife and went straight to her place. She got out her instruments to listen for the heart-beat and there was nothing. She said, 'Maybe the baby's in an odd position or something. Let's not panic, let's just go straight to the hospital'.

Brad and I hopped into our car and we went over a couple of speed bumps, and I said 'I think maybe she moved'. I was desperate for there to be something. I think I knew already in my heart. By this time it was 11 pm. They put the machine on and I'd had enough ultrasounds during the pregnancy, as soon as I looked up at the screen I knew there was nothing. She was just lying there. There was no heartbeat. I turned away and I lay on the bed, and I looked up in the registrar's eyes, and she had her eye on the screen and she kept moving the ultrasound around, looking. Then she looked down at me and her eyes welled up with tears and she shook her head. I started wailing. It was so surreal because they all went out and left me alone with Brad, and we were in this really kind of generic hospital room, and the walls were this sickly nothing colour. There was this moment where I thought, 'Oh man, this is the worst night-mare I've ever had. Come on, wake up, wake up.' But it was real.

My immediate reaction was that I just wanted them to cut her out. She's dead, I don't want her in there. The staff talked it through with me. They seemed to be making excuses, and having spoken to them subsequently, I know what it was now. Quite often if women don't go through the proper birth process they never quite recover from the experience—not that I think you ever do. Because if you have a caesarean it's kind of like going to the dentist and getting a bad tooth pulled. And the other thing was that caesareans are a major operation, and they didn't really want me to have a higher risk in subse-quent pregnancies. So Brad and I went home and it was the loneliest night of our lives. Heart-aching. To go back to our nice big comfy bed where we'd made her and to lie there with her inside me, knowing that she was dead. To lie there and think about what we still had ahead of us. Then to think about how to ring our parents, and tell them that all their hopes and dreams were shattered too. So we didn't have much sleep that night. Then we got up and had to start making the phone calls. Just horrible, horrible. I was full term so everyone's expecting you to ring them with good news.

It was decided that I'd be induced and go through the full labour process, which was really fucking with my head. To have to go through what as a first time mother you're so incredibly scared of, knowing there's not going to be any reward at the end. My mum stayed with us through the whole birth, massaging me, and I think it must have been especially hard for her—and for my dad too—having to watch me, their baby, go through it.

Suddenly I was in labour, and was still doing all the things that we'd learned in birth class and that I'd read about. Brad was wonderful, incredibly supportive and encouraging, but it got to a certain point where it's like, 'Whoa, this is really hurting'. Obviously at this point nothing we did was going to affect the baby, so we decided that my comfort would be the priority. I had an epidural, which was something I'd always been against. It was sensational. I can't recommend it highly enough. I fell asleep for about four or five hours, and then I woke up and I was fully dilated. From when her head descended it only took me about twenty or thirty minutes to actually push her out. And there she was. She was very tightly bound up in her cord. They unravelled her and we thought that was what had happened, she'd got tangled in her cord, and cut off her own blood supply.

Brad had caught her as she emerged and cut her cord once it was untangled. He lifted her up on to my chest, and she was warm and soft and big, and there was this very brief moment where I thought, 'Oh you've all made a terrible mistake'. I was waiting for her to open her eyes and look up at me. Willing it to happen. But she lay there and she was limp. I looked at her and she was so beautiful. I know every parent thinks their child's beautiful, but she was just so angelic and peaceful. I lay there looking at her and I was kind of calm for a moment, and then it hit me and I let out the most tortured howl. You never think that you're going to have pain like this in your life. That you're going to be sitting in a hospital, covered in blood, holding your dead child in your arms. Nothing can prepare you for that. I take some comfort sometimes in thinking that she never suffered. That all she knew was the inside of my tummy and her mum and dad's voice. I like to think that being inside your mother's womb is like being in the best hotel in town. You've got everything laid on, room service, everything. I hope that's all she ever knew.

Anyway, we cleaned her up and our parents came in to see her. It was a very sad time. We laid her out with everyone around us and we dressed her in the clothes that we'd brought with us. My parents were madly taking photos, which seemed a bit intrusive at the time, but I treasure those photos so much now. We washed her together, and we did prints of her hands and her feet. And cut off a little lock of her hair. It was very kind of ritualistic in some ways, and it took on a lot of importance to try and do it properly. To actually spend that time with her and record her. Because there's a lot of feeling generally among people who don't know better that if a baby isn't born alive or dies in the first week or something, that they don't really exist. But it's just not true. She was inside me, and boy, was she alive. She was already a part of our lives and she was certainly a part of our future that we'd been planning and our hopes and our dreams. And that's what was also lost. By the next morning when we woke up, she was quite blue and cold, and we could accept that that was just her body and that she as a person wasn't there. It was very hard leaving the hospital, leaving her there.

We had a full funeral for her. People were like, 'Oh I guess you just want your family there'. I said, 'No, I want everyone I know there, because I need to have her acknowledged, as a person, and as a terrible, terrible loss.' In life you know you're going to lose your grandparents, and your parents. Obviously you don't want to have it happen, but that's kind of how it works. But losing a child is just different, it's wrong. It's like the natural order of things has been fucked up. I think it's the hardest thing that anyone has to do, to bury their child.

Organising the funeral was terribly difficult. Neither Brad nor I are religious by any stretch of the imagination. After what we'd just been through, we were certainly questioning the existence of anything fair. But then you get into, well, just in case there is, I'll pray to everybody just to look after her. There ended up being about 120 people at the funeral and we'd organised a hotel around the corner to have a bar tab and some food. And that was good. But the morning of the funeral, Brad and I sat down to make a CD of music. I mean there's somewhere you think you're never going to be. Picking out music for your child's funeral. Brad kind of laboured on, being the musician in the family. We picked out three songs and I don't think I can ever listen to them again now. They're Maddie's songs. It'd just break my heart to hear them.

We picked 'Forever Young'—Bob Dylan, 'Box of Rain' by The Grateful Dead, and the one I chose was 'Brass Buttons', the Gram Parsons version, which he actually wrote about his mother. It's got this line in it that says, 'And the sun comes up without her, it just doesn't know she's gone'. It's just so true. It's like the world keeps turning and the sun does keep coming up and it keeps setting, and meanwhile you're broken-hearted and in a state of disbelief. At the funeral both our dads got up and said some words and Brad's best friend Jeff read a poem. Then I got up and spoke, which shocked everybody. There were things that I wanted to say and that I wanted people to hear. So I got up and poured my heart out. I'd just given birth two days before. My milk came in that morning. And yet I didn't have a baby to feed. I wanted to tell people how much I loved Brad, too. How important he was to me and how proud I was of him for being so brave and being so strong for me. And then—and this is probably one of the saddest images I'll ever have in my life, Brad picked up her coffin, just this tiny little white coffin—so small—and he carried it out himself and put it in the car to go out to the crematorium. We kissed her goodbye, kissed the coffin, put big lippy marks all over it. We didn't go to the crematorium. Just wanted to end it there.

We found out some stuff about what happened that really shocked us. We thought it was a simple cord accident. But we got the pathology back about two months later and that showed a really high level of bile salt in my blood, which is indicative of a condition called obstetric cholestasis. It's a malfunction of the liver that occurs in the last trimester of pregnancy, and if it goes undetected and the pregnancy goes past thirty-seven weeks, it has a very high incidence of still-birth. They're not sure exactly why it happens but the malfunction of the mother's liver causes a biochemical reaction with the baby, which makes the baby's heart stop beating. Finding that out was devastating because it means I had this condition that could have been detected with a simple blood test. We would have known and we could have got her out and she would have been okay. Brad found that especially hard. Because he'd kind of accepted the cord thing as like being struck by lightning. But this was something entirely different. We really tortured ourselves with that, and we went through feeling very bitter towards every doctor or midwife we'd seen. But I didn't have a classic presentation of the condition. It usually causes very strong itching on the hands or feet, which I didn't have at all, although I had insane itching on my stomach, where I was tearing at my skin. I wasn't particularly concerned about the itching, because the book that I looked it up in said itching on the stomach is normal during pregnancy because the skin is stretching so much. But it's like what's done is done with Madeline. She's dead. There's no use torturing ourselves or going, 'If only you'd done this'. We can't save her, but we can save our next baby.

So I became very adamant that I wanted to find out everything I could about the condition. Because I never wanted to be in the position again where a doctor or midwife could be dismissive of me. After doing weeks of research on the Internet—because there's very little information about it even though it is quite common—I found an article out of America that suggested that one of the possible symptoms was vomiting. When they first gave us the results I asked the doctor what causes the malfunction of the liver and he said hormones, oestrogen. I said, 'Don't the high levels of oestrogen cause vomiting and nausea?' And he said, 'Yes, but the two aren't linked'. I was like, 'How can you say that? They might not be caused by each other, but they've got a link there because they're caused by the same thing'. Right then I knew that was one of the signs. But it's still early days of research which they haven't quantified and qualified. So in some ways I kind of felt vindicated. It ain't going to change it, but it makes me feel okay about another pregnancy. I'm scared about it, but I feel strong, because I know what the problem is. There's something there that we can control, that we can test for, that we can do something about.

Thinking about having another child, it just opens up so many Pandora's boxes really. I had this incredibly overwhelming desire to have a baby right now, I want to get pregnant right now, I want to have a baby. I'm sure part of that was hormonal. My breasts were leaking everywhere and I felt this physical ache in my gut. I felt so empty. I'd gone through this whole long process of making a baby and yet I didn't have one. My body didn't really seem to know that. My breasts still leak every now and again now, when I think about her. But Brad couldn't even contemplate it. I went through a very weird thing with Brad, feeling that I'd led him down this disastrous path in a way, because when we were first living together he was quite adamant that he didn't want to have children. Then as the years went on, I wore him down. We've reached the point now where we definitely want to have another child. But we really wanted to avoid having a baby that was going to be due around the same time as Maddie, because it would just mess with our heads too much. So we thought we need to have the time to actually grieve, to regain some strength, for me physically, and for both of us mentally and emotionally. And for Maddie to have time that's hers and the respect and peace that are due to her as a person.

Brad and I have reacted very differently to what happened. We've been going through things at different times, and even though we've gone through this process together it's kind of like witnesses to a murder or a crime. They always see things from their own perspective, and their stories never match up. Obviously Maddie was inside me, and she died inside me. So

I've gone through a whole emotional thing of feeling that my body failed her, that I wasn't able to fulfil my primary function as a mother and keep my baby alive. That tortured me for a while. I think sometimes Brad feels more that the system failed us. But I think we've managed to talk all about those things the whole way through, and act as a sounding board for each other. I convinced myself a few weeks after she was born that it was my fault because I'd started eating fish and given her too much energy and that's how she got bound up in the cord. In my head that seemed so logical, but once I said it out loud and saw the look on Brad's face, it was just like okay—stupid. But I feel we can't be separated now. That we've gone through this incredible thing together, we've survived it so far, and we still love each other so much. I gained incredible strength from it. I went through this terrible fear of losing him for the first month or so after Maddie died, I was having nightmares every night that Brad was dead and I had to go and identify his body in a body bag. I think that was probably from losing a dear friend, then my grandmother, then my baby. It just kept getting closer and closer. I had this terrible fear. Either that he would die or that he'd run off with some nineteen-year old blonde bimbo or something like that. He'd be looking at me going, 'Don't be stupid, I'm here, I'm with you. We're together.'

There comes a time when it seems that some people think you should be over it. My immediate friends, no. But I was at a gig a few weeks ago and I ran into a friend there who's been one of my best mates since I was sixteen. I hadn't seen him during my whole pregnancy, but we're still kind of close. He's like, 'So how you doing?' and I was like, 'Oh, I'm really fucked'. And he went, 'Oh, still?' And I just looked at him and I went, 'Yes, still'. And I walked away. It was like fuck you. How dare you? Still. Yes, still. It's going to be there forever. Sometimes I get worried that I bore people with talking about it, but I've made a point right from the beginning and this was a vow that Brad and I made together, to be really open and honest. I think it's the only way that you can really get through it with any level of mental health and integrity. Because if you try and bottle all this stuff in, I think it would just drive you mad. I mean there's moments where I've felt that I was going completely mad with grief.

I just want people to acknowledge that it happened. No one can make it better. That's the hard thing. When people see you for the first time, they don't know whether they should say anything. It's a horrible position for them to be in, so some of them just choose to ignore you. Or they come up and pretend that nothing's happened, and talk to you about work. Then there's the ones that don't know at all, they're probably the hardest. I'm getting very good at dealing with it now. I think the best thing that anyone's said to me was my friend Petra, at a concert. She walked straight up to me and just looked me in the eye and said, 'I am so, so sorry. I know there's nothing I can say. I just want to let you know I've been thinking about you and Brad and my heart goes out to you'. It was simple and nice; to the point.

We have moments every day, obviously, that we think about Maddie and get a tear in our eyes, and we feel sad for her and for us. For everything she's missed out on and we've missed out on. But there'll be moments when we have fun and that we take pleasure in each other and we don't feel guilty about that. Whereas in the early days if you laughed at something, you felt, *I can't laugh, my baby's dead*. I don't want to be a person who is so overwhelmed by grief that I don't have enjoyment and pleasure in life, because then there's no use in being here. I want to enjoy my life, with my husband and I want to enjoy my life hopefully with my future children. I know that Maddie will always be a part of my head and my heart and that basically everything that happens in our lives is always going to be tinged by this tiny bit of sadness. Some days that'll be worse than others, especially days of importance, such as Christmas and birthdays and Father's Day. But I want there to be a place where Brad and I have an acceptance of what's happened and that the bitterness has gone, and that we can live life to the fullest. I feel as though we owe her that too. And we owe it to her brothers and sisters. And hopefully there's going to be hundreds of them.

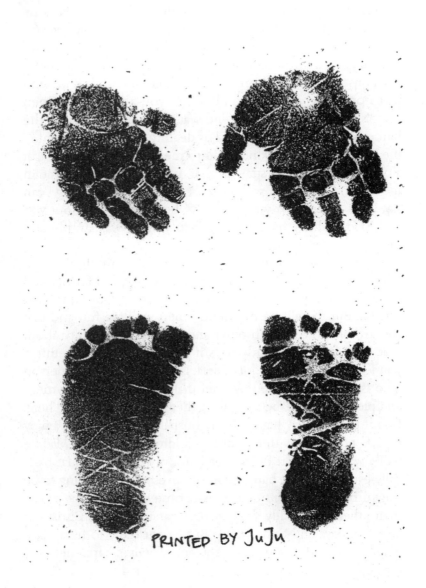

PRINTED BY JuJu

# JUJU

## Lea Batalha Trindale

*The happiest moment in my life would have to be giving birth to our baby boy Juju. The saddest moment in my life would have to be giving birth to our baby boy Juju. Never did I think it could be possible to experience such a moment.*

*It's been two years now and as I look back , from the day I went into labour with Juju to the day we scattered his ashes into the sea, I can honestly say there is not one thing I would change. It was as if it was meant to be.*

*It was a birth just like any other birth starts out and everyone was there and excited. Mum, Dad, sister, husband and best friend. It was actually quite special.*

*But Juju slipped away from us just as quickly as he had slipped in. It was a devastating experience as it took no more than the blink of an eye for such a happy moment to be so sad. Everyone did the best they could but it was too late.*

I had a wonderful pregnancy with Juju. I loved it. I was only twenty-five years old, but I love children, always have loved children. And of course it's never the right time. But when you do get pregnant, it's more than the right time. You just start to live around being pregnant and looking forward to having a child and you dream about your future with children. And having a baby with somebody you love is even more special. Miguel, my husband, was also excited and happy to have this baby so it was absolutely wonderful.

I was very healthy and all the signs were good. I went to the doctor regularly and we did the prenatal classes. You never hear about the possibility of something going wrong, that for example the baby's heartbeat can stop within the space of a minute. In the classes they give you a quick briefing about stillborns, but of course you don't want to be too traumatised about it before you give birth.

My labour started one night and we went into hospital the next morning. Many hours into the labour there was a change of shift and two midwives came to give me a routine check and everything seemed to be going well. Then they checked for Juju's heartbeat, and it was difficult to find, quite weak in some positions. It was as if he was hiding. He had turned around so his spine was on my spine, and his feet and hands were facing the outside. Then a moment later, we found his position in strong force. They monitored me for a safe period of time.

Soon after, I had one really bad contraction and it was like I knew something happened, I felt it happen, but I didn't know what it was. At that point I started to think I would maybe need some drugs, and I suddenly wanted this labour to happen fast. At first I had thought, 'I don't care if it takes one or two days. I'll enjoy it, and the pain doesn't last forever so I can handle it, I can do this.' But now I just wanted it over; and I had a really weird sensation, so Mum and my support person, Simone, called the nurse. She did a check-up but she couldn't find the heartbeat of the baby. The midwife didn't panic, but she was very concerned. She got out the bigger machines and I started to worry. I said, 'Oh my God, what are you doing? He's still there you know,' and she said, 'Yes, it's all right. I just can't find his heartbeat at the moment, but we'll find it.' I felt strangely detached. I didn't want to know the reality. So I just sort of zoned out.

The nurse rushed me to the labour ward and there they brought in the ultrasound from the theatre and it was more chaotic. Other nurses came in and specialists, and the ultrasound confirmed that there was no heartbeat to be found. I wasn't able to show any emotions and I felt really bad for the people who had to tell me. At first they couldn't tell me, they just didn't want to believe it, and they kept re-checking. I looked at the ultrasound specialist and said, 'It's OK, it's OK.' He was just so nervous and kept searching and searching for any sign of the heartbeat from Juju. My family didn't want to believe it, either. It was too tragic, and it had happened so very quickly that it was just unbelievable. One minute everybody was happy and making jokes and laughing, and then the next minute it was confirmed our baby had died.

The family stayed optimistic for as long as possible. All the staff, the nurses and doctors were very upset. They were in tears, just like my family. They tried not to show me their sadness, but for my family I know it was comforting. It was only right that everyone be so emotional.

It got to the stage where I needed some rest. By then the labour had gone for twenty hours, and the shock of it all had made me even more exhausted. Plus I still had the pain of the contractions coming in, and I had to continue the labour and deliver him. So I was given an epidural. And finally I could rest. My father and sister went home for a bit of sleep, but Mum, Simone and Miguel stayed at the hospital and they hardly slept. Mum didn't sleep at all. Every time I woke up I could see a few bodies on the floor and Mum standing in the corner watching me.

I don't remember waking up in the morning, but by then baby Juju was ready to come and I had to continue the birth. The midwives asked me how I wanted to deliver the baby— vaginally or by caesarean section—and I told them I still wanted to have him vaginally. I asked if they could stay and help me deliver Juju because they'd been with me all through the night and through my pregnancy, and they had been beautiful. They agreed, even though their shift was really over. Dad and my sister Bianca arrived soon after, so everybody was there and the birth started and it was time to push. They guided me through it, and it was amazing. The crown of his head, then the little face and eyes, and then the rest of his little body. Once again for a few moments it brought happiness and smiles to everyone's faces.

It was still a birth, whether he was breathing or not, and he was still there, definitely in spirit. After Juju came out Miguel cut the cord, and he felt happy to finally be a part of the birth, even though he always was. I just looked at Juju, and wanted to hold him immediately. So the midwives put him on my chest, and we all cried, laughed and joked for a while about whose features his little face and body resembled. He looked so precious, and his face so peaceful, as if he was just sleeping, and would wake at any moment. But of course he didn't. Everyone felt his presence though, as if he was letting us know that it was all right for us to be happy in such an unhappy situation.

The nurses said we could do whatever we wanted to do, and they suggested we spend time with him. We went back to the birthing centre and bathed and dressed him. I put him in all the little items that I wanted to dress him in. The hospital made this beautiful little book of when he was born and took some hand and footprints, as well as hair and fingernail clippings. It was a very positive and happy gift to keep his sweet memory. We cuddled a bit longer, then it was time to say goodbye. This was the hardest thing to do.

When I got home, I chose some clothes that I wanted Juju to wear for the funeral. Mum was going to take them to the hospital and she asked if I would like to go, and I said, 'No, I don't think I can do it.' Then at the last minute I changed my mind and went with Mum and Miguel. But this time it was different and really sad. I didn't like it much so Mum helped the social worker dress him and put some special things on him, a bracelet and a few other things like that.

Two beautiful friends of ours organised all the funeral arrangements for us, as we didn't know where to start. That morning before we left home Miguel went to buy the latest Café del Mar CD, Volume 6. We listened to the CD and the third track really stuck out at us, 'The Messenger', so we took that to play at the funeral and since then it has been Juju's song. The funeral people arrived at the crematorium with Juju in a beautiful white coffin and huge arrangements of flowers. There were bouquets of flowers everywhere, from friends all over the world who had found out about Juju's death. It was so beautiful.

It was a stormy day, raining, even though it had been sunny for ages up until then. It was like the day he was born. I had said to my mother that he would be born in a storm...I just had this feeling that it would be pouring and he'd be born in a storm, and he was. And then after he died, the sun came out for a few days, then later it was stormy again for the funeral. That was comforting to me.

I felt the funeral was important not only for us but for everyone who wanted to come and give their respects to our family and baby Juju, as they had also been waiting to meet him after the nine months of pregnancy. So I imagine it was hard for them to cope with it too, and it helped people let their emotions out.

We had our own little ceremony as well. A friend of ours organised to get a boat, so we took Juju's ashes out on the harbour and then out to Tweed Heads, with a group of very special friends. We had a very nice ceremony, played his song and emptied his ashes into the sea with beautiful petals of all sorts of flowers.

We decided not to have an autopsy on Juju's body. It didn't seem right. We agreed to an external examination, but I didn't want them to cut him up. It wasn't going to bring him back, so we left it at that.

Juju dying and his heartbeat stopping wasn't the fault of the midwife, and it wasn't my fault either. Perhaps he wasn't meant to be born. Some things do happen for a reason, sometimes to protect you. Of course none of us was glad when it happened, but what can you do? How can you bring him back after he's gone? I'm not going to look for reasons so that I can blame somebody. I have to accept that he couldn't be with us, and that's it. Maybe that's why I didn't want an autopsy. I'll always remember him and hope that everybody who was there will remember him. I don't need any answers to make myself feel better, because I think I'd just feel worse if I blamed myself or others. The guilt would be too much. And I'm quite a spiritual person, so I have my own beliefs about what happened.

My aunty in Macau told us that the same day Juju died, my grandfather who'd been very sick went into hospital. Two days later he started to ask 'Where is my great-grandson?' Then he started yelling at everyone and saying, 'I know they're behind that door over there, why don't you let them in? Why can't you bring him here so I can see him?' The next day he became non-responsive. He wouldn't speak to anybody. It was if he couldn't hear anybody, as if he were in a coma. The doctors expected him to die that night.

Later that night, my aunty telephoned us so we could speak to my grandfather in Macau. I so much wanted to tell him what had happened, but I couldn't. I broke down and cried, and told him that I loved him and that everything was going to be OK. The next day he died. So in a way I feel like Juju came into our lives and left to help my grandfather go peacefully. My grandfather was petrified of dying, he didn't want to die, he was afraid of not knowing what death was, he didn't want to go there. Then, in the last days he became calm and quiet. It was like he could feel some sort of presence that was going to help him on his journey.

That thought comforts me. It's what I believe and I'll always think of that. I feel somehow that they are together, they're looking out for one another and they're fine. A young soul and an old soul together. Sometimes we joke and say, 'Grand-father, don't teach him too many naughty things, OK?'

I did go through a stage, though, where I felt my belief was really shaken. I mean, when something like this happens, who or what do you believe in? It doesn't matter what your beliefs are, you tend to question 'How could this happen and why did this happen to us?' So I went through a stage of spiritual questioning. I accept it more now, that there is no answer. But it's not easy.

After Juju died, I still had my maternity leave, which was six months. It took a long time just to get out of the house and speak to people, and then actually go to a few dinners or lunches with friends. I can't say I got bored at home because I didn't. I spent time reading and painting and doing things around the house. But after six months I felt like it was time to move on and occupy my time a little more, and start inter-acting with people again. It was very scary going back to work. Just to speak to people who knew what had happened and those who didn't was very hard and awkward. I wasn't able to concentrate very well at first. It took time.

There's not enough awareness about stillbirth. If your pregnancy has gone well it's almost guaranteed you'll go home with your baby. You don't realise there are other complications possible. After this happened we talked to a few people and just realised 'This happens all the time, and more often than we think, like two in 100, 2 per cent.' It's because death is not an easy subject. People are more open talking about someone who has lived and died. But when it's a baby it's a lot more personal, people haven't met this baby or known it as a person, so it's a lot harder to speak about. Only people who went through this experience with you are comfortable talking about it.

So it's hard for people when something like this happens. At work, people who didn't know me very well would say, 'Oh don't worry, you're young, you'll have another one.' They thought that was the best thing to say but it's not. Whether you have another baby or not, the baby you lost was still a person. A new baby could never replace that baby.

Sometimes I feel like I haven't fully recovered, I'm still going through it. I look back and wonder how I ever managed to get out of bed in the mornings. I know that I am surrounded by great people who have helped me when I am sad and depressed. My mother, for example; she's such a positive woman, full of energy. She helped me believe that things would be OK and that it is all right to feel the things I feel at times and just go through it.

At times Miguel and I reacted differently to Juju's death, because we were at different stages of the grieving process. He tried to be stronger for me and I just let it all out and went with it. His grief was the same, it was just the timing was different. Miguel can be very reserved at times, and at first I was afraid of how he would cope. I wondered if he would talk to me about it all, but he was absolutely brilliant. We tell each other how we're feeling. If we're upset, or want to cry, we don't hide any feelings from each other. And if he's thinking about Juju he'll say, 'It would be so good if he was here.' I do the same. I think we're going all right. We seem to have healthy minds. We've accepted the death in a positive way, so I think we're lucky in that way.

And then there's Titi. He's a little tiger cub, very small and very cute. When we first found out that I was pregnant with Juju, I had the day off and I stumbled across this little tiger in a shop. It was just so cute, calling out to me. 'Oh please take me.' So that was the first present I bought for Juju. I wrapped it up, didn't even show Miguel, and kept it in the drawer. When we were packing his things away, I came across a little wrapped-up present, and asked Miguel to open it. Miguel thought the little tiger was really sweet and so we decided to keep him, and we called him Titi. We've always kept him close to our bed. We've taken him everywhere and he's like a special symbol of Juju. Having Titi has made it easier to talk about Juju.

After Juju died, we had to pack all his things away. We had everything set up for him. His cot, and a little place for him to get dressed. My father was very protective and concerned about how it would make us feel to arrive home with all Juju's things still there. He wanted to pack everything away before we got home but my mother convinced him not to, saying, 'No, they have to do that themselves.' It took quite a few weeks before we could bring ourselves to clear Juju's things away.

At first losing Juju was pure pain and it was impossible to let go and start grieving. It leaves an emptiness, an ache that seems will never go away, but gradually the space between the pain gets longer and now it's not so much an ache as missing him and wishing he was here to share things with us.

Later we'll try for another baby, but not right now. I feel I can't try too soon because then you feel like you're having another baby purely because you lost one. At the moment I'm just concentrating more on my work and where I want to go with that.

Our lives have changed and I've changed a lot too. I've become more patient, and so has Miguel. We look at life in a different way. During my pregnancy I looked after myself, but it was more for the baby than for me. We try not to take things for granted anymore. Just going for walks on the beach and enjoying peaceful times together, and liking every moment in life. Sometimes it's really difficult working in TV news because you see so much disaster and unhappiness. But I feel if I'm happy within myself and if I can make other people happy at some point, that's happiness for me. I try hard not to get upset over small things. Why put yourself in a state when you don't have the power to change it? If you do have the power, change the situation. Sometimes it's better to change your attitude towards a situation rather than try and change the situation itself.

I still want children, maybe two or three. Family is very important to me and I want it to be important to my kids also. Later, when the time is right it will happen again. Definitely.

# MIDMOONLIGHT

## Amanda Collinge

### 1. *Wangchuk Tashi, 1998*

High in the Himalayan mountains lives an old man, a Tibetan refugee named Wangchuk Tashi. When the Dalai Lama escaped from Tibet to sanctuary in India, Wangchuk followed him, and now lives in a refugee camp in Ladakh—a remote corner of the world, where religion and land have become one. Where monasteries rise like mountain peaks and even the rocks are carved with prayers. It was there in the late 1990s that I interviewed Wangchuk for a television documentary.

During our encounter, Wangchuk Tashi tells me about his time as a Tibetan warrior in the 1950s, when he fought for a free Tibet. Then came years in a Chinese prison, where he was repeatedly tortured. But there is only one wound that has never healed. Wangchuk was forcibly sterilised by prison guards, and could never have children. He tells me this with the camera rolling, and I am overwhelmed by the pain in his eyes. For the first time in my professional life, I break down and weep. The camera stops, the translator looks confused, and Wangchuk Tashi and I grip hands. I can see he has never stopped wanting a child. I have wanted a child for nearly ten years, and have none, but his right to parent was brutally taken from him. And despite his loss, it is clear he embraces life with energy and goodness. Later, when Wangchuk takes me to his hut for sweet yak tea and comfort, I can only tremble at his resilience, and feel ashamed of my own self-pity. We've been friends ever since. I send him photos and money, he sends me amulets of the Dalai Lama and sacred dust for my health.

## 2. MidMoonlight, 1999

I lost a tiny baby daughter three years ago. If she'd lived, she'd be a toddler now. I still sometimes hear her footsteps, or start to rush home to get her dinner, or think how the child down the road would be a lovely playmate for her.

My husband is Italian. His cousins are young and fecund and already on their third child each. They give me strange smiles and tell me, 'We'll be retired by the time you start'. I want to explain that I did start, long ago, but that things kept going wrong. I'd like to tell them about MidMoonlight.

MidMoonlight we called her because I lost her in the shower at midnight when the moon was full. So intact and gleaming that I could pick her up and marvel at the beauty of her precious sac, even though my heart was breaking and I knew this was one brutal birth/death scene that would haunt me for life. But I can't tell the cousins this. They'd think I was mad. Most people would. MM was a seven-week embryo, and that apparently is not old enough to be mourned. Not old enough to be anything, other than a 'good sign that you'll get pregnant soon'.

But I didn't fall pregnant soon after and I am not mad. I've been close to it, with grief, so I know the difference. I've been staggered at the intensity of this grief, but have come to understand it, in part. Once you have felt life within you, and wanted that life to continue, it remains etched on your soul forever. What makes the grieving difficult is its illicit nature. Plenty of women I know carry the same dark secrets. We've just learned to keep quiet.

## 3. The Longing, 1999

I am a television reporter. I travel to China and India and rural New South Wales and look into the camera earnestly, telling other people's stories to a trusting audience. But lately I've been feeling a fraud. I should tell them my truth. I am a childless mother. My husband and I have been trying to conceive for four years now. We've tried everything our doctors, friends and books suggest—boiling herbs twice a day, headstands after sex, boxer shorts, temperature charts and ovulation kits, wanking in glass cubicles. Staying busy, being relaxed, not touching alcohol, getting drunk. Our bedroom has become a clinic, forlorn and desexualised. He had an operation to make his sperm swim faster. I've been through five cycles of IVF. But still no baby. I have failed to live up to my good reputation for achievement and shattered my own sense of self. I am defective.

After the miscarriage, there is a second miscarriage six weeks later. Or so the doctors say. It is all so impossible and crazy and hideous that I continue to work, numb. On an Aboriginal community in Arnhem Land, on a politician's cream leather couch, I am working and bleeding at the same time. Bleeding without stopping, huge clots of blood like liver. But worse is the psychic pain I can share with no one. I am still mourning the loss of MM. I long to share with her the beauty of the tropical coastline where I am filming, dabble her tiny feet in the water. Finally, I seek medical advice and find myself weeing on a Darwin doctor's testing kit. I am pregnant, it says. The doctor, who is young and pale, with clammy hands, tells me I'm 'a fascinating case'. But I know the silent leak of death. Back in Sydney, I bleed for twenty more days, and the diagnosis is reviewed. The new verdict is 'a miscarriage in two parts', like a play in two acts. Like a tragedy in reverb.

My husband and I try desperately to feel better. He takes me to Fiji, to a paradise hut. But I spend most of the time sick, felled by a strange fever. I've always been big on running from pain ... go for a swim, take a holiday, change cities, change countries. But this time nothing works. I learn that this is a pain that follows you everywhere. Returning to Sydney, we pull out the last card and decide to move house, leave the cottage and garden that has become the empty nest. We move to the beach, to an apartment where the sound of the sea takes over at night, and friends live nearby. The sea is my nourishment, and a slow recovery begins. I join a gospel choir, and the singing soothes the chaos in my soul.

### 4. Betrayed: the past

My longing for a child does not abate. In bed at night, I battle with insomnia and self-recrimination. Am I being punished for a wild youth? Too many drugs? Too much hard work, long hours and putting career first? Or was it too many boyfriends? The wrong sort, perhaps? Why did I stay with men who weren't committed to the idea of children? And why was I seduced by feminist thinking which led women to believe they could leave baby-making till their late thirties? Foolish, foolish girl. You do not deserve to sleep.

I remember being twenty years old, a university student. I hear repeatedly that we young women must not let babies get in the way of career. That women these days can do both ... have family and profession, and I am relieved to have this very good news. Because I definitely want both. I collect stories of women who are thirty-nine, forty, even forty-one! who successfully pull off high-powered jobs and then produce gorgeous children. I think to myself ... great ... plenty of time. But I also hear talk that unsettles me a little. Derision of women who have children young, or decide to be stay-at-home mums. Smart talk about babies being a millstone round your neck and tying you to the kitchen sink. I am not so sure of this talk, because I adore children, and have always imagined myself one day as a mother. Looked forward to the lightness of baby breath on my arms, to passing love and stories and songs down the line. I hear nothing of plummeting fertility rates after thirty-five, increased miscarriages and women who simply miss the boat. Instead I grow used to being lucky and happy. Foolish, foolish girl. You do not deserve to sleep.

Ten years later my father dies and I am bereft. All I can think of is creating family. I am thirty now and I feel I must act for my father's sake and for mine. Betray the mother within me no longer. But my situation seems hopeless. I am in a relationship with a man who has had a vasectomy and shows no inclination to have it reversed; who promises to start contributing to a medical health fund to cover the cost of the operation but instead spends the money on alcohol and drugs. Friends console me, saying the hunger is a grief reaction to my father's death and there is still plenty of time. That old refrain again. So I sublimate the longing, focus on my career, finally leave this partner for good, and travel to Spain, where I live and work for three years.

## 5. IVF, 1998–2000

My husband, my true love, wants children as much as I do. Sometimes even more so. We take turns in falling apart, and decide we must try IVF. For me, the decision alone feels like a defeat from which I will never recover. I had always felt so sexual and fertile. Never needed doctors much. To now subject my body to still-experimental medical technology, and surrender myself to an industry that delivers success to less than half its clientele, is shocking to me. I sense well in advance that the loss of control and dignity will be enormous.

Our first attempt at IVF is disastrous. Clinic One is lax in monitoring my hormone levels and ignores my warnings that I feel the hormone dose is too high. Within three weeks I am swollen like a cow with bloat, unable to walk and breathing with difficulty. Hyperstimulation they call it. A condition that affects 5 per cent of IVF patients. We have produced six embryos by this stage but at the last minute the doctor informs us it is too dangerous to transfer them back into my body, as this would exacerbate the hyperstimulation and I would probably end up spending Christmas in intensive care. The cycle is cancelled and we spend Christmas in intensive depression instead.

In the New Year we feel compelled to remove our six frozen embryos, our potential children, to a better clinic, more expensive, but where the science is more rigorous.

Clinic One relinquishes responsibility for our microscopic offspring the minute they leave the hospital grounds, and Clinic Two will only accept responsibility once they arrive on their premises. So my husband and I carry the liquid nitrogen tank gingerly down in the lift, into the car. We look like we are carrying a fire extinguisher. No one knows it contains our frozen dreams. As we head off across the city, we try and joke about it being our first family car trip, but the rain outside turns threatening, the traffic is savage and we end up arguing in fear. Take it out on each other. Can only find a parking spot vacated by a mother my age and her newborn babe-in-arms. We feel like freaks with our esky of hope.

Our second attempt ends in the conception of MidMoon-light, and we are delirious with joy. I am pregnant at last, and breathlessly we bounce around making plans and imagining her soft head, her dark eyes. My husband dreams of a girl. My eyes are opened to a happiness I never knew existed, to another, better world. They are three precious weeks, for which I remain permanently grateful to MM. As you now know, there is a shower scene which ends it all, tops off a day of excruciating cramps and clotting. Somehow, we manage to get through the night, and take her in a clean jar into the clinic the next morning for testing. It is only then, at the moment when I hand her over to science, that I lose control, lose my mind and lose the closest thing to a child I've ever had.

The tests show two chromosomal abnormalities and confirm she was a girl.

Many, many months later, we return to the clinic. Three more IVF cycles, three more failures. I always knew when I wasn't pregnant, days before the clinic results came back. I would wake sobbing in the night, gripped by the emptiness in my belly. Not a flicker of life. Just the familiar hollow nothing. A bleak ache. By day, I alternate between grief and anger. The anger sometimes grows to a wild rage that lashes out at innocent targets, most often myself. I want to die in a car accident, be run over, disappear.

I become absorbed with the extraordinary effort required to stop the sense of failure leaking into every other aspect of my life. My relationship, career, my friendships and my sanity are all under serious threat, so harrowing is the cycle of optimism and loss. I am suspended in a state of perpetual hope, future unknown. I decide that determination and tenacity are the only way through. What I can't escape are the nightmares.

I dream we take our dead embryos to the gynaecologist,

because he is the best in town, and maybe he can help us. He tells us to bury them in a freshly ploughed field at night, that this will ensure they grow again. We do so, and watch over them with our lives, until one dreadful night during a storm, a wolf-sized dog digs them up and devours them. We are powerless to stop him. Then I dream I have cancer, but I hardly care about this, so focused am I on getting pregnant. My GP asks me to come in, she has some good news. She tells me that the cancer tests have come back negative, I am not going to die. 'But what about the pregnancy test?' I scream at her. 'That's what I need to know!' She tells me I am not pregnant and I collapse on the ground, howling uncontrollably.

In yet another dream another doctor has our dead foetus in his tea cup. It is a huge white tea cup and our baby is inside, swimming in red blood. Slowly, this doctor, another specialist, starts to eat her, limb by limb, dabbing the corners of his mouth politely as if to remove crumbs. He is smiling at us all the time.

## 6. Breakthrough, 2000

By the sixth cycle, we are battle-weary and sceptical. I don't even bother to stop work this time, I no longer care if my stress levels are high and we are starting to pursue adoption. I do, however, demand more control. I ask for a curette before the cycle starts, because I've been feeling as if I needed one ever since I lost MM. I also tell the clinic I will do this cycle in conjunction with a course of herbs and acupuncture, carefully designed by a skilled Chinese medicine practitioner I know and trust. To my surprise, they agree. The herbs are to enhance the effects of the IVF drugs, minimise their side-effects and make the lining of my uterus as inviting as possible. I am also high on love...just one month on from the wedding my husband and I celebrated in defiance of grief and in the name of our devotion to each other.

I fall pregnant and we are quietly ecstatic.

*Amanda Collinge and Lucia*

## 7. Little sister

In the early days of the pregnancy there were terrifying bouts of bleeding and cramping and sinister clots in the toilet. Threatened miscarriage and two panicked trips to hospital. We remained cautious and bought nothing for months, holding our breaths until the first and then the second trimester passed without disaster. Waiting until we had our child safely in our arms. The baby, however, never faltered in her resolve to survive. Every check-up revealed the same strong heartbeat, textbook dimensions, excellent position. Unaccustomed to good news, we left the hospital each time wordless and dazed.

But as seven months became eight, I started to feel bolder, then exultant. The nightmares had gone. In their place came exquisite dreams of my daughter. Weeks before she was born, she revealed herself and smiled, reached through the skin of my stomach and held my hand. The night before the doctors discovered she'd turned, she herself showed me how she'd flipped, and lay peacefully in my uterus, ready to be born. Showed me too how she would take my breast straight after birth and how she would love trees and birds and talking. Assured me she was perfect and safe.

When my daughter was born early one Sunday morning she was just as I dreamed her. Small and dark and knowing. Born exactly two years after MidMoonlight. Pure light. Lucia.

We have been blessed. Lucia is strong and very much alive. Out of hardship, you also find unexpected joy. Right now, I'm bursting with it.

# WHITE TEARDROPS ON MY EMPTY BELLY

## Jo

*A curette they say.*
*Funny how it sounds like an exotic French cigarette or Swiss*
*    chocolate.*
*Not what it is at all; a scraping of foetal remains from the uterus*
*    a suck and vacuum for the debris.*
*It should be called something else.*

When people talk about miscarriage it has no connotation or meaning for the physicality of it, or the hormonal and mental devastation that comes with it.

It's just like, 'Oops'. The very word 'miscarriage' implies that not much has happened except a little bit of a mistake and that's all right. That's how all the doctors like to talk about it, and all the professional people you deal with, 'Oh, it's just a miscarriage'.

When I had my first miscarriage I had no experience of them at all. I had no knowledge. So when I found myself in hospital bleeding and all this stuff, organs and things were coming out of me, I was in a state of shock about the gruesomeness of what was happening to my body. I was completely unprepared for it.

The hardest thing about those years of not being able to sustain a pregnancy was the gore and the guts and the blood and the whole totally bovine process. I don't want to sanitise what happened. It's not often described in its viscerality, in its bodyness, and the people I know who have had miscarriages all gush out at me about how dreadful and revolting the whole thing was.

What's weird about this whole saga is that I always felt that

I'd never have children. I never wanted to have children. Then when I was twenty-seven all of a sudden I just got this ridiculous need to have children. It was a completely illogical thing. I didn't want to feel it, I didn't want it to be part of my life; I was resisting it even as it crept into my psyche. And then I realised there was nothing I could do about it, I just had get it over and done with.

It's the way I do things. Once I decide there's no way round something I have to get on with it. And I was prepared to do it with or without John. It wasn't anything to do with our relationship or a need to have a family with him or anything like that, it was entirely personal. After a while he realised I was serious. We talked a lot about it. He said he didn't want to, and I said I really have to. I didn't threaten him but it was implied that if he didn't want to have a child, then our relationship couldn't keep going, and it was true.

It really wasn't a threat, it was the reality of the situation, and he begrudgingly gave in to the idea so we tried once or twice and I got pregnant straight away.

Then at three months I started bleeding, and I froze, I panicked, I can't really describe how I felt. So I went to the doctor and had an ultrasound and we saw that there was still a heartbeat, and the doctor said I just had to lie down and relax. He said the bleeding should stop in twelve hours or so, it should be fine.

The bleeding didn't stop, it got heavier and heavier, and I got really severe pain, really severe cramps, and all this mucusy stuff came out, and big clots that looked like livers. I sat on the toilet and it all came out and I looked at the bottom of the toilet bowl and I'm sure there was a little foetus at the bottom, and I couldn't pick it up. I really wanted to pick it up and I always feel sad that I never did. The thing is it was so kind of grotesque that I couldn't bring myself to, because it was so revolting and I didn't want to face it. But that's what it was and that's where it was. I was bleeding, bleeding, bleeding so they said to go into the hospital.

When we got there I had all these internal examinations which really hurt and every time there was a new shift there'd be a new doctor who would do another incredibly painful examination. Then they gave me some morphine and I remember spacing out in my head and being really obsessed with this smell. I kept on wondering what the smell was. It wasn't until several hours later that I realised it was me. It was the blood and stuff coming out of me and the smell of dead baby. I was revolted by the whole idea of it.

Then they wheeled me away and gave me a curette and I came back and the smell had gone away.

I felt like I was a lump of meat. There was a lot of indignity, a lot of lying there with no clothes on with your legs open, with people looking up there. The whole thing was a violation, and you're completely out of control.

You're never sure exactly what the doctors are looking for. They want the foetal remains to test it. I don't know what it is they test but they test it. They want to see that there's actually foetal tissue in your blood to prove that it is a miscarriage. Maybe they were worried that I'd bleed to death.

For my second miscarriage I was in there for ten days. Every morning they'd take me down to the ultrasound and the little heartbeat would still be there hanging in, and every night I would be bleeding, bleeding.

There was a clot forming that was causing the bleeding and every day it got bigger and bigger and this tiny little heartbeat was still there, hanging in there. That was horrible. Waiting. Every night I had to wee into a pan then the nurses would peer in it with a torch to check if there was any blood and loss. One night there was all this tissue-y stuff in the pan and they said, 'Look, this is it.' But the next morning we went to have an ultrasound and the little heartbeat was still there, it was absolutely agonising and tortuous and it was nobody's fault, but seeing it there every day for so many days was horrible.

*Alex was the name we gave that baby.*
*The first one was Rose.*

So I went back to work. And everyone started making comments like, 'Oh, you're too thin. You should take time off work. You shouldn't exercise so much'. I know they were trying to help but I felt like I was being blamed. I had to work, otherwise my brain would just absolutely go crazy, I would've been completely obsessed, even more than I was.

It took me a long time to recover. The hospital and being pregnant had taken a lot of physical toll. Then I started to see babies everywhere, and I was getting this mad feeling that my whole life had become dominated by this absolute need. Everyone else was having babies and there were beautiful babies and pregnant women everywhere, which I'd never noticed before in my life.

What really drove me insane was the feeling that people thought that I had no capacity to know what was right for me, like I was some kind of idiot. What I would have liked wasn't advice but support, people just saying that I looked nice or something, not making me feel inadequate. The whole process of getting pregnant and losing the babies was a gradual disintegration of my sense of myself and my confidence in myself and my body to do this thing that seems perfectly natural for everybody else. It felt like a fault in me. I was having this problem because I've got psychological problems, or there was something wrong with me. That was the beginning of the slide into despair, really.

*Poor little titties*
*Hard and round*
*Looking for baby*
*Dripping white teardrops*
*On my empty belly*

It was the beginning of a time of feeling physically shattered that went on and on for months. I got the worst asthma in my whole life, I just couldn't breathe, I couldn't sleep; I was in a really bad state of madness. I could carry on with life, I could go to work, I could smile at people, I could talk and have coffee but underneath I was grief-stricken and alone, because it seemed to be so something that I just wasn't supposed to be so devastated about.

But it had ramifications for my entire existence. The way I felt before this had gone, and I don't think I'll ever have that easy self-confidence again because this sense of loss was so great, and so lonely that I couldn't ever see my way out of it. I had this sense I was causing myself to miscarry. I felt like I was expelling these things, and that it was my head that was doing it. It was a secret that I couldn't tell anybody, because I felt like it was too hard to talk about, to tell anyone.

I thought I was really mad, I thought that there was something more that was happening to me, because everybody else, even when they had miscarriages, they seemed to be OK. I tried to talk, I tried to seek mainstream counselling but I found it completely useless, and worse because I'd gone seeking help and had come away feeling even more ridiculous. I don't know why that happened, but I just felt they were not equipped at all to deal with it. And that's when I got onto the SANDS (Stillborn and Neonatal Death Society) people. In their newsletter there were stories that people had written to babies they'd lost years and years ago, and it was obvious people still remembered the anniversaries of babies that were never born, that they still felt it. Reading them I felt enormously relieved. I thought, 'Oh, my God, it's OK'.

After the second miscarriage we went away. We left Canberra for Darwin, and we tried to get pregnant, and I couldn't. I thought I was pregnant twice but the tests never showed anything. I started to get desperate because I'd never had trouble getting pregnant, and I thought 'Is this psychological, is my head stopping me from getting pregnant?'

And then there's what happens to your sex life. I have this image of cartoon dogs fucking with a caption that reads 'We're trying, We're trying'. Sex certainly became mechanical. I tried to make sure we did it every night in the middle of ovulation and it wasn't fun.

I can't feel sexy or want sex if I'm not feeling good about myself, and throughout this whole time I didn't feel good about myself at all. Not to mention work. I felt like I should work part-time to lower my stress levels but I was getting really stressed because I enjoyed working hard. I found it difficult to get part-time work that was satisfying without having to explain, 'I'm trying to get pregnant, I've had these miscarriages and I need not to work too much'.

So we decided to come back to Canberra and I did get pregnant again. It was a little bit like the second pregnancy. I bled almost straight away, and I bled and bled and bled until I bled it out.

I thought I was feeling OK about it until I went down the coast for a holiday and my friend who'd just had a baby, had her sitting on her knee, and she was the most beautiful baby I'd ever seen in my life. She had peachy skin and blue eyes and she was bouncing and smiling and I was overwhelmed by madness. I had to lock myself in the bedroom. John came in and I said, 'We have to go, I can't stay here'. I was either going to steal that child or bash it to death. There was this mad-woman feeling in my head. I was crazy, and I felt I couldn't cope with being crazy, and I was trying. The more I tried to be normal the worse it got. It was a tiny two-bedroom flat and it was obvious that something mad had happened to me, and my friends didn't have any idea what it was. It was so humiliat-ing. To this day I hate to think what they thought.

I didn't try to get pregnant for a whole year. I tried to get on with life. I tried to pretend that I'd do something else and forget about it. But of course you never do, you never forget about it, never. I spent a fortune on cures. I went to everybody, and they all said they could cure me. They looked in my eyes, they looked at my liver, they manipulated my spine, they gave me vile herbs and vitamins. But the thing that kept me sane was a homeopath who massaged me. It wasn't the medicine or anything she gave me, it was that she touched me. I was so tortured physically and she made me feel normal again.

I was driving everyone away from me because I was embar-rassed by my madness and I couldn't share it with anyone. John was getting fed up, and during all this time we were going to the obstetrician and having genetic screenings. So the medical intervention was continuous as well.

To be truthful I don't know really what happened for the next year, but after that I got pregnant with Jackson. It was an awful time, a mad time. I was going to see the obstetrician every day. I was having injections every day and my levels were supposed to be going up and up and up, and they started to plateau, and then they started to drop, and I had to have extra injections. Then we got to three months and we felt like we were over the bad time, and on the first day of the fourth month, I bled, and I bled and I bled and I bled.

I just thought, I can't do this again, I can't cope with this, but I had to, there was no turning back. So I went into hospital and had more ultrasounds and checks and bleeding and waiting, waiting, trying to be relaxed. I was in an abyss, waiting for this baby to die. For two months I was flat on my back not moving, watching the foetus peel away and come back and peel away and come back.

I had anxiety about going to the toilet all the time. I'd try to convince myself not to look down into my pants and see if there's blood, just once, just don't do it. And I couldn't. To this day I still do it because of this memory of that time. I had to throw out all my underclothes because they were all stained, and I couldn't bear it. It was like remnants of babies every-where. Remnants of failure.

But at about six months I started to feel better. I went home and I stayed quiet. I did some gardening and I walked the dog, and somehow the time seemed to go. I was sick too and I was uncomfortable, I couldn't walk very far, I couldn't sleep and I was always exhausted, so I didn't do much, and I didn't work. I went into labour on Christmas Eve, and John and I were absolutely convinced that if it was a baby, because I couldn't believe that there was a baby in there, that the baby would die.

We were just terrified and convinced that I would be muti-lated and that a horse would come out, or something that wasn't a baby. When Jackson was born John and I looked at each other in total shock and went, 'Oh, fuck, it's a baby'.

We were the most neurotic parents. We thought he was going to die. We still do. It's easier now, but with both our children we've had this constant anxiety that because we were both such failures at this, that these children were going to die.

Having Jackson made me feel, at least on the outside, like

one of those other women with babies, and it was enormous. I think had I never had a live baby, I would always be mad, and it was such a relief that the madness could stop.

The horrible thing was he was sick a lot. Every time he was in hospital we thought he was going to die. We didn't know how else to be so that was a really hard and isolating thing too. And of course I got post-natal depression. I was so exhausted. Mothering didn't come naturally to me. John was working really long hours. I was alone with a baby who never slept. The baby I'd wanted for so long, and I didn't feel I could deal with him. It was like, 'She's got the baby, but what's wrong with this woman now? Can't she get it together?'

My confidence, which had gone up a bit, hit rock bottom again. I knew I should be grateful and I was grateful, but I just didn't know how to live very well with it. The thing is all this reproductive difficulty is so ordinary. I feel like I'm over-dramatising the situation because so many people have been through all these things and many, many more terrible things than me. Every woman who's been involved in reproduction has experienced difficulty in some way. But it is harrowing, and it was, and it continues to be harrowing as a memory.

Even my second child Georgia's birth and early life were difficult. It felt like John and I weren't fit, that there was some-thing inherently bad about our wanting to be parents. When John had a vasectomy we celebrated because it was the end of it. It was as if we'd accepted that if our children die it's beyond our control now.

The thing that kept me lonely all that time was my fear of going mad. Once I stopped thinking I was mad and realised I was deeply sad, I started talking. Other people's stories came to me and that was a real healing process.

It's not that I'll never forget. I carry an aching heart with me all the time that I never had before. And a sense of mortality. Before this, I was an immortal person, I was convinced I was invincible. Now I have a strong sense of my own mortality and an even stronger sense and a great fear of my children's mortality.

They're gorgeous kids. Every day we say we're so thankful

that we've got them, and I just hate to think what I'd be like if I didn't. I would have lost my relationship, I would have probably lost several other relationships, I probably would have been driven crazy by the obsession to have a child. What's good about what's happened is that I can get on with my life. It was on hold for a long time and now it isn't.

# BIRTHING JACKSON

## John

It was Friday 23 December 1994, my last day of work, and I was really exhausted. I had been at Parliament House since June; it was the hardest and longest I had ever worked, and the Christmas parties and late nights hadn't helped. It was so full-on that I felt that I had not had time to prepare mentally for fatherhood. Just as I was leaving the office to go home I remarked to a workmate that I was really looking forward to a good sleep and a few days off work to 'batten down the hatches' with Jo, and get focused on the fact that she was about to have a baby. The baby was due on 1 January, but we'd been told to be ready two weeks either side of that date. So when I hit the bed that night, it was with a sense that one chapter of my life was closing—but I was not prepared for how quickly the next one would open.

'Something's happening', Jo said when she came to bed that night. 'No, it can't be,' I said supportively. 'Just go to sleep.'

Something *was* happening, though. The 'contractions' (at that stage neither of us knew exactly what a full-blown contraction was) continued all night. There was little sleep for either of us, and I remember thinking to myself 'Not yet, please, let me get some sleep; give me a bit of time, I'm not ready for this yet!' I could sense something beyond my control was about to start.

Jo's obstetrician, who had been fantastic during the pregnancy, told us the week before that he was going away for Christmas. Of course he was going away for Christmas—as if anyone would be stupid enough to have a baby at Christmas—and our birth helper, Robyn, was also away until after Boxing Day. Fortunately our other helper, Louise, was able to make arrangements to be available just in case she was needed on Christmas Day.

By the Saturday morning the contractions were regular, every five minutes and I started cleaning, don't ask me why— the laundry mainly—then in the early afternoon the contrac- tions became irregular and I was relieved. I just wanted things to stop, at least for a week or two. By late afternoon, though, the contractions had become much stronger but less frequent. Was there something wrong? We had no idea, so at about 5.30 we decided to go to the hospital. I drove rather quickly.

When we got to the delivery suite we were told that a midwife would be with us soon, and after about five minutes a middle-aged woman appeared and introduced herself as Pauline. She talked to Jo about the contractions and about what we wanted from her. She had read our file and was aware that we wanted as little intervention as possible, although Jo also explained that she was not fanatical about intervention and was prepared to accept that it might be necessary later on. This was fine by her, Pauline said; no one was going to force anything on us. This first conversation was so important. It established the ground rules for the next eighteen hours, and I instantly had a very strong sense that Jo and the baby (and me too) would be in good hands. As it turned out, Pauline is someone who has left an impression on me that I will remember forever. She was very, very good at her job and we were so lucky to have her.

After a brief examination, Pauline told Jo that she was in the very early stages of labour and that the contractions would have to be much stronger before anything serious was going to happen. This was a bit of a disappointment for Jo, who looked at me as if to say, 'How much more is this going to hurt?' but at least we knew everything was OK. Pauline said if we wanted to, we could go home and wait for things to happen there.

We are both really glad that we were given this option because in retrospect this was one of the best things about the birth. It was our first baby—how the hell could we know what was happening? I certainly felt very vulnerable and in no position to argue with anyone; if an obstetrician had suggested a caesarean I think we would have agreed on the spot. But once we knew Jo was OK and it was only a matter of waiting, we decided to go home and do just that. We set ourselves up in the lounge room with take-aways and videos (*Waiting* with Noni Hazelhurst, what else, and *Four Weddings and a Funeral*) while the contractions became stronger.

At about ten o'clock Jo went to the loo and noticed some bleeding. I panicked—three miscarriages had taught me that blood was a very bad sign—and rang the hospital to tell them that something was wrong, we were coming in straight away. This was greeted by what I considered to be a rather cool response. The person on the end of the phone wanted to speak to Jo about the amount and colour of the discharge. 'What the fuck does that matter?' I was thinking, but Jo spoke at length to this voice (it belonged to a midwife called Robyn, who was also fantastic) and when she hung up she looked at me and told me that we should stay at home. I couldn't believe it. I was so worried and, once more, I felt so vulnerable.

We went back to the lounge room floor.

After another hour or so there was more discharge and again we rang the hospital and again were told there was no need to come in. I couldn't believe it, again! All the stories we'd been told said that Woden Valley hospital were really interventionist and here we were, seeking intervention, and they told us not to come in! But their advice was spot on. We stayed home until the next morning, and in retrospect this time was very special.

The contractions continued and Jo started to feel serious pain. I started applying hot nappies to her lower back to ease the pain which, she tells me, was remarkably effective. We turned off the lights, lit candles and incense and put on some mood music. It was an amazing period of time, one I will always remember. While the rest of the world was having Christmas Eve, Jo and I were having a baby. The tiredness left me and I reached a plateau where the panic and anxiety gave way to a feeling of resolution: we were going to do this birth, and I would give whatever it took. It was probably the first time I really started to believe that the pregnancy was a goer. Up until then, there was a part of me that felt that this pregnancy would also lead to disappointment.

I also began to focus totally on Jo's needs. It is not something that I do very often, but in doing so it became very much 'us'. The birth was something that *we* were doing, she and I, and by definition the baby too. Those hours on our lounge room floor were very special indeed.

At about 4 am, with the contractions getting more severe, we decided to go in and this time I didn't ring the hospital, just in case they told us not to come. When we got to the delivery suite we met Robyn, the voice on the phone. She was superb. She sat with us briefly while the room was prepared. She put her hand on Jo's stomach as she was contracting—I don't know what she was feeling for, but she obviously knew. I remember thinking that this was women's business, and that there was a bond between them, an empathy. When we went into the delivery room, we put the mattress on the floor, turned the lights off and the music on. It felt really good, like we were in control and the midwives were there to help us, not direct us. Robyn came in and talked to Jo, told her that there was a long way to go and that Jo should try and go with the contractions rather than fight against them—let her body do what it wanted to do. It was working well. It was excellent advice, given very gently.

For the next few hours I kept on applying hot nappies and Jo kept having contractions as the sun came up. At 6 am there was a change of shift and Pauline appeared again. Fantastic. But when she made it clear there was a long way to go, I was devastated. All this work and not far gone; how much longer could it take? I began to recall all the horror stories about sixty-hour labours followed by emergency surgery and babies delivered half dead. In short, I got the shits.

It was time for reinforcements: I called Louise.

Louise is one of Jo's best friends. I hadn't been sure I wanted her at the birth because she can be pushy and talks too much—she is, after all, a journalist—and I was worried that she might take over. On the other hand I knew that she would be strong if I fell to pieces. Up until now we'd resisted calling her in because we wanted to do it by ourselves, but by this stage I decided that I needed help.

When Louise arrived, Jo was still on the mattress and Louise produced a bottle of oil and began some gentle massage. I was told to go and find some breakfast, part of me feeling like a failure because I needed a break. As I was leaving the room I looked back at the two women on the floor. Louise was talking (of course) and massaging, and it hit me: Jo has needs that can be met by other people and I don't have to be everything to her, even in childbirth.

I found the staff cafeteria and wondered how much longer it would take. I was really tired and I knew Jo had not slept for days, as well as already being exhausted from the pregnancy. When I got back to the room I must have said something about still being here tomorrow, because Pauline said she would not allow that to happen. It was the first time that I had ever seen intervention in a positive light. Up until then my image of intervention had been gynaecologists waiting with the golf clubs in the delivery suite, trying to persuade every woman to have a caesar so that they could get a round in before dark. It had never really occurred to me that intervention could actually help if administered carefully by people who were on our side, trying to get the best result for all of us.

In the meantime the hot nappies and massage continued for the next few hours until about ten o'clock, when Pauline did another examination and announced that Jo was fully dilated. It was time to start pushing. I knew from our childbirth classes that this was the beginning of the third stage of the labour, the time when I had been warned that Jo would become abusive and hysterical. As it turns out she became neither, but it was hard work for her. She pushed and pushed, went red in the face; she screamed and yelled and pushed again. She tried different positions and pushed and pushed.

In the lead-up to the birth, one theme that was constantly on my mind was how I would cope with Jo being in such pain. I had sat beside her during three miscarriages, two of which were extremely physically painful. I can still clearly remember waiting outside the cubicle in the casualty section of Woden Valley hospital and hearing her scream as some doctor did an internal. As it turns out I didn't crack up watching her give birth because this pain was different from a miscarriage. In retrospect the reason is obvious—this time there was a positive outcome. A big strong beautiful baby boy at the end of the day is a million miles away from the numbing emptiness of a miscarriage.

After an hour or so, the pain was really starting to get to Jo and I started to wonder if all the pushing was achieving anything. So, apparently was Jo. 'It won't come out this way,' she screamed. 'Get the doctor!' Pauline was wonderful. She talked about the various options (drugs, episiotomy, forceps etc) and at one stage when Jo started screaming for a caesarean, Pauline said she would get the doctor and left the room. I followed her and asked her whether she was really going to get the doctor. 'Of course not,' she said. 'Jo won't need him.' When we got back to the room Jo had forgotten why we'd gone. Pauline suggested gas, and things really started moving from there. The gas helped Jo's awareness of the pushing and for the first time she felt the baby move up the birth canal. After about an hour it was obvious that the birth was close and Pauline began to prepare the birth kit.

This is it, I said to myself, this is really happening—and I immediately started to panic. What if it's deformed? I noticed that the floor of the delivery suit was tiled—what if I drop it? What sort of a father will I make? Will I ever sleep again?

The 'what ifs' never really left me, but they were pushed to the side. Jo was lying on her back and Louise and I were holding a leg each. To encourage Jo, Pauline kept telling her that she could see the baby's head. I thought she was joking so at the next contraction I looked and there it was. A very white piece of skin with black hair on it. It was Jackson. It was happening! Oh, my God!

Jo kept on the gas and kept on pushing. Pauline kept working—encouraging, coaxing, joking, urging and much more. Louise and I tried to do the same. 'Come on, Jo, you can do it, push, here he comes...' Several times during this process Jo said she'd had enough, the baby wouldn't come out this way. She was off with the fairies and she was in great pain; every time she pushed she went red and her veins stuck out. But there was progress. With each contraction Jo said she could feel him move and every time she pushed I could see more and more of the baby's head. Pauline asked if it was OK with us if she delivered him, which we were delighted to agree to.

She told Jo that he was coming and that after the next contraction she should pant. And with the next contraction his head came out and Jo panted. Pauline twisted his head to one side; another contraction and he was out. 12.20 on Christmas Day, 1994. A boy!

The next few minutes were a bit of a blur. There was a lot happening—an extra midwife had arrived to help. Pauline sucked out his mouth and put him on Jo's stomach. She was in shock; I think I was, too. All the classes we had done, all the books I had read could not have prepared for this moment. I don't know what I was expecting to feel at the first sight of my first child—maybe I thought it would be a meeting of two individual travellers; maybe I thought there would be a bolt of lightning or the heavens would part and angels would sing. There was none of that—he was just so fucking ugly!

And it wasn't because of the blood and gunk, because there wasn't much of that. His head had crowned and he looked deformed, he was long and dangly, his face was squashed up and he had a flat nose. But the biggest shock was that he was a boy. None of the ultrasounds had showed signs of any crown jewels and we'd been certain it would be a girl.

Louise kept telling us to bond with him. I felt like telling her to shut up. Neither Jo or I wanted to touch him. Pauline asked if I wanted to cut the cord but I didn't want to have anything to do with him. Louise took a picture of Jo and the baby which tells it all—Jo and I are looking at him and he is looking at us and we all have this look of absolute horror.

In retrospect I think I was expecting to feel about him then as I do now. I thought that it would be something innate, something primaeval that would click the minute I saw him. It wasn't the case, and I was disappointed. But that's fairytale stuff—like all good relationships, ours has taken some time to develop.

The doctor came in about three minutes after he was born, had a look at Jo, saw there was no tearing, said, 'Well done', and left. In all he was there about two minutes (and later sent us a huge bill for his 'work'). Pauline had to go home for Christmas dinner and the new midwife, Genevieve, told me that new-born babies like to be nursed by their fathers. So she wrapped up this ugly screaming mass and I walked him around the room, and after a while I realised that it was quite nice nursing your own kid. His head went back to normal, he stopped crying and he opened his eyes. I began to think that perhaps it would be all right, provided I didn't drop him.

We stayed in the birthing suite for about three hours while Genevieve showed Jo how to breastfeed. When it came time to leave we gathered our gear and headed out. As we passed reception one of the midwives asked if we'd forgotten something. I counted the bags—they were all there; looked at Jo who was in a wheelchair—she had all her gear; no, nothing missing. 'What about your baby?' she asked. Jo and I stared at her. Ah yes, the baby.

It is hard to know how and when to end this story, because hopefully it will be ongoing till I die. About three weeks after he was born I had a bit of a crisis—what sort of parent will I be, will he hate me, will I fuck him up? My friend Patrick rang me around that time, and as always, provided the very best of advice. He talked about the concept of 'acceptable parenting'. That I don't have to be the perfect parent: my obligation to Jackson is to provide food, shelter, clothing and an emotional and physical environment in which he can develop and grow. The rest is up to him.

It is difficult to get past the idea that he is on loan to us, that it is all temporary. I often lie awake at night, sometimes for hours, making sure that he is breathing. Someone once wrote of parenthood as the 'weeping sore that never heals'. For me that means that there will always be something to worry about with Jackson if I let myself. Today I worry about cot death.

Tomorrow it could be one of these terrible drug-resistant viruses or a sudden attack of asthma. In the future he might get hit by a car like my sister Monica or get struck by a bolt of lightning—whatever.

He is just so beautiful. Every day he changes. He gets curious, frustrated, angry, tired, joyous (in fact sometimes over-joyous) and a whole lot more. In short, he is just like a human being. And I would like to think that our relationship gets better by the day.

Jackson, welcome. I will try and do everything I can to make your stay here as positive as possible. I hope that you enjoy your life in the lucky country and that you will have a positive impact on it. I wish you well on your journey, and I hope that you will love your life as much as I do mine.

Love, Dad.

# WE WANT MILK

## Heather Grace Jones

*Childless on just such an afternoon I am picking up pieces of cliff and throwing them over the edge. I am a blue wrapped Virgin, no Bellini baby at my breasts. She is beyond me, sleeping in the arms of Mary or some other woman who has no difficulty conceiving. When I leave here I will grab my lover's breath as she passes me tea, hold it, and imagine a child and the smell of fertility.*

*If I am ever a mother I will be as happy as the spray of salt on your face after a day filled with computers and telephones. Motherhood a small miracle like winter afternoons at Bondi, cold and happy and full of conflicting desires. Walking by the water I will look at the grey horizon and not be afraid. I will want coffee, to go home, to swim in the ridiculous sea, to stay out late with the wind rushing inside my coat and my nose red with anticipation. Darkness will settle over me the way a parent smoothes a blanket inside a cot, for comfort.*

*If I am ever a mother I will spray Betadine and good intentions everywhere.*

### Her finest accomplishment

I have been trying to get pregnant since May four years and five months ago. I never imagined the difficulty that pregnancy would pose or the time it would consume. May seemed an auspicious month to begin, the season of change, the smell of leaves sharp in the air, the bite of cold as yet uncertain. Perhaps spring is more obvious but the cycle seemed more courageous in May, more in tune with the inherent contrariness of trying to fall pregnant without a male partner.

I was not a lesbian when I was young and full of eggs, but I have always wanted a child. At seven my favourite game was choosing names for my baby. I still play it. My lover and I lie in our lofty bed and speculate about the degree of damage we could inflict on our baby if we called her Winifred or Agnes. We giggle and discuss whether she should call us both 'Mama'. We wish we could create a child together. 'Conceive comes from the Latin *concipere*, To take in'.[1] I take her in me as sweet as wedding cake. I hold her tight fist and wish a baby could, would flower from her fingertips, the brush of her lips against mine. We are maternal bodies who fuck for pleasure and comfort and in order to exist. During our first years of trying I thought my pregnancy as inevitable as the tides. Lucky that we had two wombs instead of one, but lately I have come to understand that if my lover has a child, I will be excluded. The baby will not be mine in the same way as if my body had grown large with her needs, her ankles twisting below my heart.

My yearning for the physicality of motherhood is as inexplicable as it is immense. Biology must play its part in this little drama. My body born with the potential for half a million progeny in stored oocytes, is slow and sterile as these eggs age alongside my sagging butt. They grow less adventurous every day and must be encouraged, like astronauts with drugs and exercise, to launch themselves into unknown reaches.

Each egg pure and self-sacrificing as mothers should be. As I will be, if ever I thrust wrinkled skin and flailing limbs out between my legs, and begin the domestic and social rituals that constitute the raising of a child. I am dreaming of being the perfect mother—a role that seems within the grasp of any modern girl, her finest accomplishment. In the last three centuries 'the mother' has grown more saccharine than soap opera. She has shifted her bulky body, her brood, her principle desires to fit within the confines of a Rousseauean vocation.[2] Maternal love, previously an unspecified emotion, has become axiomatic. Infants, who once routinely languished with wet nurses, are reified in popular culture while a woman such as Lindy Chamberlain who is thought to show insufficient maternal affection suffers the consequences. Even economies are partially dependent on the mother as we know her and my desire is as malleable as any other sucker's. I disappoint myself by wanting what I have been taught to want. By wishing for the stereotypes of the maternal, the first glance between mother and child. The vernixy breath of my newborn sticky on my chest.

Even today as I write this I want a child. You only get so many primal experiences: birth, food, shit, sleep, sex, pregnancy, death. It feels real, my instinct. As solid as the stones they use to cement bridges. Tangible. But I know that instinct is as mass marketed as romance; the ways I think about it peculiar to my culture and history.

According to Freud instinct has four central components. These can be illustrated, embarrassingly, by my own desire to bear a child. First there's the drive, or in my case the urge to make a baby. This combines with a need to actually satisfy the urge, the baby itself and finally hormones, or itchy fingers when looking at an infant, or whatever it is that's the physical source of my yen to procreate. In a Freudian world view these practical forces work together to determine the unconscious desire of the individual.[3]

After pop versions of Freud became commonplace and psychoanalytic theory more opaque, the philosophical distinction between need and demand and desire becomes less obvious and we're left with an even more scrambled subjectivity; mine in this instance, a sense of self that's further complicated by gaps and tensions. In longing, one is forever fragmented, and it's in these gaps, this brokenness, that desire flourishes. It manifests regardless of whether or not you believe in instinct. I am driven towards maternity and the fantasy of wanting to be. I experience a hunger that is both real and imaginary. I see my squalling, bawling baby as if she is already here.

Grasping at the slippery edges of my desire to be a mother, I try on these theories like buying new clothes, ideas following ideas that do not logically connect. There are too many reasons for wanting a child. If I desire to be a mother, it is because at a given moment Freud's four operations are in synch. If I desire to be a mother it is because I have tucked Freud under my toddler's arm and run headfirst into the world of the symbolic, the social world of language and culture, where I stay because I cannot leave. If I desire to be a mother it is because I am a creature of my time caught lusting after immortality. No matter, my longing remains. I am compelled by a desire that is as awkward as it is certain.

### Longing: to 'wish earnestly or vehemently for a thing or to do'[4]

The women in my family have always had trouble conceiving. I have never believed this would happen to me. I am not like the women in my family. Each month I have waited, hopeful, as urine soaked across the litmus surface and presented another minus. This is a lie. I have waited month after month, hope hidden, anxiety trapeze-tight and the tiniest suggestion of a pregnancy enough to propel me forward. Each month I have balanced the hormones in my body, dreamed my baby flying, placed my hands on my swelling belly and cooed songs to my unborn. I have thrown away so many pregnancy tests I am an environmental hazard. I have not cried whenever I could avoid it.

There are people who don't want children, have never, will never want children. My friend, L., who is many years older and smarter than me, says her clock never struck midnight. She tied her tubes at twenty, saved on the inconvenience of contraception and made her life. She refuses the assumptions of femininity not only by her lack of desire to mother but by refusing the 'naturalness' of sexuality or gender. As a single childless dyke with a great big ute, she repudiates taboos around homosexuality as she reinscribes the clichés of queerdom. Her identity is formed in a context where 'female-ness' is no longer a given, where it is possible to challenge the basic categories of identity and where the yearning for a body that has birthed a child is not inevitable.

Perhaps my yearning to live in a maternal body is a longing for a stable category of identity, for a fixed position on the sex/gender continuum. If I could only be a mother I could be satisfied. I could be fulfilled in the simplicity of one role. Meanwhile I stop short of being as desperate as the fairytale wolf who deceives the child in order to possess her, but only just. The illusion of the perfect state is always present but out of reach. During the night I wake startled by the cry of a cat or a neighbour's child. In the dark I try to remember that one is always in flux. I feel for a moment the fragility of my own life. I do not change the sheets that are spotted with my menstrual blood.

I feel myself lurching between body and self, between what I think I know and how I feel. In this lurch is potential for transformation. It is possible to allow ourselves to be remade by the unexpected. To encourage our identities to shift as we metamorphose. Each change is not a new age 'life-choice' but a potentially dangerous movement away from the safety of the categories that contain us: white, women, lesbian, professional, sporty, whatever. It is easier to stay still frantically trying to freeze the confusions of daily life and selfhood into fixtures, but listening to the night sounds around me I want to be more than my physical limitations. I want to question the rigid expectations of identity and subjectivity.

When I was ten I had a recurrent fantasy that I would find a baby, or better still give birth to one and get in the newspaper. At twelve I knew where babies came from, the luxury of imminent impregnation fading. These days when I pick up the bundle who is my second nephew, failure crackles in the air around us. Anyone looking at his baldy head, his Simpson's fingers, knows he is not my child. My inability is obvious. I do not watch him grip the nipple in his mouth. When I hold him I am aware that other people see me as less. It is conceivable I am paranoid. At the gynaecologist's we are counting days, studying mucus, looking at statistics that tell me I am one of 25 five per cent for whom there is no reason pregnancy doesn't happen. I am still waiting to be a part of the hoopla that links girl to woman, nature to culture. To truly grow up, one must bear fruit. That much is given.

### Spilt, or there's no use crying

Some days I know I have always been a mother, that the viscerality of a baby will not substantially alter my self-perceptions. I share this wishful prescience with many other infertile women. Maggie Kirkman's research (see 'I'm Going to Be a Mummy When I Grow Up', p 185) shows that being a mother is a central identity for many young woman long before their bodies start to swell. In other words, our sense of self is projected into forthcoming events as much as it is reconstructed from our pasts. A role, a birth, a child that does not yet exist has substance in the blood and dreams of your present.

We imagine ourselves in control at the same moment we are veering into the unimaginable. Looking forward, we condemn ourselves to long for the impossible; looking back we invent yearnings we haven't had, constantly remaking what we want. I remember my mother's tears. I remember my lover's sadness.

By the time I was seventeen, I didn't want children. I worried about overpopulation and the end of the world. Aware even then that my desire could allow me to consume a child in the same way I might collect new furniture, I was conscious of avoiding the ultimate narcissism of producing a child. This year infertility is a disruption of my whole sense of meaning. Dry as the desert I imagine Baby, Happiness, Love as if they are inevitable. Desire a low-grade infection that disrupts me.

Lately my best outcome is to see desire as a collective, not an individual, force. Better to view it as a way to unravel the social and political codes that produce maternal longing. To imagine desire as a way of understanding the subtleties of yearning, both personal and collective. Yearning: 'filled with longing or compassion or tenderness'.[5] Longing: hopeful as the bruised mouth of the lover. Like love, like desire, longing is disordered, melancholy, solitary. It is, I hesitate to admit, a selfish preoccupation.

As the rain drips off the roof I wonder whether it's possible to calibrate the differences between love, desire and instinct.

I don't know how to measure what really matters. If the instinct to reproduce is separate from the instinct to mother, is separate from passionate desire, not to mention love, how do I understand the loss of milk from my breast? Motherhood, whether a metaphor for perfection or for ambivalence and transgression exists; the infertile woman by contrast is curiously absent from popular culture, the infertile dyke by inference a simple confusion. It is as if the emptiness of the barren womb is illuminated by its invisibility. Longing a literal lack. Unlike the more obvious freak, the bearded lady or the chicken child, the infertile woman is visible only by degrees. She is lucky to be a social oddity and not a sight gag.

*Late, I write my name on the bottom of the list and go down to Pathology, surreptitiously brushing my hair, pulling out the knots with my nails. Alcohol and crescent fingers swab the soft skin of my elbow. My blood is sluggish, like old tomato sauce crusted around the top of the bottle. 'You should drink more water,' she says. The young woman with the needle up my arm. We look for a vein. Tighten the tourniquet. A rivulet of red runs up the butterfly and into the vial.*

*She is dewy-skinned and twenty, this bangle-sparkle-bodily collection girl. All the other woman in the waiting room are over-thirty tidy. Our birthdays falling stock. We purse our mouths, our lips. Bunch the muscles in flabby thighs, conceal the slits that any moment now will open nicely to the slide of stainless steel.*

*We will lie on our backs, bend knees and chat as a nurse enters us, train into tunnel, waves crashing, horses rearing, Alfred Hitchcock in full cinematic abandon. My womb has wandered, left its secure lodging and found its way into my throat. I am breathing uterus and bloody pulp. I am keeping my hope fresh as the green grass smell that accompanies new mothers.*

*At home we tried the eyedropper, syringe, cake-decorating methods all to no avail. JJ wanking in the outside toilet while we watch TV inside extra loud.*

*Queuing up with strangers who don't smile is easier, more difficult, easier, than shy holding a jar warm against your skin hustling the boy out the door. We speculate about his thoughts out there in the damp backyard with the snail killer and the reminders of other bodies' functions but we don't really care. We are as optimistic as fresh toast.*

*He has a beard, this boy John, in the beginning we ponder a hairy baby. Later we forget to ponder and briefly consider doing it the natural way. Even now, we talk to our baby as if she is here. We imagine her sturdy legs, bad temper, as we suck up frothy sperm, hold hands and try not to spill it on our clothes.*

*In the clinic I try to relax. Stressed women never conceive unless they are junkies, teenagers, Catholic, sex workers, really poor or my friends who it just keeps happening to. I am visualising blue skies, golden beaches as I press down on my heels, breathe deep into my stomach and nod to accept a number, a letter, a height, weight, eye colour, a maybe-baby in a purple straw.*

*Spreadeagled, I worry my bits are weird as another doctor gloves up and rubs cold lube on my genitals as if he is kneading bread . . . We do not have eye contact. When it is done I fold the disposable gown as neatly as I can and place it on the dressing-room chair. I am trying to leave a good impression.*

*I imagine sperm interior swimming, homing, I spend the day happy, keep my feet up, defy gravity a tiny pad soaking up the freefall. JJ says maybe our bodies just don't work together. Maybe my body just doesn't work. I am a hen who lays no eggs, a long-necked camel, a half a man. Will you pierce me with a stork's bill to quieten my hysteria? I am awash with rusty blood, sitting in a saucer of milk, exposed. My womb is back tight in its pedestal of bones. It flexes.*

*I give up coffee but not alcohol. Take vitamins, owe my naturopath money, owe the clinic so much money they send me to the receivers. I plan to steal a newborn but the next one I see is so ugly I am thwarted. In the oval office the doctor has his family photos. He says he doesn't know if I am viable though my eggs release and hormones surge with monotonous regularity. In Mengele's kitchen time passes. I try to remember I am nowhere nasty.*

*The only things worse than the baby hunger are big business, road rage, police brutality, torture, starvation, the welfare, art galleries, the greenhouse effect, earthquakes, depression, deforestation, the anti-hemp movement, scabs, pastoralists, economic rationalism, war crimes, our treatment of refugees, the state of Indigenous health, and ten-year-olds dripping in someone else's cum.*

*But I am thirty-eight and without child. I am obsessed in that
shameful, hateful way of absolute longing. I want no one to know how
hard I am grieving. I want everyone to know.*

### Dry as the desert

Many women see their infertility as failure, and I am no exception. Its smell follows me, visible in unfortunate lights. My
feelings are as obvious as peroxide and disturbingly universal.
Failure is an experience that crosses cultures, women across
the globe lament their lack of childbearing capabilities and are
persecuted for their infertility. Folkloric accounts shame the
infertile woman for her witchcraft, sin or choice of career over
family. In Western folklore it is either selfishness or neurosis
that has generally prevented a woman becoming pregnant. As
late as the mid 1970s leading psychologists, conflating the
medical and the moral, saw nothing odd in the notion that 'as
Harlow's disturbed monkeys could neither reproduce nor
effectively nurture, that seems true for people too. It is as
though to some extent nature's fail-safe mechanism is infertility in those who are not psychologically healthy enough to
nurture.'[6] Even today women are labelled desperate, obsessive,
hysterical if they try too hard to have children, have 'too many'
interventions, or let their physical inadequacies affect their
personal relationships. We are castigated for wanting to have it
all, a career and motherhood, as if the very greed of such
a combination is bound to be punished by difficulty in
conceiving. This punishment is generally, though not always,
figurative in the West. Women elsewhere are not always so
lucky. As Germaine Greer has pointed out, barrenness is associated with lechery in many cultures, fruitfulness with
modesty and virginity.[7] A woman who is perceived as licen-
tious and unfruitful is an easy target. Infertile women often
suffer brutal treatment. This manifests in all the obvious ways,
not the least public humiliation.

It seems I may not be a viable unit. My doctor tells me this
as if he is ordering meat. The photo in his office of the baby in
one hand the forceps in the other is perhaps after all, not a

joke. At dinner I pull the bones from fish and drink a toast to patent tubes.

'In India a childless woman is an inauspicious guest at a wedding or chauk (infant blessing) ceremony.'[8] In Egypt she is '...an eyesore to her husband.'[9] In the China of the one-child policy, recent comments about childless women in a magazine belie the suggestion that fertility is problematic in that culture: 'Although she looks smart and healthy she is pitiably useless.' 'Keep a dog and it can watch the door, keep a cat and it can catch mice. But what's the use of such a wife?'[10]

In Western religion such a wife has prayed to St Anne or St Elisabeth. My prayers have gone to pagan goddesses and fertility drugs. In another time I would be a witch, night flying, enjoying my pact with the devil and the taste of children's flesh. Such a woman is dangerous to know. It might be catching, this sterile streak. My friends do sympathy with a touch of fear, the history of anxiety about infertility as infection echoed in modern folklore.

In Andersen's 'Thumbelina', the much-desired child escapes without a backward glance from the strangeness of her adopted mother's home. In Basile's sixteenth-century fairy tale, retold a thousand times in modern parlance, we are expected to feel no pity for the childless hag who is Sleeping Beauty's rival for the prince's love. She has brought nothing to his house despite years of marriage. The infertile woman is despicable, the embodiment of both lasciviousness and asexuality.

They say that women perceive the world through their wombs. Georgia O'Keeffe drew flowers and I still see uteruses, the origin of life and hysteria. She is rumoured to have thought her flowers were not sexual but functional; a view of the female body influenced perhaps by Freud who believed that a woman's desire to have a child was the foundation stone of her sexual desire. This conflation of sex and procreation is constantly re/produced by church, state and popular culture. The woman is allotted a sexual role that she fulfils in order to be part of a socially sanctioned feminine pleasure. Thus sex and birth twine between desire and what is understood. For most heterosexual women, this merging of the sexual and reproductive organs happens early and happens hard. The separation is a process that involves politics and abandon.

For us dykes it is possible maybe to inhabit a space where fucking is separated from reproductive desire. Maybe. As an unwillingly childless woman you become primarily identified not by your sexual organs, but by that which does not function, your empty womb and that which does not exist, your phantom child. Negotiating the distance between passion and children reveals desires that are not only entangled but thwarted.

This revelation is a sadness. In every self-help book I have read on the subject, which is too many, for the authors, mostly women who have fought the demon of childlessness, infertility is to be mourned. It is true that grief is a constant in this narrative, yearning a full-time occupation that bears little resemblance to the glib consolations of institutionalised therapy. Loss and the nostalgia for that loss tear the self apart as you grapple with the constant shift of possibility and another lost hope.

I dream of climbing and falling, climbing and falling; what I know at odds with what I feel. I feel my infertility as the division between longing and being. It seems a hollow place. To long is to be in the future or in the past, it is to be always directed outside the moment in which you are currently located. Intent I catch the waft of fontanelle in gardens and books. Dancing, I am afraid my darling will leave me for a younger woman with a womb that bounces healthy on the ultrasound. I am afraid I cannot fix what is wrong.

I know I should reconsider my infertility as a point of departure. I should assemble the pieces of my barren womb, take my desire for a baby and make it as valuable as any newborn. I need to make and re/make reality, encourage movement, any movement even if it isn't logical or forward. I know my body is capable perhaps just of other things. It is possible I should take up rhythmic gymnastics or archery.

It is doubtful that I need to procreate, there are plenty of children in my family, in the world. The history of need manufactured. The language of desire predicated on emptiness, as if that emptiness is a given rather than a creation. As Michael Ignatieff has argued 'need is bounded by the idea of the necessary or the essential. Desire is unbounded even by the idea of utility.'[11] But my grief even if it is not necessary is hungry. Augustine said, 'It is yearning that makes the heart deep'.[12] Perhaps it is this absurd hunger for something I have never known that makes me who I am. How do you grieve a death that has never happened? Is it motherhood I desire or conception, birth, the raising of children, the walking in the park with my stroller and the dog? Inconsolable, I'm still hoping for the ministrations of stork or sperm. My grief evaporating in the passage of time. I am mourning future losses and losses already incurred. I am mourning nothing in particular. My arms are empty.

## Endnotes

1 Gabis Rita. (1998). *Oracles* in *Wanting a Child: Twenty Two Writers on Their Difficult but Mostly Successful Quests for Parenthood in a High-Tech Age*. Eds: Bialosky Jill, Schulman Helen, New York: Farrar, Straus and Giroux, p 82.

2 In his 1762 novel, *Emile*, Rousseau articulated the idea of motherhood as a 'vocation'. Mothering in this version was a virtuous and noble activity. He emphasised the sense of devotion and sacrifice that a true woman and mother not only felt but enacted. The modern family was launched at this time, sailing into the future on a Rousseauean sea of maternal love. For the record Rousseau placed five of his own children in foundling homes.

3 Fuery, Patrick. (1995). *Theories of Desire*. Melbourne: Melbourne University Press. p 18.

4 Sykes, J.B. Ed. (1982). *The Concise Oxford Dictionary Seventh Edition*. Oxford University Press, Great Britain, p 596.

5 Sykes, op cit p 1249.

6 Bardwick in Phoenix, Ann, Woollett, Anne and Lloyd, Eva. (1991). *Motherhood Meanings, Practices and Ideologies*. London: Sage, p 60.

7 Greer, Germaine. (1984). *Sex and Destiny: The Politics of Human Fertility*, Picador, Great Britain, p 51.

8 ibid, p 52.

9 ibid, p 52.

10 Chen in Handwerker, Lisa. (1995). *The Hen that Can't Lay an Egg; 'Bu*

*Xia Dan de mu Ji' Conceptions of Female Infertility in Modern China* in Terry, Jennifer, Urla, Jacqueline, Eds, *Deviant Bodies Critical Perspectives in Science and Popular Culture*. Bloomington: Indiana University Press, p 366.

11 Ignatieff, Michael. (1984). *The Needs of Strangers*. London: Chatto and Windus, pp 18, 27.

12 ibid, p 35.

# AFTER FIVE YEARS

## Elisabeth

After five years it is hard to remember exactly how I felt when Rosie first talked about having a baby. She'd decided she was going to have a baby and she said if I wanted to I could be involved. Our relationship was young, a year and a half old, and I was in lurv. Having children was somewhere in the misty future for me. I didn't feel quite ready but I couldn't see how I could really have a relationship with her and not be a parent to her child. The idea was scary but exciting as well. So I mentally gulped and said, 'Yes' and told myself I would deal with it when it happened.

I had no idea then what the mechanics of getting pregnant involved as a lesbian couple. How to get pregnant? Find some sperm! Sperm is in men, find a man. First we had to find a man who was relatively healthy and prepared to stay healthy. Someone who was prepared to fit into our picture of a family, etc. After months we did find our man and then for reasons that will always remain a mystery a baby wouldn't grow.

Those first attempts at backyard pregnancy were exciting for me. We would jump into bed giggling, trying to suck up every last drop of sperm from the chipped blue teacup we had provided for our 'father' to wank into in the backyard toilet. I would symbolically squirt it in, then we would gross out when the precious stuff leaked out into the bed and joke about who had to sleep in the wet patch. Time after time time Rosie still wasn't pregnant. We decided to try another way: this meant 'The Clinic', which has loomed so large in our lives for sooooo long. At this stage I was still pretty optimistic about the whole thing. I was getting more and more into the idea of becoming a parent and I was sure that soon a baby would

129

arrive and we would become a happy family of three instead of two.

Initially visits to the clinic were exciting in their own way. I felt sure that this would work, we were in professional hands. Going to 'The Clinic' was a process, a regulated procedure. Taking blood, waiting for results, sperm shots, waiting for results again, doing the whole thing over again as each cycle was unsuccessful. Going to the clinic was exhausting. Not an early riser, six or seven mornings in a row fighting to get to Bondi before dawn's crack was draining by the end of the week. That was all I had to deal with, though. Rosie had to put up with the constant blood taking and investigations up her clacker. Being pumped full of physical- and mood-altering hormones and being referred to as a 'non-viable unit'.

After a while I don't know if I felt removed from the process but I was not really involved, apart from driving Rosie to the clinic and waiting there. I no longer had my physical role as sperm squirter and though the clinic was kind of lesbian-friendly, I didn't feel like I was really acknowledged as the partner. I always felt uncomfortable squashed at the back of the tiny cubicle as the nurse did her thing. Afterwards I would hold Rosie's hand as we read New Idea and secretly ate croissants.

That's kind of how it was at first but after several months The Clinic began to colour our whole lives. As time went by and cycle after cycle our baby wouldn't grow, The Clinic turned into the regular awful event. It wasn't fun or exciting anymore for me and it became desperate for Rosie. All our happy expectations had faded into dull disappointment and then into despair as the reality of childlessness loomed.

My memories of that time are exhausted and claustrophobic. Riding up and down in the little grubby elevator, squashed into drab prefab cubicles, the stupefying boredom of The Clinic waiting room.

The process of donor insemination (DI) itself was dull, invasive and a financial strain, (those pathetic more than half-dead sperm were costing over $700 a pop) but something else had secretly started to grow in our relationship, something black and oozing. I don't know what to call it. It was a thing between us. One part of it was the reality of no baby coming for Rosie. It was something terrible to see this deep, darkest, blackest despair I could do nothing about. But that wasn't all; it was also slimy, subversive and twisting. It turned us against each other. Rosie accused me of not understanding what she was going through and, even worse, not wanting to understand. I was confused, guilty and hurt. It is true no baby was not the end of the earth for me—I thought I could see a future ahead for us if no baby came. And it is also true that I didn't exactly know what was going on for Rosie, but I thought: How could I? And as hard as I tried I couldn't seem to satisfy this need in Rosie.

Anyway, after four years of trying to get pregnant, there was still no baby and the relationship was in a big fat mess.

And then... but before I go on I want to talk about what it was like being the potential mother of my female partner's child. As a non-biological female parent, I am invisible to the heterosexual world. People aren't accustomed to dealing with you, so they don't. They don't have a box to put you into, which has its benefits if you want to stay out late all night and party, but if you are trying to be a parent it can be quite difficult. Friends, parents and acquaintances inquire about my role. My parents do not automatically refer to our baby as their grandchild. They have not cooed and doted over Rosie as some in-laws would. Who knows what will happen with time? I want them to be part of the joy of this, our baby. I wish for happy families with all the grandparents and extended family members involved regardless of biology.

Meanwhile, my partner and I keep having to publicly reinforce my position, saying who I am at ultrasounds and doctors' appointments. Even worse, we have to fight against a kind of self-censorship because people don't always automatically include you, and you don't always know what you are supposed to do in parent situations. I have had to learn to think of myself as someone with kids and think about my role as the other parent. It's a new part of being a lesbian dealing with additional discrimination and expectations and I'm still trying to figure out how to assert myself against the heterosexual paradigm and how to simply think of myself as a normal parent.

The Clinic, that old Clinic, was trying to be lesbian-friendly but they didn't quite make it and, let's face it, they don't really care; they are just trying to make money. At the compulsory pre-procedure DI counselling session, the social worker tried to cut and paste her spiel to fit with our sexuality. It didn't work. The concerns of non-biological fathers did not compute with me and the legalities of non-biological lesbian mothers were not mentioned. Staff and doctors were mostly friendly but always a little bit awkward, which was, I felt, ironic since the waiting room was usually chockers with our friends and other lesbian couples—let's face it, we are their biggest growth market. Heterosexual couples used to covertly stare sometimes in the waiting room.

I have wondered how different my experience would have been if lesbian motherhood were taken for granted. How much less pressure there would have been on our relationship. I will never know what it is like to be the biological parent of our baby and whether it would have made a difference to the struggles we went through. Being a biological parent, my commitment to the baby would have been taken for granted unless I actually chose otherwise. Being a lesbian parent, I have had to earn my commitment stripes. Sometimes in the depths of it all I didn't feel very committed and this I think had so much more impact on our relationship than if I was the father, but maybe I'm having myself on.

Recently I caught up with a friend and asked about how their pregnancy was going. He told me his partner had had a miscarriage. I was really sad thinking about how I would have been feeling if I was him and then he astonished me by saying that he felt all right, because he never felt a connection until the baby was born. I walked away thinking that he and I might be sociopaths for not being able to connect with potential babies when I realised I did have a really strong connection to the whole baby thing once Rosie got pregnant. It was her infertility I couldn't connect with. Watching a doco about the death of a baby I was curious to hear another father expressing ambiguity about his partner's pregnancy and their future child. It wasn't until the child was born and dying that he suddenly got it.

Ironically these stories of paternal neglect made me feel much better about my feelings when Rosie was trying to become pregnant. Biological fathers obviously didn't know what the hell was going on most of the time, so it was OK if I didn't. In fact I seemed to be doing much better than either of them. My worry about whether I would have more insight into the whole thing if I were biologically related to the coming child, blah blah, was soothed. And suddenly I was feeling fine—not only because I'd discovered I wasn't a freak but because a little miracle happened when Rosie and I least expected it. After plodding up Everest and then looking like we were going to be blown away in a storm, IVF came through and Rosie got pregnant.

God, it was a near thing though. Only a small quantity of eggs harvested and then they all carked it except one—what a tenacious little bugger that must be—and it managed to stick to the wall of Rosie's uterus. Yippee. I won't say it was happiness overnight, because it's hard to shed grief and depression and resolve relationship tensions, but things for us have improved a lot.

And it doesn't end there, wish I'd known. While the fact of pregnancy was unbelievably joyful the practicality is so tenuous it's excruciating. They don't tell you about the threat of miscarriage, spina bifida, Down syndrome, etc. I'm learning that from here on in that it won't be smooth sailing either, but that that isn't necessarily bad. I don't know how others have found the experience of getting pregnant by artificial means, but for me it has been life-changing, and my baby hasn't even been born yet.

# WHO SAID YOU HAD TO BE MARRIED?

## Leesa Meldrum

*Leesa Meldrum was denied access to IVF clinics in Melbourne, under Victorian law which banned fertility treatment for single and lesbian women. In 2000, she took her case to court and won, on the grounds that she had been discriminated against as a single woman. Prime Minister John Howard tried to reverse the new ruling, and the Catholic Church has challenged Leesa's case in the High Court.*

I was so surprised at all the fuss over my case. I just thought it was a natural thing for a woman who was infertile to want to have a child and be able to access fertility treatment in her own state. I couldn't believe it when my house was surrounded by media—they camped here. I never really expected it to get to that level. Here I am, just a woman who wants to have a baby, like big deal.

When I won the court case it was definitely a victory for me, and for all women in Victoria. Why should women in Melbourne have to travel interstate for IVF? I mean, it's a cosmopolitan town, why shouldn't we be the same as the other states? I was really happy with the outcome. The problem with the media coverage was that a lot of people missed the point. They didn't realise I am infertile; they just thought I was a single woman wanting a child. I think too, they wanted to miss the point, because everybody thinks that all women should have a husband and children and to me that's a thing of the past. I guess I'm representative of what is going on now. It's very hard to meet the right partner or find a husband, and if I waited I'd be far too old, so I had to do something.

I still don't understand why people have a problem with

single women having IVF. If I was fertile and went down the pub and met some guy and didn't even get his name but fell pregnant, people would probably be OK with that. But because I want to be responsible, and I want to pay, and I want to do it all the right way, they seem to want to punish me. Maybe they think I'm a closet lesbian, or I want a designer child, I'm not too sure. I don't think there's anything shameful in doing IVF, whether you're single or married. I don't care if I've become the public face, because I'd made up my mind to be a single mother and I don't care who knows. In some ways it was a relief to announce it publicly.

Everyone assumes that getting a husband is the solution. Even doctors have told me that. In 1999, one gynaecologist told me repeatedly to go and get a husband. I remember saying to him once, ' Where am I going to go? To the husband supermarket?' That day I left his surgery crying, because I thought to myself, 'Well, I'm never going to have a baby, because no one is ever going to help me.'

I always suspected I may be infertile, because I'd been in long relationships and never fallen pregnant. But it was only two years ago that I had it confirmed. When I was a little girl I wanted five kids, and I still would want five. But I'll be lucky now if I have the one. That's all I've really wanted to do, is to be a mum. And I've always been maternal. My boss at the RSPCA is always saying, 'I wish you'd hurry up and have a baby,' because I keep wrapping the little baby birds up like they're babies, with their little heads sticking out. I think I'd be a good mother, but whether my dream will come true or not is another thing.

When you're single, the medical profession treats you differently. I've been discriminated against for the last eight years that I've been trying to get pregnant. When I first thought about doing IVF, I rang a few hospitals in Melbourne, but no one really wanted to know about me. Once I went to one of the major womens' hospitals in Melbourne and I didn't even know I was infertile then. I just wanted to have a laparoscopy to check. They told me to come back when I had a husband. When I complained, they simply put me at the bottom of an operation list, so if somebody dropped out one day they could ring me at the last minute. That was clearly discrimination.

When I first started trying to get pregnant, the IVF clinics wouldn't even accept de facto couples, so I had no hope. All I could do was get into relationships that were unloving, and I'd stay there and do anything to keep the relationship going, even when I was unhappy. Eventually I decided to go overseas, and I went to Northern Ireland, because I knew IVF was more accessible there.

In Northern Ireland, single women can have IVF and the first three cycles are free. I was just about to start IVF, but my visa ran out and I had to come back here. I mean, even the Catholics in Northern Ireland have IVF. They believe in having children, so I don't know what the Catholic Church is doing down here in Melbourne.

I came back and finally begged a gynaecologist in Sydney to do a laparoscopy. He told me he didn't usually treat single women, but he agreed to do it. He put me into hospital, did the laparoscopy, and discovered that my left tube was damaged. Later down the track, though, I found out there was a lot more wrong.

*Leesa started IVF treatment in 1999, but under Victorian law at the time was barred from Melbourne clinics. She had to travel to Albury, on the New South Wales–Victorian border, for each IVF cycle.*

I made the trip to Albury six times. It was really lonely. When you're doing IVF, you've got anxiety already, you're distressed and worried about what you're about to do. I had a four-hour train trip and sometimes I'd arrive really late at night. I'd have to go and find a hotel, get up in the morning, get a taxi, go to the clinic for the transfer then come back to the hotel. I had no one with me, nobody. I didn't know anyone in Albury, so I'd have to get up and go and get food. It was awful, a very lonely experience, at a time when you really needed your family.

My mum and father are very supportive. Deep down, my mum probably would have liked me to marry and have children, but she understands now that it didn't work that way, and she knows my desperation to have a baby. She would do anything too, to get me a child. So I've got very good support. It was just impossible for them to come to Albury with me.

All up, I've done sixteen artificial insemination and IVF cycles. It takes a real toll. I find it almost impossible to do IVF and work at the same time. I've done it, but it's ghastly because I have to say to a supervisor, 'I've got to go and have the transfer and I won't be in for two days,' and they're ringing up saying, 'We're short-staffed, can you come in?' and I don't even want to move, I just want to lie still. It's distressing, because the workplace doesn't really understand. I've had to tell men that I'm on IVF and 'I need this day off' and 'I got my period today, I've got to go to the doctor'. It's pretty humiliating. I feel like an open book. Everybody around you knows, because you know what a work-place is like: even if you tried to keep it a secret you couldn't. And you feel a bit of a failure, because everyone else is falling pregnant and you're not. At my workplace, nearly everyone around me seems to be pregnant. Except for two older women, everyone's in their twenties or thirties, so they're all having their babies, and they have them so quickly. Like they just plan to have the baby, the next thing you know they're pregnant. They talk about how fertile they are, and it really hurts.

People don't realise what women go through for IVF. They think it's simple. I mean, if I just wanted to be a single mother and go on the dole, why would I put myself through all this pain and all this money? It's cost me over $30,000, and I'm injecting myself for fourteen days, and having a general anaes-thetic, and taking time off work. My whole life revolves around IVF. I have no social life, I'm just dealing with IVF all the time, just trying to become a mother.

The hormone drugs really stuff me around, too. Like I used to be really skinny, then I started taking all the drugs and I put on stacks of weight. And with the hormones you get big mood swings, it's a real emotional roller-coaster. For example, at the RSPCA, people ring up and say their cat died and I start crying. Usually I wouldn't do that, but on the hormones, life's just not normal. Each month when my period comes I find it

*Leesa Meldrum*

devastating. I describe it as a death. I have to grieve for the loss of the embryos, because really they are potential babies and they were my babies, so it is a death. Then I have to get strong again and start another cycle otherwise I'd probably end up in a mental institution. I've got to keep positive the whole time.

Of course, since I won the court case, I've been able to go to the Melbourne clinic, and that has made life much easier. I simply have to get up, catch the tram down to Richmond. And there are people here to come and pick me up, so that's great. And also I've got a new doctor, one of the top specialists, and he's wonderful. I have great faith in him. So hopefully I am getting closer to success.

In fact, he's the one who's discovered what's really wrong with me. I've got a few medical hurdles to overcome that I didn't know about till I met him. He fixed my damaged left tube, but he's found that my cervix is very narrow and that I have antibodies in my blood which means my blood's so thick that it can stop the embryos from implanting. I'm about to get that seen to, and I might need more surgery before I do another IVF cycle.

When I finally found all this out I was really angry, because eighteen months prior to this laparascopy, I had the other one in Sydney, where they'd picked up that the left tube was a bit stuffed but they did nothing about it. So why didn't they? I mean, I could have gone on like that for the next ten years. I consider it malpractice in a sense. It adds to my dilemma about falling pregnant, because I could have had this fixed years ago. But you feel so vulnerable at the IVF clinics, you just do what they tell you to do because it's your only hope. Especially if you were single and going across the border was your only hope. You did whatever they said.

The old law was ridiculous. I know a girl who married twice and divorced twice just so she could get on the IVF program in Victoria. She does IVF, gets say, thirty eggs and then gets divorced. That was the only way that she could get into a clinic. She calls me her hero because I've changed it for her now; now she doesn't have to get married a third time. I never even thought to do that, I would just constantly be upset that I was discriminated against. And I always wanted to do something about that. In fact about three years ago I said to a woman at work, and she keeps reminding me of this, I said, 'I'm definitely going to be the girl to change it for single women,' and then it happened.

When the Catholic Church responded so badly to my case, I didn't feel hurt, even though I'm Catholic myself. In fact, I was furious the priests showed up at the court. They don't get married and have kids, so what would they know about it, anyway? They should read the Bible more closely, because back in the Biblical days, there were a lot of women who didn't have a man but they had a baby. It was often described in terms of divine intervention, it was planted like a seed, like artificial insemination and IVF. So personally I don't think they know what they're talking about.

So many other states have had IVF for single women and lesbians, so where was the Catholic Church, then? I think they're just looking for media attention, or maybe some politician is putting them up to it. There must be something going on there because if they were so concerned about single women and lesbians, why didn't they do something in Sydney, Adelaide, Surfer's Paradise, where all the clinics accept single women?

I don't have a problem with God, I just have a problem with the Archbishop of Melbourne, and all his mates. I still pray to God to help me fall pregnant. God himself hung around with all the people that didn't fit into society back then, so I'm sure he's a loving God. It's just these bishops that have created rules to suit themselves.

John Howard, the prime minister, seems to have backed off a bit. If he was to spend a week in an IVF clinic, I'm sure he'd change his mind. How would he have felt if he didn't have his children? That's what these politicians are not looking at. We have the right to have babies, and bring them up, and be good mothers. I think originally he was opposing me just for votes, to make him look good.

One Christmas I had a very sick dog who was dying, and a friend of mine who's also a single woman on IVF came with me to the vet clinic. But I felt I spent the whole day comforting her because she was so upset that it was Christmas Day and she didn't have a baby. We spent the day sitting in the lounge room consoling each other. We'd both been invited out, but everyone else has children, and it makes it too painful because my biggest dream is to have my child run out on Christmas Day and see all the gifts.

Then on top of everything, on Christmas Day my period came. So I had a dying dog, an upset single IVF woman, and I had my period. People have no idea how hard it can get. Soon after Christmas, the dog died and it was horrible because I'd had him for fifteen years and he was like my baby. I did everything to save him, it cost me thousands of dollars, but at the end of the day he just died. So it was really difficult. I had the double dose of losing the babies and losing my baby, my dog.

I've looked into overseas adoption, but again, that's a lot of money and it takes a long time. I've looked into adopting here, but it's not babies here, it's only older children who are not really wanted by their parents. If I have to, I'd do it, but unfortunately you can't adopt here if you're on the IVF program, so there's always obstacles. I thought about fostering, but then I know myself too well. I'm so desperate to be a mother I don't think I could give the child back. So I don't think that's for me.

I know I'd be a good single mum because I've always wanted to be a mother, and for many years I've collected clothes and articles and to me it's a career. I want it to be my career. I'm not going to go to work at first, I want to stay home with the baby. I just want to do everything for the child, nurture it, teach it the realities of life, make it happy. I've been working for fourteen years at the RSPCA, but I also had another job where I went around putting sick people to bed, and I could do that part-time. So I've got things up my sleeve, to support a child. People always ask, 'How will you do it?' but I'll survive. I think any woman can make a good mum, if that's her dream.

The reality is I hardly know anyone who's got a husband. OK, there's my cousin, she's got a husband and a family, but most women I know are single or divorced. The whole thing about happy families is a myth, and people have to start realising that. Who said we had to be married? Is it such a crime not to be married?

Even though I've had to do all this IVF on my own, when I'm in the IVF clinics I don't feel any worse than someone who's sitting with their husband. Sometimes they start fighting and the husband looks really tense, and I think it could be harder with a man than without one. And I never had that dream of getting married—I've never really liked the white dresses. I've been in de facto relationships, and it was a nightmare. When I've been by myself I've been quite relieved. But I have always had the dream of having a baby, always.

In fact, an IVF baby is probably more wanted than that of a normal heterosexual couple wanting a baby, because of what we go through. I think every woman should be shown what people go through for IVF because then they might donate— if they're fertile and they've finished their family, then they might donate embryos for those who need them. As women we're not educated enough about fertility and infertility, not at school or in the community.

I know I'd donate eggs if I could. I'd carry a baby too. If I had one baby, I'd carry a baby for somebody, because I know the desperation. I've already donated one of my embryos to a girl who's got none, and somebody said to me, 'You might have needed that,' but so does she and I've already got some in storage. I hope she falls pregnant with it.

I'll definitely go to court again if I have to. Even if I fell pregnant, I would fight this battle because I wouldn't like any other woman to go through what I've gone through, having to go to Sydney or Northern Ireland or Albury. I've done it all, and it's just not fair, and it also makes me think too, that women haven't progressed in life, like we're still really second-class citizens. You look in the paper and there's advertisements to help impotent men; nobody kicks up about that. But if a woman's infertile and single, it's a totally different scenario. I think women need to unite and show that we are just as valuable as the men in our society.

All I can do right now is keep on with the IVF and deal with the grief. Sometimes I get inspired because I meet people who've been in similar situations and been sucessful. One of my friends went through IVF fifteen times and they've just had twins. And I met another lady, she'd done it twenty times. So there could be hope at the end of the day. I try not to give up. I try to stay positive and inspired.

# SECRETS OF THE
# LITTLE ROOM

## Tom Morton

It's not easy shooting your bolt into a specimen jar. Few women will believe this, of course, and why should they? Why should an activity that seems to come to men as automatically as sneezing or yawning suddenly become a problem just because they're serving up a sperm sample in an IVF clinic?

The little room is equipped with a leather rocking-chair, a washbasin, a bottle of whisky and a stack of magazines, mostly *Penthouse*, *Black Label* and the like. The chair squeaks, and just across the corridor the technicians are working patiently away, listening to classic hits FM station and waiting for you to hand your contribution across the counter. The whisky is supposed to be for after you've done the business, but over the course of a number of visits to the little room, I took to pouring myself a slug before I'd taken off my trousers. It's hardly a romantic setting. A friend of mine who had spent some time in the little room himself, a loving and devoted husband, said he sometimes wondered what it might mean that at the crucial moment, just as he was producing that one precious wriggler from which would come his darling son, he was thinking about Miss Dominican Republic 2001 and not his wife.

I spent the worst and the best day of my life in the little room. If it's possible for someone who's lived such a comfortable, privileged existence to know what despair is, I think I found out that day. It seemed like the end of everything, but it turned out to be a beginning.

I couldn't say exactly when I first knew I wanted to have kids with Eury, but it was pretty early in our affair, much earlier than I would ever have dared admit to her. An affair was all either of us thought it was. She had a boyfriend in Sydney, I was a convicted serial monogamist, a recidivist with a lot of form. It was January and the nights were hot and still; we were just keeping each other company without our clothes. One Saturday we drove down to one of the beaches past Geelong. Eury lounged in the passenger seat with her feet up on the dash, singing along to a mixed tape she'd made, early Elvis, Smoky Robinson, excited as a kid. I loved the way she got a kick out of things that were so simple, even if she was rude about the Melbourne beaches when we got there. She was a dag, and she didn't care.

Well, you can guess the rest. There's a great poem on the subject called 'Story of a Hotel Room' by Rosemary Tonks, about a pair of English lovers in Paris. They too think they're temporary 'guests of one another's senses', having nothing more than a fling. Idiots, says the poem, for '...without permanent intentions/You have absolutely no protection'. Before I knew it I was in free fall, skydiving without a parachute. I had no idea what I was doing, but one conviction was growing stronger and stronger in my mind: this reckless, wild, often infuriating woman was the one I wanted to mate with (her choice of words, not mine). I'd met my match in more ways than one. One day, as we were lying in bed, she was telling me about the longtime boyfriend in Sydney, how she wanted to have children but he couldn't come at it. Without thinking, I blurted out, 'You could have a child with me'. Not a smart move. But as I've discovered, the smart moves are not always the right ones.

It took a couple of years for her to even start contemplating my offer. In the meantime a lot of bad shit went down, as they say in the movies. Bad, but character-building. Eury found it harder to let go of the boyfriend than I'd guessed. He didn't know what he wanted, or couldn't make up his mind. She moved back to Sydney, I followed her. I've never been much good at pinball, and for a while I felt like one of those silver balls, perpetually bouncing back and forth between the ringing, pinging pins. A kind of blind determination kept me going, a feeling that this was the one thing in my life I had to give my all to.

Sometime towards dawn one morning, after a few hours of shallow, alcohol-attenuated sleep, I dreamed I was walking beside a wide, wide road in Melbourne, a little like the Punt Road where it passes Collingwood Town Hall. There was no traffic, only a kind of pale grey radiance, so pale it wasn't even light, like a very fine mist covering the world. On the other side of the road I saw three figures: Eury and two small children, walking in the opposite direction, away from me. She didn't look my way.

I woke from this dream with a terrible sense of regret and failure. I was sure it was all over.

Around two years later I made my first visit to the little room. In the meantime Eury had made the final break with the boyfriend, and we'd moved in together. We stopped using contraception. After everything that had happened, both of us assumed that getting pregnant would be the easy part.

Nothing happened. Eury had herself checked out. Both of us assumed, somehow, that if anything was wrong, it must be with her. Infertility is automatically assumed to be a female problem; it's discussed endlessly in the popular press, while male infertility is shrouded in a discreet, embarrassed silence.

The gynaecologist gave Eury the all-clear; no blocked tubes, no endometriosis. Eventually, I took myself in hand and got my sperm seen to. A week later, I emerged from the fertility clinic like a fish gasping for air. I had sperm all right, but the little buggers weren't swimming properly. The technical term is 'low motility'.

Over the ensuing months Eury and I learned more about human reproduction than either of us had ever wanted to know. I had an operation to correct a varicocele, a varicose vein in one of my testicles. As far as I understood it, the increased blood flow through the vein heats up the testicles, which affects the sperm, making them sluggish and listless. I remembered reading about some British actor who'd spent months dipping his balls in a bucket of iced water every day. The operation seemed preferable, but you had to wait at least six or seven months afterwards for any improvement.

In the meantime, both of us had acupuncture and Chinese herbs. The doctor was a British woman who'd done a master's in genetics and then stepped off the track of a conventional scientific career to study in China. The herbs tasted foul, but I was reassured by her calm, dispassionate open-mindedness: she saw Western science and Chinese medicine as complementing each other, the claims of each to be assessed on their merits.

During this time I also started to tell people about my sperm problem. I found this hard to begin with. Female infertility gets talked about all the time; not least, I think, because women's bodies are considered the rightful property of science, an appropriate subject for public discussion—by properly qualified male gynaecologists, of course.

Going on IVF wasn't an easy decision. IVF is hardly a democratic kind of procedure: the woman has to submit to repeated examinations, hormone injections with all sorts of unpleasant side effects and the actual procedure itself, which can be very painful. Shortly before the procedure, there's a final injection that triggers ovulation, which has to be given into the muscle of the buttock in the middle of the night. I learned a lot about the extent of Eury's grit and determination the first time this had to be done: the alarm went off, the light went on, and she'd plunged the needle in without so much as a murmur before I'd hardly opened my eyes.

All the man has to do, by contrast, is give himself a quick one off the wrist in the little room.

Despite misgivings and a justifiable sense on Eury's part that she was getting the rough end of the pineapple, we went ahead. The first time, we tried our luck with GIFT: gamete intra-fallopian transfer.

The scene in the operating theatre resembled a scene from the manuals of the alchemists. Four figures in blue coats, masks and cotton caps moved about the room in a trance of intense concentration, little more than their eyes visible. My darling Eury lay with her legs in stirrups; I sat by her side, both of us facing a video screen that showed what was going on inside her. Jenny, the doctor, inserted the ultrasound probe, illuminating Eury's uterus and then her ovaries. We saw the follicles which hold the eggs—dark, finger-like or globe-shaped smudges, a little like nebulae. Despite the pethidine she had had beforehand, Eury tensed with pain when Jenny punctured the follicles and drained off the precious fluid in which the eggs were swimming—we hoped. Jenny was very calm, talking to Eury, explaining every step.

On the other side of the room Joe, the technician, bent over a microscope in a kind of glass booth with transparent walls. He was looking for eggs in the fluid Jenny had already drained. Another video screen showed us the view through his microscope. We had already been told we could get a video of the whole procedure afterwards if we wanted one.

While Jenny was still harvesting from the other follicles, Joe gave us the good news: first two eggs, then three, finally a fourth—more than we'd expected or dared to hope. Eury was happy and relieved that the pain was over, at least for a while. Jenny asked whether we wanted to put all four eggs back, or save one or two for later, just in case—but we decided to go for broke and put all four back.

Now came the difficult part: getting the eggs back into the fallopian tube along with 150,000 sperm. We had already been told that my sperm had washed up OK—the teaspoon or so I'd managed, not without some difficulty, to get into the specimen jar had been centrifuged and the most promising selected for re-insertion. At first, the catheter went up easily into Eury's left fallopian tube, but that was just a test run. When Jenny tried to put the catheter bearing the one precious drop of fluid that held both eggs and sperm into the same place, it wouldn't go. Eury was moaning softly with the pain, but she was very brave. Another catheter had to be fetched. Jenny tried a third time, this time aiming for the right-hand tube, but again no luck. By now everyone was on edge: I looked over at Paula, the nurse, and saw she was clasping her hands tightly together, squeezing the knuckles. The fourth blue-coated figure, an Indonesian doctor who was observing the procedure, averted his eyes modestly, but he looked worried.

Eury was in a lot of pain, so I asked if she could have more pethidine. That, too, had to be fetched. Finally, Jenny tried with a fourth catheter. Everything inside me was tense, willing it to succeed, willing her to find the right place. If I could have prayed, I would have. Instead, I thought of my Uncle Jim and my Gran, and Mum and Dad. All of them are dead, Mum when I was fifteen, Gran four years after her, then Dad's brother Jim, then Dad the year I turned thirty. I remember Mum holding me by the hand as a little boy, and the day she and Dad told us we were going to England to see the family, not long after she found out about the tumour. She was wearing a floral dress that day, and I remember thinking how young and fresh she looked, glowing with life. Just as I saw Mum in my mind on that day, Jenny found the spot and released the little drop, with all our love and hope swimming in it, into Eury's fallopian tube.

Everyone breathed a sigh of relief and looked glad and smiled. In this little cave, cut off from the daylight, surrounded by all the machines, the luminescent screens, the peeping of the machine that monitored Eury's pulse, in this thoroughly artificial womb, I felt as though some kind of mystery had passed through us.

That evening I cooked the dinner while Eury was resting, and finished scribbling the poem I'd started in the clinic, while the pethidine wore off and we waited to go home:

Nautilus and Argonaut

Light which is not light pearls in your inner sea,
To navigate, a singing too high for our ears.
Islands and archipelagoes unfold, whole dark continents
Up on the ghostly screen.

In this room without windows, you are opened
To the light. Up goes the tube, you wince,
I squeeze your hand; a filament, sheltering that single drop
Which holds both you and me, seeks a still haven.

What is that singing? It is the shades, the ancestors,
Guiding the boat through the dark waters, steering
The doctor's hand, they are all there singing
To the blind specks tipped from the boat into dark water.

'Swim', they sing, 'swim', as a gloved hand
Squeezes the rubber bulb and withdraws the tube,
'Mingle and come forth'. Above the crescendo, glowing
With pain and pethidine, you murmur 'Say a poem, Tom,
   say a poem'.

Two weeks of waiting. A couple of days before we were due
to go back to the clinic for a blood test, Eury got her period.
There's something elementally final about that smear of
blood. You can't question it, or wonder if someone's done the
test wrong. It's just there, as implacable as the tide going in and
out.

Over the next few months, during which we had another
unsuccessful procedure, we tried to talk through what it would
mean for us if we didn't have a child. Sometimes all the old
tensions in our relationship would reignite, and Eury would
become angry and withdrawn or declare that she couldn't see
any point in our staying together without kids. I didn't feel that
way. Why didn't I go off and find someone else, she asked me,
someone younger, more fertile? On one occasion, after she'd
repeated this question, I burst into tears. I felt she was deliber-
ately trying to hurt me—but I came to realise there was a kind
of frustration behind Eury's anger, a sense that I wouldn't face
the truth.

I was reluctant even to contemplate the prospect of failure—
that was the word that seemed to come unbidden into my
thoughts at times like this. Just as I'd been determined that
Eury was the one for me, I was determined that we would
manage somehow to have a child, and sometimes I think Eury
felt this determination was something blind, unwilling to
admit doubt. I started to unbend a little, to accept that enter-
taining doubts didn't mean admitting defeat.

Having a child by IVF seemed in many ways a selfish thing

to do. The year before, we'd been on a holiday together to Madagascar—a beautiful, haunting country, inhabited by people living in the most savage, bare-arsed poverty I'd ever seen. In the capital city, whole families lived in rubbish skips, lighting fires in them at night for comfort rather than cooking, because most of them seemed to have nothing to cook. On the main highway, a dirt road comparable with some of the more impassable dirt tracks in Central Australia, children stood by the roadside holding out baskets of fried grasshoppers and chicken heads to sell to tourists. How could it be right to indulge our desire for a child with a medical procedure costing thousands of dollars when the living children of living parents existed like this?

It didn't stop us. But both of us felt that if the IVF didn't work, and we couldn't have a child naturally, we'd have to change our lives somehow. Sitting in a cafe one Saturday morning, surrounded by other middle-class couples drinking their coffee, I saw the next twenty, thirty years of Saturday mornings stretching out ahead, drinking coffee, returning to a comfortable home, grumbling about our comfortable, secure jobs, going to the movies, having dinner. An overpowering sense of waste and futility came over me. What was the point of it all?

Around the same time, I realised I had very little idea of what having children was really like. In a hazy, idealised way, I had an image of myself and Eury with a couple of kids, playing in the park, or at home in the sitting room, laughing and making up silly games together in the evening. But I hadn't tried to imagine what our lives would be like, what sort of parents we'd become, how our relationship with one another would change.

After our second attempt at IVF, I wrote another poem.

Imaginary Child #1

Rewind the tape. You tumbling upwards through bright air
Onto your feet. The ball sucked backwards to my boot.

Your limbs unfurling from my arms as I
Unhug you. The sun moves eastwards
Over the winter park.

Earlier still
Nappies unsmear and fold themselves
Into the wrappers. That's the better part.

The last glimpse I catch
Is the bloody cord, winding you back,
Like a fish flapping, back
To the inner sea.

By the time our third attempt at IVF came around, we'd pretty
well agreed that it would be our last, or at least that we'd take a
long break before attempting it again. Both of us felt worn out,
drained, as though everything else in our lives was on hold.

The day came and we arrived early at the clinic. It was barely
light outside. As usual, four or five other couples sat in the
waiting room flicking through the magazines in edgy silence.
I signed the familiar forms and sloped off to the little room. I
knew I was a little nervous, it being potentially our final go,
but I'd managed to do my part both times previously. I had a
belt at the Johnnie Walker, sat down in the chair and studied
the magazines.

Nothing happened. There was flesh and fur by the acre on
display, but none of it produced even the mildest stirring in
the requisite area. I had another drink. A particularly embarrassing fantasy about the singer-guitarist from an Australian
rock 'n' roll band produced no results. I put my trousers back
on, went out to the waiting room and asked Eury to come in.

Eury was very tender and sensual. Between us we tried
everything, but every time I started to forget myself and my
steadily increasing panic the chair would start creaking loudly
or the technicians would change the station on the radio or
Eury's caresses would change and I'd be jolted back into self-
consciousness. There seemed to be a voice in the back of my
head saying It won't work, you're no good, you can't do it. Every

moment of sexual anxiety, of fear that I couldn't get it up, of physical and spiritual impotence I had experienced came flooding over me. My pathetic prick got half-hard and subsided five or six times.

We tried it in the little room and in the ultrasound room away from the technicians. I couldn't do it. Eventually I said I'd go and see the nurse. At the very beginning of our attempts at IVF, we'd had some of my sperm frozen at the clinic, insurance against just such an eventuality. The nurse said, yes, they could thaw it out, but it would take an hour or so, and time was short, the egg harvesting and transfer had to be done within a certain window of opportunity.

I said to go ahead and went back to Eury. Walking into the waiting room I felt as though I was in the middle of a huge amphitheatre and the whole of Sydney was laughing at me. I told Eury they were going to try the frozen sperm and she ran into the darkened ultrasound room and began to cry. I said, 'I'm sorry, I'm sorry', over and over, she said, 'I don't need you to be sorry, I need your fucking sperm'.

I started to cry and the words of a prayer came into my mind, one that had drummed its way into my memory in countless tedious church services as a child. 'We are not worthy, O merciful Lord, to come to this Thy table...'

I'd never seen Eury so furious and frozen and cold. She wouldn't speak to me or look at me. An hour or so passed, and just before the nurse came to lead her off for the procedure the doctor appeared, and reassured us that the frozen sperm had thawed out and appeared to be of good quality. 'Sometimes if they've survived freezing they swim that little bit harder!' he declared jovially. I didn't believe him.

A few weeks before, I dreamed that Eury and I went to Hell. We fell for a long time down a dark shaft, knowing Hell was where we were headed. We landed, not in a fiery lake, but in a small, cramped room. In the room was the father of my best friend, a former Anglican priest, a great drinker and sinner in his own way. I heard him preach once on St John's Gospel and thought he was one of only two priests I'd ever heard who didn't sound like a mealy-mouthed used-car salesman. In the dream, he seemed to be protecting us in some way. Following this dream, I bought a copy of Dante's *Inferno*, and on some whim I'd taken it with me to the clinic to read. Now I sat in the waiting room while Eury was being prepared for the anaesthetic, reading my way through the circles of Hell.

After a while I couldn't take any more. I was convinced that I'd lost Eury, that she would never forgive me for my failure. Shame, self-loathing and self-pity blanked out any other emotions or sensations. The dream I'd had years before, or Eury passing by on the far side of the road with our two children, came back to me. I knew I'd blown it. I knew this was the worst day of my life, worse even than when Mum or Dad died because it was my fault.

I decided to go out for a while. As I emerged into the daylight, I had a sudden overpowering feeling that everything would be all right, that somehow the procedure would work, despite all that had happened. It was as though I'd been struck by lightning. But the feeling faded again, and I wandered around miserably, buying some flowers, trying to eat something. In a terrible numb daze I went into a church and prayed to God in his mercy to give us a child, and I cried.

Praying didn't some easily. I remembered years ago, at the Anglican private school I went to, some bishop or deacon waving a finger at us and telling us that no matter how much we might doubt the Christian faith there would be some time in our lives when we'd pray. I took this to mean that there was some time in our lives when we'd be forced to submit to the stinking foul hypocrisy of the Anglican Church, and I hated him, like I hated the rest of them, with the exception of one curate at our local church and my friend's hard-drinking father. Praying always seemed like the final admission of defeat to me. I didn't know what God I was praying to now, but I couldn't help it.

After Eury emerged from the anaesthetic we went home in a taxi in exhausted silence. Eury went to bed. I made some soup, watched television and went to my bedroom. I got down on my knees and prayed again before I got into bed, something I hadn't done since I was about ten.

A little later I head Eury crying and went into her. She told me it would have to be all over between us, that she couldn't rely on me, I wasn't strong enough. She felt abandoned, let down in a way I'd never let her down before: not because I'd been unable to do 'that one thing'—though she still couldn't understand what had been the problem—but because in that moment I'd thought only of myself and my 'failure'. I'd been afraid, afraid for myself, instead of trying to understand her disappointment. She told me then that they had harvested only two eggs from her ovaries, barely enough to give us even a reasonable chance of success. Mixed with her anger was a bitter seam of self-reproach; she felt she'd been too hard on me, too cruel, but felt that meant she mustn't really love me after all.

I can't remember now what else we said, but sometime towards morning we fell asleep. I woke momentarily to feel Eury's arm around me and slept again.

That day neither of us went to work. We wandered aimlessly around the house, saying little, tiptoeing over eggshells lest the recriminations of the previous night break out again. In the afternoon we went for a walk. By evening I felt not all was lost, that there was some way our relationship might continue. Eury was forgiving, more than I dared hope for. Though I couldn't have said it this way at the time, it was as though something had broken in us both, like the spring in a wind-up toy, but to our surprise we were still walking and talking.

Nearly two weeks out from the dreadful day we went to stay with Eury's mother in the Blue Mountains. On the Saturday we walked for a long time, afternoon sun softening the brisk, chill air. Both of us were taut as violin strings, not daring to hope. We talked about taking a long holiday, maybe leaving work. Eury was sure she'd get her period the next day.

The following Wednesday we went to the clinic for the results of Eury's blood test. We'd never made it this far before. Speechless with excitement, we waited while the nurse phoned through for the results. Pregnant! We wept, or at least I did, and laughed and couldn't believe our luck. A day or so later I went back to the church and thanked God, a God I didn't know and still couldn't bring myself to believe in.

I don't think I stopped holding my breath completely until Angelo was born, six weeks ahead of time and weighing not much more than three pounds. Again, we were lucky; Eury had pre-eclampsia which wasn't detected until very late in the pregnancy. Another few days and Angelo might have died in her womb. When the obstetrician lifted him out, he looked like a tiny rabbit, covered in blood. As the air rushed into his lungs, he let out a huge howl. From that moment on, I was pretty sure he'd be OK. Anyone that small who could yell that loud must be a tough little feller, I thought, and indeed he is. I can't imagine the world without him now, or his brother Georgie, born two and a half years later—all our own work this time.

I couldn't say what the meaning of this story is now, except that I wouldn't wish it had happened any other way. I think I learned something about love in the little room, and about something else. I feel blessed, though by whom or what I don't know.

The Stars, Baby, the Stars
*With apologies to Dave Graney*
Soon, it will be your first Christmas.
Coming home from a party
We carry you to bed, both
A little drunk and drowsy
From the warm night and Brereton's Runway Red.
Your Mum lays you in the crib, and I think
We are like constellations to you, wheeling
In the bright sky the other side of myth.
Reliable, comforting, but still
Light years away, beyond speech.
Parents are always old, by the time
You know them, they tick and chime
At the appointed hours, predictable
As the tides. Perhaps, though
Half a lifetime from now, when you are
Coming home from a party, kissing someone

Or slipping down the long dark slope of sleep
You'll glimpse, just for a moment
Two faces bending over you in darkness, alive with gratefulness
And the stars, baby, the stars.

# ALWAYS PART OF ME

## Joanna

When I decided it was time to have children, we had lived together as a couple happily and studied together and travelled together and I guess all of a sudden it felt that, yeah, now the time is right. We both felt like that and it was a natural progression because I'd always thought about myself as a mother. It was always a part of me.

Having said that, I didn't daydream it very much, and for a time there during high school it probably wasn't something I dealt with because careers were pushed far more, but it was always in me. I never pictured myself without children.

When I imagined being a mother I related it to my own childhood. I'd be raising children as I had been raised, replacing a little bit of what I'd been given. I wanted to stop thinking about me a little bit and start giving more to others. Motherhood meant a chance to be a teacher, a chance to nurture, a chance to be a family in a fairly traditional sense.

I saw myself having a career, a partner, a home and then the children. Fairly orderly, isn't it, but I never thought that privilege wouldn't be mine. Particularly once it was taken away. Then I realised having children was something very special, it was something that life really did revolve around, and the loss felt horrendous. I felt like I'd been betrayed. I also felt very angry that it had been taken away, that it wasn't going to happen to me.

In the beginning we decided we'd do it in some romantic city overseas. So I came off the pill but while I was travelling I didn't get a period for three months. Being a midwife I knew this wasn't a very good sign, but we also felt that we'd got plenty of time. It was weird, though; when we got back an urgency set in because I felt that there was something wrong and I also knew that often you needed to try for twelve months before anyone really paid any attention to you. I knew I could be waiting around for another twelve months and have nothing happen, so when we got back I made some doctors' appointments and after much messing about and being sent to the wrong doctor we found out my hormones weren't at the correct levels.

No one really ever knew why, but they were just all over the place and it looked like nothing was going to happen in my body. I could have waited and waited and hoped, but I felt strongly about it. I wanted to do something. Every obstetric appointment I was eager to get there, I was eager to hear what was to be said. I'd come home and go over every word, replay in my head what was said, the positives, the negatives. Then I'd go over it with my partner until I drove him mad. It was total emotional fatigue, sometimes I'd walk away from an appointment very happy and positive and other times really drained.

It became my focus, but I tried to keep it in perspective and there was also always some hope, and distractions occasionally as well, and the distractions helped. I think within myself I was very, very desperate. It went on every minute of my day, and when I was getting close to a period or feeling more hopeful, I became even more desperate. In the end I took the hormonal path, tried different dosages over the months and eventually it took an extra injection of progesterone to kick start my system. The thing is, though, it isn't just the hormones, it's the blood tests and the visits to the doctor and the clinic and the whole process.

And you're thinking 'People do this so simply'. It happens by accident, it happens and people don't want their babies. It's so unfair and it made me appreciate a body that worked well, a body that just did it. Just like when you've got the flu and you don't notice how smoothly your body's working until suddenly it's broken. Luckily for me eventually it did work, but there were huge ups and downs. When you thought you were getting close you could be on a wonderful high and then you'd get the news or a telephone call or a visit and you weren't pregnant, again. I can't actually even remember how horrible I felt, I can't. I don't want to, ever.

So much crying, but also a lot of support from friends and my mother and my sister and my husband. A lot of my grief I kept private, but I needed that support. I tried to picture my life without children and convince myself that that's OK, if I'm going to go down that road I will, but during that waiting time I did get angry and distressed, even when I was trying to stay positive.

And even though it was only two years, it wasn't like it was five years or ten years, I can't tell you what it was like. I'm not sure if it was real for my husband in the same way. I was lucky he always said he would be quite happy if it turned out to be just us two. If it wasn't to happen that it would be fine and I believed him, I really did believe him. Although it would've been a loss for him as well, I think he would've dealt with it differently than me. For me it was excruciating. No one else can see your loss, but that doesn't mean it's not there.

Everyone else sees you as a whole person or the two of you as a couple but within you it's monumental. You have a plan for your life even if it is never spoken and for that to be shattered isn't easy. You have to go through the disbelief and then the anger and then the acceptance. People often seem to feel the need to do something to compensate for not being able to have children, like saying this is OK because now I can spend more money on myself, I can go overseas, or I'm freer. For me that was thinking that my husband and I were a family anyway and that I would hang onto what I had and not ruin it because we are a fabulous couple.

One of the other things that's important for me is the relationship with my immediate family. I always felt that I would've liked to provide grandchildren for my mother but I don't think that was expected of me, even though the stereotype is that an Italian mum would put the pressure on. She didn't do that. She was simply there.

I think if it had have gone on for much longer, there would have been some expectations from our more distant Italian infrastructure. Our close contacts were very much in the same mould as Mum, supportive and understanding.

Even given that, I do think people find infertility hard to understand. What I don't think is that they take it lightly. The problem is people don't know how to come to terms with it for themselves so it's easier if you appear as if you've gotten over it. You really lay yourself open if you do share it with too many people and you can be easily wounded. I think I was fairly protective about who I shared it with and how much I let out.

I found it hurtful enough to see friends fall pregnant and have children and not be able to share in it or feel that they felt that I couldn't share in it. For me it was enough to be in a room with a few pregnant women to feel wounded. No one was ever intentionally nasty but on top of that I also felt responsible because my partner was in the same boat and sometimes even a conversation would be hurtful. We might be with someone who didn't know we couldn't fall pregnant and find them saying to your partner, 'You're shooting blanks,' and the guys might be laughing, but in fact that's huge. Depending on how you're feeling you can take it to heart and walk away and later you just bawl. You feel like a failure. Useless.

It's funny, though, I never felt jealous. The midwife in me was my outlet. I was happy to do that and I think that some-where I always felt that it would happen and I hung onto that so, so, so strongly especially because it was only two years. For two years you can still be fairly positive. It's the failure after failure that wears you down.

And then there's hoping for the pregnancy. I had one very bad experience when I'd gone on well over my due date. I had breast tenderness and a few early signs and my husband and I were really convinced that I was pregnant, and I probably got to twenty days over. So I drove down to the hospital, had my blood taken and then as soon as I got home I got my period. We felt that that was probably a really early miss. I kept thinking, 'Well I got that close, it could happen again,' but when I remember that devastation, it was terrible. Then the following month the same thing happened, my period was late, my breasts sore, all that so when I went for my blood test I was going, 'Don't get your hopes up' and then I got a call to say that I was pregnant and I just bawled. I just cried. I just howled. I howled from my gut.

Mothering is not like I thought it was. You have to be very clever as a mum. You have to actually understand each one of them and as you have more children you also realise how different each one can be. It's through a lot of love, a lot of understanding, and a lot of being with them that you get to know them and you understand that yes, they are your children but they're human beings in their own right as well. Why am I crying? It's such an important job, it's so lovely to do and you don't always get it right. And I'm so lucky speaking now from the perspective of having children. If I was talking about this in the middle of the second year it would be very different. What makes me appreciate the kids even more is knowing that there was a time when they weren't going to be there. They feel very, very precious.

# BOX CONCEPTION

## Sophia

I'm standing in my sister's kitchen. It's a big kitchen and this is my big sister. I am little but I have big ideas and dark thoughts. I like to let them out with her here. Where the light of her and her kitchen gives them insect wings and lets them fly for a while.

Then she starts talking. She tells me she cannot have children. That nothing she has tried has changed this fact.

I'm probably gulping hard on some tea at this point. I'm probably finding her kitchen a lot less airy. I'm probably wishing I was a better sister, a bigger sister and a little less lesbian.

My sister tells me she cannot conceive of herself without children.

I can't hear her.

Because I am shit-scared.

It's hard to describe this sort of fear. It's gulped like hot tea and it numbs me on the way down. So now I don't know why I'm reeling when it's her tragedy. It strips away the bench space and strips the polished floorboards from underneath me. It takes my words and it even takes my empathy. I am dumb and stupid in her empty kitchen. I don't know what to say and I can't taste my tea.

My sister is telling me she cannot have children and cannot be happy without children. That each of us can be granted a singular fate. An empty gift. A small ribboned box of torture that we have to hold. Very close.

So here is my sister, calmly insisting on accepting this dark gift. Letting it be delivered into the foyer, letting it strip this kitchen with its contents. Stripping us of any bigger (little-

163

sister) ideas. Making us face what's imperative and what's impossible.

So I am shit-scared.

From within my dumb and mute skin, I imagine airlifting my beautiful sister high above it all and dropping her into different skins. Maybe a gypsy child in a Baltic wilderness or a chairman of the board with less complex concerns.

But there's no choice for either of us. We have to stand here with this little box of blackness. We have to hold it. We have to hold it. Very close.

Standing stupidly here, I remember how this little box of child came to exist. It is not an accident or a whim, this desire for a child. It has been crafted by each of us over the years and it's not fair that my sister, big as she is, should have to face it alone.

Of course, we were children once ourselves. But we were always more than that. We were children of a beautiful mother in a hopeless marriage and so we carried hope with every bit of our growing limbs. We saw our otherwise unsmiling mother brighten in our presence as we helped her pack the car to leave our father. We saw her almost laugh as she discovered us in the back seat of the car with the full range of stuffed animals we felt it was necessary to bring to our new life. We heard her insist that she had learned more from us than she could ever teach us in a lifetime.

In the war zone, we held the flag that stood as a reminder of what was worth fighting for. And that's how we understood ourselves, and all children; as the keepers of life and the reason to keep living.

The task of re-making these babies fell to my sister. I think the prospect of giving birth to a 'keeper of life' weighed too heavily on me. I was relieved to be rendered barren by my sexual preferences. Maybe I wanted simply to keep being the child waving the flag.

Either way, this was my sister's box and it came with her story. All I could do was hold it carefully and stay beside her in the kitchen.

She didn't talk about wanting a baby much in the months

that followed, except to tell me how stupid people were when they didn't understand the weight of an unborn child. She would re-enact the callous interactions with extended family, the latest stupid suggestion that she had somehow brought it all on herself. She might mention an adoption seminar and how she lost her hope there or the renewal of hope with the new round of hormone therapy.

My big sister also cried a little. And I often didn't know what to say. I didn't know a lot of things then.

I didn't yet know she would conceive.

The hormone therapy eventually worked for my sister and she was soon ovulating with the best of them. She fell pregnant and quietly told us that she would be having a child. We eased open the box and held the dark and beautiful images of the ultrasound to the light. We thought they were Art and threatened to frame them. We thought they were Grace and leaned in with hushed tones to look. We saw them as gifts and were deeply, deeply grateful.

Much remained mysterious.

Except that, in time, I would come to know three of my sister's children. And from them, in turn, I would learn how to change trajectory whilst sprinting on the polished floorboards. How to deliver the perfect dive bomb, quietly observe insects and live within the shape of a certain space. Both dark and light.

# THIRTEEN

## Graham and Dee Burge

*Graham*

It started twenty-five years ago, in 1976 when I was twenty. Although I was still living at home with Mum and Dad, the thought of having a kid was starting to grow on me. Why? I suppose, then, a selfish reason was more overwhelming than the paternal call of nature. I wanted to have a kid whose company I could enjoy while still young enough to be active. So when 'he' was twenty, I would be forty. We could go to the pub, play cricket, go to the footy and enjoy life.

At twenty, I was playing footy and cricket and being educated in the ways of mechanical engineering. Not a lot of responsibilities, not a lot of money, and very little worldly experience. In fact, the desire to be a father was, in retrospect, a very selfish ideal. As time would prove, I really did nothing to promote the desire beyond talking about it to a few friends. But the desire was always with me.

It was around this time that IVF was first brought to the public's attention, or at least I became aware of it. There seemed to be outrage in the community—IVF was against nature and our scientists were tampering with 'things' that should not be tampered with. It was all right to do it to other animals, like sheep, but not humans. We are a taboo target for such science. I suspect the community at large had almost no supportable knowledge of infertility and was more concerned about its ability to limit the exposure of new technologies. No one wanted two-headed deformities. (Thalidomide? What was that? Agent Orange? What was that?) Anyway, at twenty, I was pretty oblivious to that. I was young, strong, fit and having a good time growing up. What more can a young bloke really want? Life was a party interrupted by sleep. In the 1970s, a young bloke could get a good free education, a job, set his sights on a progressive career path, and he belonged to the Baby Boomers. No problems.

By the time the 1980s struck, things had turned for me. Mum and Dad wisely kicked me out when I was twenty-four. This was the time for me to grow up and take on the responsibilities of an adult. By the time I had finished uni, jobs were getting harder to find, interest rates were on the rise. My mental makeup had also changed significantly. Capitalism had taken a firm grip on my mindset. A very high priority was to build wealth, and my initial career ambition was to become a millionaire as an employee. All the business philosophies were studied and became part of my principles of life. Work was hard and enjoyable. I was still fit, still playing football and cricket, and the parties were still a happening thing. My thoughts of children had waned, my need to secure a future was the priority.

Around this time I became aware that the age for couples being married and having kids seemed to be increasing. I remember meeting for the first time a young man who was married and was about twenty-four at the time. This sticks in my mind because I was shocked that he was married; none of my other friends were. Not long after this time, my elder brother got married to his short-time girlfriend. Another learning curve to go through. Life was still a party, just a little harder. At this time, I cannot even recall what community thoughts were on IVF, and as a healthy young adult I was not concerned.

In the summer of 1984, I met my future wife. We met in a pub in Richmond—another party. We had a tremendous time getting to know each other and finding out how we thought about things. My career was still the highest priority, but many of my friends were settling down and thinking about extending their families to include children. A natural progression, but I am sure exceptionally difficult. To go from playing up to being responsible is an absolute mind-twister.

Over the next eighteen months Dee and I fell in love and got married. We were thirty and we knew it was time to have kids. We had designed and built our home to incorporate all the components for four or five people. Our design even considered children's needs as they grew from babies to young kids to young adults. Everything was going according to Hoyle; now for the kids. It was 1988. It was the year of celebration in Australia. For both Dee and me, it seemed it was inevitable we'd have a couple of rugrats to disturb our sleep and financial plans and generally provide us with the reason for our existence.

Nothing happened.

The next twelve months, we did everything to conceive—the right time, the right position, the right posture, the right direction. If there was something we should have done, we did it. Nothing. What was going on?

Or more accurately what was not going on? We were very concerned. It was 1989 and we were not pregnant. Friends were having kids all over the place, but not us. We had not really discussed infertility, but I think Dee had a better idea of what was going on than I did. As a bloke, well, we're not really trained in these things and it's all news to us. Medical things are foreign to us. Our GP went through his paces but determined nothing. To proceed further we were directed to a specialist. I had never heard of him but Dee was impressed. Apparently he was good at what he did, whatever that was.

This was still 1989, and then cutting-edge technology was awesome. These guys could do anything. Well, that is what I thought. After tests and examinations for me, Dee was subjected to the same and more. We were desperate to have kids and as we approached our mid-thirties the desperation grew.

Reflecting on what we thought about and how we reacted in 1989, it shows how things have changed. We daren't talk publicly about infertility—we did not want others to think we were defective, or be embarrassed. We were asked frequently, 'How are the kids?' or, 'Are you planning to have kids?' Questions were always based on family life. We had a family life,

Dee and myself, just no kids. It is amazing how that can push couples into different social groupings. We had many friends in 1989, we still do, but we did lose touch with some of those who had kids—for all the obvious reasons.

In 1990, the waiting period over, the 'counselling' done, we were ready to have our kids. IVF was the method to help. I was very confident we would do this IVF thing and have our own child in nine months and we could get on with our intended lives.

### Dee

#### 1990
#### 6 May

*I've been feeling very unsure and concerned about this whole IVF procedure. So many questions and uncertainties. I've always considered IVF to be the last resort, but our GP Andrew said just to think of it as the next, not the final step.*

#### 12 May

*Our first attempt has been abandoned because my hormone levels weren't high enough. I can hardly believe it, walked out in a daze. Graham wanted to hug me but I knew I'd cry.*

#### 10 August

*Parts of the last ten days have been my worst over the last three years. If our next attempt ends the same way as the last couple, Prof said we'll have to look seriously at whether IVF is for us. I guess that's what knocked me. What else is there?*

#### 23 October

*Well, one egg and sperm got together! Spent a nerve-racking day waiting to hear the results. We're feeling quite excited and, I guess, hopeful. But I think our chances are fairly slim with only one embryo. At least we got over the hurdle of fertilisation and now we know it's possible.*

## 24 October

*Forty-nine injections for nothing! The poor solitary embryo didn't continue to develop properly. We just hugged each other and cried.*

## 1991
## 21 January

*My thirty-fifth birthday. If I'd been told fifteen, ten or even five years ago that I wouldn't have children by this time, I would have been horri-fied and disbelieving. We've been trying for four years this month.*

## 28 February

*A forward step at last, we made it to embryo transfer. I keep having to remind myself the embryos are in there and theoretically I'm pregnant.*

## 4 March

*My laparoscopy incisions had been oozing clear fluid all day on Satur-day and all the hospital said was, 'Apply pressure,' which did nothing. During our dinner here for eight people (stupid timing) I had to change my saturated clothes twice. Twice during the night I woke up completely soaked. I tried not to panic and wondered if I should ring an ambu-lance. Graham, who had celebrated being able to drink again after 'sperm-protection' abstinence, was next to useless, said it was 'only plasma'. At eight-thirty next morning I rang the hospital again and was told to apply pressure – again it did nothing. I finally rang Prof at home, and he said what had happened was 'quite unusual' and happened in about one in twenty cases. My condition was finally given a name – hyperstimulation. Recently I've learned how potentially serious this can be, and IVF clinics now take extreme care to avoid the condition and warn patients of the symptoms.*

## 12 March

*I got my period early yesterday. On Saturday night over dinner we'd talked about 'our' names, Emily and Paul. Dangerous, I guess.*

## 20 December

*Four out of five eggs fertilised, transfer in theatre. I casually mentioned to Graham that I'd like him to come in with me and he went pale. Wish I'd had a camera—Graham in white hospital shirt and pants with nothing on underneath, and bootees and cap. The embryologist put our three embryos up on the monitor (the fourth hadn't continued developing). I felt quite strange seeing them—those three potential children with all our genetic make-up. A catheter was passed up through my uterus and into my right tube. A strange feeling—not exactly painful, but uncomfortable. We watched on the screen as the embryos were passed through the catheter and deposited in the correct place in my tube. I felt worried about them falling out, but was assured they couldn't.*

## 31 December

*I got my period today as I did on day thirteen last time … cried and cried. It's such a sudden, harsh disappointment after the long, slow and involved build-up. We both really felt I could be pregnant this time and now that hope has just evaporated.*

## 1992
## 1 January

*I've given up wishing for a baby at midnight. Went to a party last night. Didn't feel well with my period and felt more and more out of place and sad. The girls spent a lot of time talking about children, one was pregnant, and I was the only one without children.*

## 27 June

*Twelve eggs. The biggest pick-up I've had. Prof put the three 'best-looking' eggs back in my right tube with Graham's sperm and the remainder will be fertilised (we hope) and frozen.*

## 1 July

*Some great news. The three embryos from the remaining eggs have all frozen successfully. I'm starting to get a good feeling about this attempt …*

### 12 July

*Feel sure my period is coming …*

### 14 July

*I'm in a state of shock! At 4.15 the phone rang and the nurse said, 'Doreen, it's positive.' I was absolutely stunned and said it couldn't be right. She continued telling me my hormone levels were good and she hadn't been able to wait any longer to tell me. I just kept saying, 'I can't be. I don't believe it.' All I wanted was for Graham to get home. I thought of all we've been through and how long I've dreamed of and imagined this day. All I could manage when Graham walked in was, 'I'm pregnant' and then I started sobbing. We stood there hugging each other and crying with Graham saying over and over, 'You're pregnant, I'm going to be a dad.'*

### 18 July

*Yesterday I had the most severe headache I've ever had—learned later this is caused by a sudden drop in hormone levels—then I noticed some spotting.*

### 19 July

*By three o'clock I had a very heavy feeling, backache and felt very cold. The heaviness turned to more obvious cramping and pain and I got more and more concerned. Went to the toilet and started bleeding heavily and passed several clots. I just couldn't believe our baby was falling out of me and being flushed away. I sobbed and sobbed. We wondered how we could ever go through all this again and why it had to happen this way. Graham goes away early in the morning for a week and I feel petrified at the prospect …*

### 20 July

*Graham left in a taxi at 6.45am. I was determined not to cry. In for a blood test. Felt strange walking past the hospital, looking up at the room and thinking it was there where 'our baby' was probably actually conceived. But … I'm still pregnant! Can't believe it after what happened last night. Graham was on the phone almost as soon as I'd hung up from the clinic and the relief and joy in his voice were so obvious.*

### 21 July

*Down the rollercoaster again. Prof rang and he's not at all hopeful. He did leave me with a little hope, though, saying that sometimes the hormone levels pick up. I'm feeling quite calm and philosophical about it now. I guess if there is a problem, it's better for nature to sort it out now.*

### 22 July

*I feel that whatever happens now is for the best … Graham rang me late last night and sounded terrible. All he wanted was to be here; said he needed to hear my voice. He cried and cried and I just wished I could put my arms around him …*

### 27 July

*Blood test again. Rang for the result and it took the nurse a while to decipher the figures. I was left in suspense while she checked with the lab. Heard her in the background saying, 'So they've dropped a lot' and I knew. All that hope just evaporated.*

### 29 July

*Went for the compulsory ultrasound yesterday. It could have been such an exciting day, seeing a heartbeat. As it was, it was a fairly sad experience, seeing an empty uterus and having the ultrasonographer say there was only one tiny shadow left. I'm glad Graham was with me. We were able to joke about how it would have been if we'd seen three heartbeats.*

### 10 October

*I'm constantly vacillating between 'maybe I'm pregnant' and 'I'm sure I'm getting my period' …*

### 11 October

*Got my period this morning.*

### 1993
### 3 January

*Spent another sad New Year's Eve. At midnight my mind was flooded with thoughts of how 1993 should have been the year we became parents.*

### 27 February

*These sixteen days of waiting always seem the hardest.*

### 5 March

*The big day – and the bad news. All week I've felt twinges and at first felt convinced I was getting my period. Then, as I remembered the cycle when I did conceive, I became equally convinced that I was pregnant. It frightened me that my hopes took over my rational thoughts so easily. I knew we had only a ten per cent chance, yet I couldn't shake the feeling that I was pregnant.*

*Graham and I ended up having a terrible argument one night. I was so touchy and finally said, 'Can't you understand how I'm feeling, waiting for these results?' and he said, 'No, I can't.' I wanted to talk but Graham lost his cool and shouted and thumped the table. I walked out and by the time he came after me I was almost hysterical. I felt totally out of control. I'd been too scared to verbalise my hopes to Graham or even write them down.*

*Anyway, now I know the rational thoughts should have prevailed and I've been going over the advantages I had already prepared—I can lose weight before our next attempt, I can go back to tennis, the baby won't be born just before Christmas, we can make love again … I'm not sure what else. But all these would have faded into the background if I'd been pregnant.*

### 27 August

*We wonder how much more of this we can take. When I got past day* thirteen, then fourteen and fifteen, we felt so hopeful. But no. Can we go through all this again? When do we decide enough is enough? Why, when we so desperately want a baby of our own, doesn't it happen? I almost feel I can cope with my own sorrow, but to see Graham's face and to think what a child of his own would mean to him, I can't take it.

But even now my mind is playing tricks on me. My period, although fairly heavy, is not painful, so my mind says maybe it's not a proper period; maybe I was pregnant with twins and have lost one ... I'll know the blood tests in a few hours.

## 1994
### 2 January

Here I am at nearly thirty-eight with no children. I really start to wonder if we should pursue this goal. How would I cope with the drastic change of lifestyle? But I know Graham is as keen as ever and hasn't really considered the possibility of not having children. And when I see him with children, I feel certain we must keep trying.

### 1 May

I feel so sad and very much that the end of the road is now. Even though we've one more funded attempt, I don't feel at all optimistic. I guess when the time comes I will be. I feel so wrung out and exhausted, and keep thinking about how we would have been feeling now if the result had been different. I feel so lucky to have Graham and that we have such a close and loving relationship and above all a real friendship. We can look forward so much to our life together without children, I know, but when I think of the alternative ...

## 1995
### 22 January

I'm thirty-nine—my last year of trying to have a baby, I think. Our last attempt is approaching fast—a time I've dreaded since starting IVF nearly five years ago.

### 10 March

Quite a few changes with this cycle—nasal spray, ICSI (injection of one sperm into the centre of the egg), assisted hatching (drilling of the shell of the egg to help the embryo 'hatch') on my (old, tough!) eggs, and ordinary IVF. Again, I feel ambivalent about this attempt. But I don't know how I'll feel when the almost inevitable negative result comes along. It's been such a long and emotional road; I can hardly believe we're almost at the end, but at the same time I can imagine myself less and less with a baby.

## 12 April

Only three eggs were inseminated. Three embryos leaves very little room for anything else to go wrong and there goes the hope of a frozen cycle. I'm about to make a nervous phone call to find out if the assisted hatching can go ahead … all three are OK for the drilling to be done.

## 13 April

Took our camera into theatre … Heaps of photos: us in our gowns, doctor and embryologist with the photos of our embryos, me on the table. The embryos looked very healthy. Graham is feeling very confident and I guess I am so far. It's hard to believe this is probably the last time we'll do all this.

## 23 April

Felt all day that my period could be on its way. Poor Graham told me it'll rip his heart out if I'm not pregnant this time …

## 26 April

An inconclusive result. It's described as a pregnancy that has occurred but not fully established itself and the hormone levels could go either way. Who said you can't be a little bit pregnant? But I've felt quite different during this cycle and on the whole felt quite confident once we got to transfer. I'll try to keep that confidence …

## 1 May

Had the dreaded severe headache but still felt reasonably confident. Blood test the day before Graham's departure overseas. Felt so nervous *about ringing in for the results and delayed it a little. And then the news we've dreaded for so many years ... Graham sat with his head in his hands as I asked if there was any hope. 'No, not really.' I hung up and said, 'So that's it then.' We both just sobbed. It was terrible. To have got so tantalisingly close on our last try seems so cruel. It hit me very suddenly and clearly that my biggest sorrow is not knowing the person our child would have been. It's a grief for someone we've never known, and now we've lost the opportunity to ever know that person.*

*That brief phone call was like falling into an abyss that's been looming for years. In the past there's been something to stop us falling in; the quick optimism that we've still got another chance. It's strange that I can still so clearly see the advantages of childlessness—some would view them as mostly selfish advantages—but what a huge gap it leaves in our lives and always will.*

### Graham

When we started in 1990, we thought the technology would help us, 'save' us from being childless. The technology I considered to be black magic in 1990. Needles every day for Dee, drugs that would kill a black dog, internal hospital communications that were outright scary.

We spent a lot of money but that was nothing compared to the emotional cost. Our thirteenth attempt coincided with our ninth anniversary in 1995. We were thirty-nine and we had had everything emotionally done to us over the previous six years. Technology had gone from black magic to something that was very impressive. The learning curve for our clinicians was vertical (and still is).

It is now 2001, I am nearly forty-five, we have been married fifteen years. IVF is now a 'mature' technology and spoken about openly. Thousands, and probably millions globally of people have been helped to have full families by IVF and related technologies. Good on them. To this day I still hurt inside about not having kids. I know Dee does. We still cry and lament our childless fate. But, as they say (who is this 'they?'), life goes on. I've been trained for a career, a family, debts, and retirement at the age of sixty. I also expected to be trained to be a dad, to put up with all the dilemmas of growing children, to pass on what I know and provide a better life. That's what I want! That's what most people want.

The problem I have is, without kids, why am I here? A pretty fundamental question and one today I still struggle with. Am I here to propagate my part of the gene pool? Prolong my name? Not to have kids means the end of my family name— my family name ceases.

I am forty-five, we have a big home we do not need, many of our friends have kids who range from nought to twenty years old. We experience very little of that life. I work basically for work's sake, my career ambition has waned. Once I wanted to be the best CEO/MD in Australia; now I want to start a little factory working on renewable energy products. Don't get me wrong, I am not depressed, I have changed. My mindset is to enjoy life and experience all the things we would not have been able to if we had had kids. Many people with kids say how lucky we are. We are.

I am happy, I am lucky and I am in love with the best lady in the world. Without Dee nothing really matters. And she loves me. Only one thing is missing...

# AN ESSAY ON FATHERHOOD

## Barry Dickens

All my life long I have waited eagerly for a baby who is partly friend, mentor, tormentor and muse, who will rock me and buoy me; and never leave my untiring old heart. My heart was once misdiagnosed as more like the diesel engine of the Manly ferry than a man's. All my life long I have impatiently longed for our son, and he came home one day, to his old ancestral palace in my heart. 'Hi, Dad...'.

At night sometimes when he is asleep next to me, lying upon cool pillows that I turn over because his body is too hot on hot summer nights; why, in the sombre but never melancholy dark or half-darkness, I swear he is one of my long-dead childhood brothers, the spit of them he is, the mouth the same way, the fuzzy forehead, the same bearing, the long-dead ghost of one of my brothers, not really dead in the physical sense of the word, but religiously alive to the likeness of one of them. I prayed for him to come home and he overheard me. 'Good to see you, Dad.'

Not as a practising Christian did I pray, although I wish I were a Christian, I am not even agnostic, I am a believer in what incredibly lovely things I see, and the believer also in the most unbelievably cruel things I see each day, sometimes each second, in the street particularly, where kids are so abused and almost gleefully abandoned, you have to say.

My own childhood was dreamy and filled up with aspects of daggy working-class life, like going to the beach, learning how to mock others so you can defend your principles and yourself and your family. Learning how to draw with sharpened pencils, how to sing, write in verse, read and listen. Wait for a baby after thirteen years living with someone, marrying them, loving them more than drink, more than one's mates, one's no-hoper mates, even one's beautiful mates. Waiting in aspic together for the glittering child come to candlelight your way.

Once at a pompous party did my wife and I not flee because the pretentious woman who ran the show held her stunning daughter in her freckled arms and asked of us: 'What is the matter with you twin losers? Don't you like kids?' My wife blushed and I thought I was going to vomit. We had been trying to have a baby since we fell in love with one another. We ran off on some pretext. I still hate that stupid woman's guts for saying that stupid thing to both of lonely us way back then. Well, not hate, but it is not good the way I feel about her.

We got up and both went to work, she to the ABC, me to the theatre and journalism. I drank a lot then, I don't think particularly to do with childlessness but just boozing to ward off the Third Reich of boredom. We both drank at night, in the day, we threw boozy parties and occasionally fought, didn't have a baby and were so lost and dumbfounded it is a thing you wouldn't read about, until now, that is I walked by, it seemed to me, endless cheery crêches and chuckling schoolyards where children laughed their brains out. Where I bought petrol in our suburb was right across the road from one of these loud, alive, laughing school grounds and whole volleys of their exuberant laughter used to just throttle me with their marvellous appeal for fun.

The envy for couples with kids eats you up. You say you approve and are happy for them. That is not right, and you and they know it isn't. They give their elegant, limbed, lithe, lively kids to you to hold them. It is like holding a bouquet of flowers that aren't yours; will never be yours. In the end, after years of trying and failing, you start to distrust family life, hate kindergartens, sneer at happy contented mothers and fathers. You get nasty and all dried-up. Because of course you are duds. You can't have a baby. They are for others than you.

Once when queuing up at a hospital in our city and trying to still credit we had a chance at life, to un-ego ourselves, drop out of lower-middle-class selfishness, booze and films, smokes and lonely holidays, my wife asked of a nurse when we were trying to get home help to get her pregnant, 'Where do the losers go?' She sure hit the nail on the head with that sentence, my lonely exhausted childless wife.

Needles, tests, needles, more tests, examinations and penal servitude deep within your childless hides. Adam and Eve without the death-adder of hope for kids. No kids, not one, not ever. That is your reward after years of longing for one, let alone two or three. You kid yourselves that staying out late is better than a quiet conversation with a sober child, a chaste child, a child almost with silver wings, a child to take the sting out of life, the bitter bee sting of goading old selfishness.

When we were such happy contented, healthy, undepressed kids our hardworking happy fathers played cricket with us on the road after work, had a boot of the ball with us if they weren't too buggered after work, particularly working overtime at time-and-a-half which was extra money you couldn't turn your nose up at. It never occurred to the parents that having no kids blew your mind.

In the unplaying backyard all the bored couple can do is uglify everything they look at with truly jaded eyes. Jaded from making lazy or even frantic love trying to get the woman pregnant. Bashing one another's bodies to dust in the extreme effort of planting the seed of life and then when the love-making is over and at times everything is over, trying to think that having no baby is just how it goes. But it isn't how it goes.

Dinner-parties are the antithesis of pregnancy. Washing up dirty dishes and clogged claret glasses is the antithesis of having a baby. Doing as you please is the antithesis of a real baby and real cot and real happy infant's laughter; their brilliant wit.

Wives' best friends deciding to have an abortion because birth is too much of a hassle is a thing to scream and throw oneself into the dust about. Bored fathers with indolent children riding their trendy bright blue bicycles around in circles in the sunny park is a thing for lonely men to bang their brains into the wall about. There is nothing as awful as a happy childless couple.

One day my wife telephoned the doctor she'd been seeing, and he told her she was in for some interesting news. She cried upon learning she was going to bear a baby, and when we saw that doctor in town my wife very nearly mounted him, she was that out of it with joyousness, redemption, raptness, eagerness—call it what you wish. She overheard the redeemed. It was redeeming. 'No more loneliness!' she cried to me like a hoarse saint about to go into labour. And that is the only labour of love: to get out of human loneliness of body and spirit and soul. Apart from agony I have no other word for babylessness.

Pregnant, how about that, time for a good blush. A new book of blushes and grinning from top to toe. What are you smiling about? How about joining the Living? Will that do? For a beginning?

Dissolve the days to birth classes which were so dull they don't stay in memory or body. Expert boredom and weeks of bullshit and then the day she is told she must go in and bear it. 'I thought it was just a blood pressure test?' My wife blushed, in this floral cotton skirt really showing, right out at the front like a vast ball, a balloon-thing, never looked as beautiful. Peach-coloured, complexion of happiness, being told she'd better 'go in', so she wrote me this scribbled list of all the things she needed overnight, for the next week at least. And she told me to get the cat put down because one of my dopey brothers swore on the Bible that cats can often smother newborn babies. Why did he tell her that? People say anything.

The vet said not to put the cat down because she was a splendid and lovely creature, so I came home and fed it Snappy Tom, which I put on my toast too. I took my wife in a nightie, a favourite new book or books, rather, because she loves to read at night. New Colgate toothpaste, my brush, my sox, hers, thirty bucks—not that she could buy anything.

She had a big bed in a big room at 'The Women's'. Trees rippled outside in Grattan Street, Carlton. Possums in them having their babies in sympathy with ours. That's how it seemed. I liked the nurses. They liked me. I was given a bed and I had a baby, too, in sympathy for my wife's one. We chatted all night long, as we always do, being chronic fatalistic insomniacs. It was a short labour. Six hours. She screamed and screamed and I held her right hand, her fingernails tore through my palms. She bucked like a mule and grunted like a boar. She bore our child after thirteen years of mindless dinner parties and walking the beach at weekends. Planting trees at our beach home, but not planting a baby in town. They told her she'd have to have a caesar, induce it in the room upstairs, but he came, Lou, at seven in the morning, smelling rather like a hot bread shop, I should have thought. Like human bread our son was at birth? A laughing loaf.

I cut the cord and the nurse, the midwife, said to me, 'Have a baby' and showed my son held aloft in her right palm, he nestled right inside of that hand of hers, then to mum, lovely mummy, who cried snot and tears shot out of every single hole in her, of deepest gratefulness, deepest love, for not having to put up with movies for something to look at, to look into her child's eyes all weekend long, to cry and yawn and joke with profoundest happiness at not having to say the reason you are without children is just the way it goes. It is not the way anything goes, it is hateful and hollow and hideous to be childless. Fuck the trendies who say they don't want any.

Now Lou goes to school, I took him there today, he's heading for six, he has made a good, shy start. He is amusing and eloquent without being trendy. He is a friendly infant whose voice has charms on tap. He says he wants to be an artist and so he is. He wanted last week to be a magician, and so he was, when he got so magically born. What a flourish!

We dine at seven as a rule and Lou enjoys lettuce. He cuts his lamb chops up with considerable care. He likes a drop of tomato sauce on his lamb or beef. Yesterday he and his friends, God it was a hot day, 40 degrees in early February, and we've got no cooling, he and his friends had a run under the hose, and it was just like being with my old ghostly childhood mates all those years ago. Doing the same daggy things. Having all this fun being a kid. Gorging up the sun like fresh peaches in season. Every syllable a watermelon pip.

I make his diet lemon cordial each morning, my wife cuts

his Vegemite sandwiches, we try to add a piece of fresh fruit but sometimes he misses out and we put some shrapnel in his money-order paper bag and he has a pie and a seventy-cent white Icy Pole.

Drive him to school with his next door mates, Annabel and Boyd, who go to different schools. Peak traffic. Swearing hungover truck drivers having goes at each other in the sweltering road to their different schools. Worth the journey of thirty or so minutes because the schools around where we live aren't up to much, it is said, and we don't want drugs. Our suburb is full of them.

Once so long ago I used to wait in our bed waiting for my friendly wife to come home from Ladies' Midweek Tennis, I'd examine the shadows of the leaves upon our garden trees as they drifted in their easygoing way onto blinds or bricks, and now our baby is chatting to me, he's six, joking with me about this or that, asking me to put my arm around his waist so he can get off to sleep, or at times pushing me away as a sure sign of approaching independence. He's just like his dad that way. He will not be told. He is his own man.

# 'I'M GOING TO BE A MUMMY
# WHEN I GROW UP'

## Maggie Kirkman

I tried to become pregnant from the age of twenty-five, without success. I was thirty when I had a hysterectomy (as a result of very advanced fibroid tumours). It seemed inevitable that I would always be childless. Paradoxically, the hysterectomy came as a relief after the emotional torment of infertility: it took away the cycle of hope and despair that had become part of my life.

In my late twenties, when it became clear that my marriage was likely to be a casualty of my thwarted desire for children, I seriously entertained the idea of suicide. The life I had expected was dead anyway, taking with it the self I knew. Instead, I went back to school to improve my HSC results, and was accepted into the University of Melbourne to study Arts, majoring in psychology. I was determined to develop a challenging career. The second year of my degree had just begun when I was admitted to the Royal Women's hospital in the middle of the night. The hysterectomy followed a few days later, and I spent the rest of the semester either in hospital or convalescing. At the end of that academic year, when I was awarded first prize in both psychology subjects, one professor commented that I must have been 'driven' to accomplish so much in such a short time. He was right. Academic success was my substitute for motherhood.

As a single woman, I now had a different life planned for myself, but that, too, was disrupted. I married again, at the age of thirty-eight. Sev had no sperm which, in any rational analysis, should have defined us as an immutably childless couple. Nevertheless, we are now the parents of a twelve-year-old daughter, Alice, conceived using my egg and donor sperm, who was gestated by my sister Linda.

Until I saw Alice's birth (by caesarean section) I'd never seen a baby being born. Linda had invited me to attend the births of her two children (both of which occurred before my remarriage) but I was too emotionally vulnerable to accept. On my first week back at university after my hysterectomy, our class had been shown a beautiful film of a Leboyer birth. It took all my self-control to sit through this exquisite torture and to cry only enough to seem moved by the experience. As a university tutor, I was eventually desensitised to the film by having to show it to students three years in a row six times in the one week; but even now, when I hear on the radio the Bach harp music used in the film, I have to resist a compelling urge to run away.

I could lament the fact that I had to watch the birth of my daughter rather than to give birth. I could regret never having been pregnant. Sev could believe that his inability to contribute genetically means that he is not a real father. But what we treasure is our parental relationship with Alice, who rewards us with love and delights us with her steely desire to be her own person.

It was only after I had become Alice's mother that I felt confident enough to conduct academic research on what it means to be infertile. Thirty-one women who had experienced infertility told me their stories; nineteen of them had no children. During the three years of the research, most of the women kept me up to date about what they were doing either to change their circumstances or to come to terms with being unable to have any children (or as many as they wanted). What I learned from these women has helped me to understand what it means to experience childbearing loss and the subsequent profound sense of the loss of self. I have also come to know the possibility of developing a new future and a new interpretation of who one is.

### Having an identity as a mother

The women told me that they had from childhood been telling themselves stories about their lives which included motherhood. They came to understand themselves as women who would be mothers, and made decisions about the present and the future that were appropriate to mothers. Marion, for example, said: 'I can remember people asking, "What do you want to be when you grow up?" And I would often say, "I'd like to be a mummy."' Of course, I'm not claiming that it's inevitable that women define themselves (in part) by the prospect of motherhood. It just happens to be true that being a mother was a core part of the self for most of the women who told me their stories, and this is true of me as well.

A few years ago, psychologist Liz Short asked women university students in Melbourne about their plans and anticipated satisfactions. These women, aged eighteen to twenty, saw careers as necessary to fulfilment, but 'career was almost unanimously said to be less central to one's identity and satisfaction, and to come "on top of" or "as well as" a family' (Short, 1992, p. 175). Even though infertile women may be more aware that other options are available than were women now in their fifties and older, many have still constructed their identity on the assumption of motherhood.

### Why do I want to be a mother?

The women in my research explained their desire for children along two lines: How did it happen that I want children so much? What are the benefits to me of motherhood?

In wondering how they came to want children, some women perceived social pressure in the form of tradition, expectations, familial responsibility or direct encouragement. Anne, who became a mothercraft nurse, described the 'second-mother role' she fulfilled with her younger siblings. Marion said she came from an environment where children were appreciated and loved; having children 'just seems the normal thing to do'. Assumptions that women will fulfil these 'normal' expectations help to explain how motherhood came to be part of these women's identity.

Abigail and others drew on biology to explain their desire for children, saying that it was 'some sort of instinctual, inbuilt thing... although some people seem to miss out on it altogether.' Abigail then provided a third explanation (after society and biology) for the desire for children: meeting Mr Right. Meeting the right man can be seen as a trigger for dormant desires, or children can be understood as the natural consequence of a loving relationship. Una, for example, described children as 'an extension of us'.

Underlying these explanations was a common need that is the foundation of the mother-child relationship; as Zoë said, 'I think the nurturing, wanting to nurture, is a strong thing, too, for me'. The need to nurture may be one of the most powerful features of a woman's identity as a mother. According to Geraldine, 'having children, and providing that sort of nurturance for them, was an important part of my self-esteem, almost'.

When I was in my mid twenties and suffering anguish over my failure to conceive, I used to imagine what it would be like to be a mother, and the stories of events and relationships that emerged became my reasons for wanting children. Tania described going on a camping holiday with families including children: 'I think that was the point in time that was the most difficult... going on that camping holiday and feeling like I wasn't quite complete because we didn't have a child with us'. This sense of incompleteness illustrates how an identity as a mother exists even before children are born. When the time is right for the imagined children to be born and they are not, the identity of that woman is in fact incomplete. This is very different from claiming that a woman is not complete without children. What Tania and other involuntarily childless women are saying is that the development of their own long-held understanding of who they are has been obstructed. The person they are now forced to be is an incomplete version of the person they know as 'I'. As Yvonne said, 'Once you start to try and have children and do not get pregnant... your children still exist in your mind.'

Even though we can generalise about women's assumptions that they will be mothers, I want to make it clear that women are individuals. Virginia, for example, consciously resisted the pressure to be the stereotypical woman, hating the idea of 'the white picket fence' and all that it stood for. In her thirties, she tried to fulfil her identity as a mother in her own time, on her own terms, and in a satisfying adult relationship, but infertility intervened. In spite of her ability to withstand the pressure to be a conventional wife and mother, Virginia said, 'I've got other friends who are childless, but they're not grieving their childlessness... You get on with life, but the grief remains.'

Jenny was the only one of the women in my research who decided (not without a struggle) that her identity did not involve being a mother. She attributed her willingness to go through with motherhood to her love for her husband and the fact that 'everybody else' has children. When she discovered that this would be difficult to achieve, Jenny was upset because control over her own destiny had been taken away. It took her about a year of thought, discussion, and stress to come to a new understanding of her past and to develop new expectations for her future. Jenny now describes herself as a woman who is voluntarily child-free. Nevertheless, her story shows the pain that infertility can cause even to a woman who sees her life story leading her away from motherhood.

### Infertility: What do I do now?

The stories we devise about our future give purpose to our lives; they explain who we are and define our goals. The most familiar story for women in our culture is that of motherhood. Infertile women have grown up believing that the motherhood story is available to them as a model for their own lives. The discovery of infertility for a woman who understands herself as a mother, therefore, is both a disruption to her life and a devastating blow to her sense of self. She must decide not only what to do next but who to be next. For most of the women in this research, what they did next was designed to forestall having to change being a mother, such as by pursuing a fertility treatment like in vitro fertilisation (IVF). The woman who, until the diagnosis of infertility was made, was in control of her life and could plan when she would have her children, had been written out of the story. Her new understanding of her self begins with a sense of insecurity, uncertainty, and loss of control.

The future sometimes seems meaningless in the absence of children. Even activities not directly associated with children can lose meaning, as though the failure of motherhood unties the thread that holds the self together. Ingrid appeared to lead a busy life in her job, but was struggling to find a new sense of her self to replace motherhood: 'Most women know what their role is, to be a mother. It's clumsily put; they're a lot more than just a mother. But they have a social role that they're reasonably secure in. Well, I haven't. What am I supposed to do with my time?'

Susan was afraid of becoming a person who was 'never satisfied with the way things are' because she couldn't accept her inability to have children. She was trying with the aid of IVF to maintain her identity as a mother, knowing that she might need to reconstruct it. Yvonne summed up the tension this generated when she said: 'Why do I want this so much? . . . Why can't I just not want it?'

After Sev and I had started trying to achieve parenthood with my sister's help, part of me hoped that it would all grind to a halt and I could just get on with my life. I was working as hard as I could to achieve a baby (and it did take a lot of work: physical, with IVF; mental and emotional; practical, with persuading doctors and politicians and hospitals and committees to allow us to do what we wanted). I yearned for success; at the same time, I was preparing for disappointment. This balancing act seems to be a common experience among women who are going through assisted reproductive technology: the need to understand who you are and know what kind of life you will lead following success or failure. It troubled me at the time, but I've come to understand it as a feature of the need to exercise control over our lives in the face of an uncertain future.

## Losing control

Infertile women commonly feel that they have lost control of their lives. Yvonne told a wonderfully embarrassing story illustrating the confusion and disorientation that can be induced by infertility. It also demonstrates how an overwhelming desire can make us blind to something that undermines that desire, and how hard our minds work to make a wish come true.

*After the time when none of the eggs fertilised [in IVF] ... I went batty! I started bleeding and ... went to a doctor and said, 'There's something wrong with me; I'm bleeding', and he said, 'Is it your period?' I said, 'No'. And he said, 'When's it due?' I can't believe I said this: I said, 'It's due today'. And I thought that the blood was from cystitis! ... Even when they told me I didn't have cystitis, I thought that I must have had a vaginal infection that was making me bleed ... I just couldn't cope with having my period.*

Ingrid supplied the refrain for those who are forced to confront the evidence: 'I used to cry every time I got a period: "It's not fair". It's not fair, is it?'

Many women felt the unfairness of life in allocating children to parents whether or not they deserved them. When I saw pregnant women smoking I used to tremble with anger at their irresponsibility, at their lack of awareness of their good fortune, and at the unfairness of life when I, who would care so well for a baby from conception, could never be pregnant. (This conviction that one would be an ideal mother has obvious ramifications for those who do eventually become mothers.)

## Exclusion from the world of motherhood

Before I had Alice, I wasn't jealous of my sisters and their children. I was glad to have four nephews and a niece to love, and grateful that my sisters ensured that I was an important part of their lives. Other people's children were a different matter, however, and I preferred to have nothing to do with them. My closest friends seemed to be people who had decided against children, or were gay men, or had grown-up families.

Childless women like me may set themselves aside from children for our own protection, but we often feel that we're excluded: from the world of mothers, from the world of adult females, from families, from the future, and even from other infertile women. (It's not unusual to feel like the only person in the world who can't have children.) Wendy told me: 'There is a whole part of life that I am missing out on ... I was recently stunned when I later thought about the truth of a casual comment I made to a friend. When speaking of a hypothetical holiday I had said, "I don't have to be back for anything in particular. No one needs me."'

When you feel confused, denied, tossed about by fate, and no longer in control of your own life, it's hard to feel at one with women who are mothers or pregnant. 'People treat you like a *girl*,' said Virginia. 'You know, that you haven't had the rite of passage into womanhood ... People patronise you. They fill you in on what it's like to have children: "Oh, children are like this".' Recurring reminders of exclusion for many infertile women are events such as Mother's Day, Christmas Day, and other family and religious gatherings. Some women choose not to join celebrations of this kind; the escape, of course, highlights the exclusion whilst avoiding the immediate emotional distress. Some of my interviews took place at the end of the International Year of the Family, which for some infertile people turned into a Year of Endurance.

Involuntary childlessness can entail a sense of exclusion from the future. Genetic continuity may be important, even though some women described it as 'an ego thing' to want 'a reproduction of my husband and myself'. Gail said, 'My two brothers have no children ... so it was devastating. It meant that this was the end of the family line on my side. All that genetic history!' The continuity of knowledge, all the intangibles that one entrusts to the next generation, and the continuity of one's treasures, the symbols of lives already lived, may be of even greater importance. Gail went on, 'There are my father's prizes at school. Who do I give those to?' Barbara told me she sometimes thought,: 'Where do I fit in? What am I here for? You know, I'm going to live and then die, and there's nothing to continue on.'

## Infertility and childlessness

All the women in my research rated childlessness as a more serious problem than infertility; most defined infertility as a problem only because it caused childlessness. Louise said, 'Not having monthly periods and things like that didn't make me feel any less of a woman. It was the not having children.' Infertility does have complex, more general significance for some women. It's impossible to disentangle the threads that link infertility and childlessness and then entwine themselves around the sense of self and the body. Because infertility takes away a woman's sense of autonomy and confidence in her body, it can reduce her sense of adequacy in many areas of life not directly associated with children. The knowledge of a defective body can affect the identity of infertile women.

Some women manage to maintain a sense of wholeness because of their partner's acceptance. Holly regretted her hysterectomy because she couldn't have children, but felt whole because her husband had married her in spite of it. Had he not done so, 'I would have been crushed. That would have made me think differently about myself. I would have thought that I was incomplete, I suppose, because I'd been rejected— for no other reason.'

## More than 'just a mother'

It would be unjust and inaccurate to imply that these women have nothing more in their lives than infertility and mother-hood. Most have careers that are important to them and recre-ations they enjoy. Some women might have been able to achieve pregnancy had they not postponed motherhood for the sake of a career or other interests. Even those who pursued motherhood through IVF resented the social pressure on women to find children a complete source of fulfilment.

I went back to being a student (doing a PhD as a means to getting back into the workforce) when Alice began school. It would be easy to devote my life to my daughter, but being the sole source of her mother's happiness would have been a terrible burden for her. I enjoy being a psychologist and I love research and writing and working with students, so I have rewarding things to do away from her now, and goals for the future. I hope this means that she won't feel duty-bound to look after and entertain a mother whose life revolves around her.

Developing my career was also part of the long process of regaining control of my life. Although women may feel powerless in the face of unresolved infertility, many make bold attempts to reclaim power. It is because they have figured as strong women in their own life stories that the disruption of infertility is so staggering. This can affect their confidence in all areas of life. Recovery comes with time and effort, often by concentrating on things over which some control seems possible. When Rosemary finished her degree, she wrote, 'This has brought a quiet confidence that if I work hard, I really can have some control over the process and look forward to a good outcome—I *can* win if I try—a comforting and reassuring thought.'

I like to think that I could have led a fulfilling life even without Alice, although I'm so grateful that I don't have to test that belief. My childlessness was a profound personal loss, not something that made me feel inadequate in relation to other people. It was obvious to me that people I admired led very fulfilling lives without children, and I knew, intellectually, that it was possible for me too. The hard part was learning to live with the big empty space inside me.

If I'd had children all those years ago when I first tried, I would have been horrified at the thought of an only child. Now it's just a fact of life. I'm thrilled to have one. I was amazed at how confident I was, instantly, about being Alice's mother. I knew I would make mistakes, but I was sure I was the right mother for her and she responded to me from the beginning. (I wonder now about whether I would have been quite so confident had we not succeeded on our first attempt at IVF; multiple failures can be debilitating.) The fact that I had no friends with babies or young children meant that I was still outside the 'mothers' club'. I didn't really join until a woman in the supermarket suggested going to a playgroup when Alice was two. From then on, I was aware of occupying a new role, almost of acting a part, although one that was legitimately mine. It's not because I'm older than the other mothers, because there are a few of us around these days. It's because I had relinquished any chance of being a mother, and can't just take it for granted. I almost used to watch myself from above: 'This is Maggie, a mother, hearing reading at school'; 'Here I am watching my daughter play football in a force 10 gale'. Tears often still come to my eyes at these moments (and not just because I'm freezing). Nowadays it's netball and discus. (Discus!) I can't get over how lucky I am.

I'm also aware of feeling somewhat awkward with infertile people who still don't have children. I know what it's like.

### References

Short, L. (1992). Gendered subjectivity: Marriage, motherhood and desire. In P. Grimshaw, R. Fincher, & M. Campbell (Eds.), *Studies in Gender: Essays in Honour of Norma Grieve* (pp. 170-187). Melbourne: Equal Opportunity Unit, University of Melbourne.

### Notes

Further details of the research can be found in the following publications:
Kirkman, M. (1999). Infertile mothers: A perspective from research and experience. In R. Jansen & D. Mortimer (Eds.), *Towards reproductive certainty: Fertility and genetics beyond 1999* (pp. 120–124). Lancashire: Parthenon.
Kirkman, M. & Rosenthal, D.A. (1999). Representations of reproductive technologies in women's narratives of infertility. *Women and Health*, 29, 17-36.
Kirkman, M. (2001). Infertile women and radical feminism: Conflicting narratives of assisted reproductive technology. In J. Daly, M. Guillemin, & S. Hill (Eds.), *Technologies and health: Critical compromises* (pp. 75–88). Melbourne: Oxford University Press.

Kirkman, M. (2001). Thinking of something to say: Public and private narratives of infertility. *Health Care for Women International*, 22, 523–535.

*The story of how I came to be a mother is published in:*
Kirkman, M., & Kirkman, L. (1988). *My Sister's Child*, Ringwood, Australia: Penguin.

I owe a great debt to the women who participated in the research for their generosity and for all that they have taught me. Pseudonyms have been used for them throughout this chapter.

# ANCIENT ART, MODERN DILEMMA: CHINESE MEDICINE AND PREGNANCY LOSS

Jane Lyttleton

Coming as I do from a family of scientists and doctors, leaving my PhD studies to pursue the ancient and somewhat inaccessible study of traditional Chinese medicine was a large leap of faith. But evidently it was a guided one because I've not looked back once in twenty years. All my years of study in Western physiology and biochemistry have stood me in good stead, however, for the sort of work I am doing now.

It was only a couple of years after I opened my first clinic specialising in gynaecological disorders that I discovered that fertility might be an issue for me personally. I still clearly remember the magic and mystery of making love with my husband when I was ovulating and there wasn't a contraceptive in sight. And then the shock and disbelief when I got a period two weeks later. How could I possibly not be pregnant? All the circumstances were fortuitous, our chemistry was firing, the timing was right and our intentions were welcoming. But so it was month after unbelievable month, and then a year had passed, and then a year and a half. The magic and mystery were soon leached out of our babymaking efforts by thermometers, charts and coital duty—although my husband wasn't too perturbed by the latter.

His sperm passed with flying colours, and although none of the tests done on my blood, cervical mucus or tubes showed any abnormalities, it was assumed that the 'problem' was mine, even though I was only thirty-three and my eggs should not have been too old. I found the whole situation most confronting and for a while became quite demoralised. It was not easy to know which direction to take, but time brought with it the distance I needed to be objective. From my perspective as a practitioner of Chinese medicine I had to agree that our inability to conceive might well lie with me; I could see many subtle influences that could be reducing my fertility.

At first I tried every remedy I could lay my hands on—some rational, such as specific prescriptions of Chinese herbs, some purely superstitious, like the African greenstone fertility symbol I wore for a while after a woman put it around my neck, saying it worked for her. I consulted with Western specialists also, but wasn't ready to go too far down that route. They wanted to do investigative surgery and I was still convinced I could do this getting-pregnant business without medical intervention. I kept swallowing the Chinese herbs even when I thought the smell would make me gag. I kept taking the basal temperatures every morning, charting the fertile mucus and never stopped trying, never stopped hoping.

Many wonderful offers came from overseas to participate in seminars but I turned them all down, 'No thanks, can't do— you see I'm going to have a baby'. But eighteen months later when the offers were still coming and I was getting very despondent about ever conceiving, I gave in with not terribly good grace. I admitted defeat, accepted an invitation and booked a laparoscopy for my return.

Along with my books and lecture notes, I packed all my pills and potions. Arriving in London several days before I was due to start giving seminars, I awaited my period with some anxiety. I wanted it over and done with and asked a colleague to give me an acupuncture treatment to hurry it up. I spent days getting exasperated with my late period before it occurred to me to do a pregnancy test! I will never forget that breath-taking moment full of wonder when the positive sign appeared.

At home, I had repeatedly done the home urine tests if my period was five minutes late, or even sometimes when it wasn't late at all but my breasts felt bigger than usual or I just wasn't as tetchy as usual premenstrually. Always the results had been negative, so now I really couldn't believe what I was seeing. But positive it definitely was, and the nausea that followed so quickly in the next days confirmed it. In fact my lectures were given through a haze of nausea and fainting spells. I sent a postcard to my gynaecologist cancelling the laparoscopy. The postcard showed kids in a tenement slum in France painting graffiti on the walls. 'Surtout La Vie' said the graffiti.

From the moment I returned to work some months after the birth of my daughter I pursued every possible lead for finding out more about treating infertility. But it wasn't until Lara was old enough for me to leave her that I was able to go and spend time in the fertility clinics in hospitals in China. There I began to gain a deep appreciation of the subject. Then the challenge was to translate what works in Chinese clinics to the situation of modern Western couples.

In China, the fertility clinics in which I worked appear extremely primitive by our standards. Dr Chong is one of several specialist gynaecologists working in a large teaching hospital in South China, treating mostly couples who have not succeeded in falling pregnant. Her consulting room consists of a small, bare oblong room partly partitioned to hide a wooden unpadded examination table. Beside the table sits a steaming steriliser for the large steel speculums. Dr Chong works from 8 am every morning until the clamouring horde of women and their partners have all been seen.

There is no sense of privacy as intimate details of the sex life and the menstrual cycle are discussed in front of all the waiting patients. Each is carefully diagnosed and handed a prescription for herbs. It's not a quick procedure. Each prescription might require that more than a dozen herbs be weighed and dispensed. There may be several dozen packets to be made up if the patient is going back home to the countryside for a month before her next visit.

The contrast between clinic settings in China and here in Sydney is dramatic. My clinic in Sydney has tastefully furnished and private consultation rooms and the patients have hour-long appointments. The contrast is even more marked if we compare with the largest of Australia's modern IVF clinics.

Most have comfortable waiting rooms, surgical theatres equipped with sophisticated equipment and laboratories staffed with scientists responsible for supervising the fertilisation of eggs and growth of embryos, genetic analysis and research.

So how can TCM work in this modern setting with couples living twenty-first-century lifestyles? It has a long tradition, more than 2000 years, of applying its techniques to infertility and recurrent miscarriage. Chinese medicine recognised thousands of years ago what modern reproductive specialists recognise—that successful pregnancy depends mostly on the quality of the sperm and the eggs. This in turn can be dependent on the overall health of the would-be Mum or Dad. In the ancient Chinese medicine texts this capacity to reproduce was described in terms of kidney function, and dysfunction described in terms of kidney yin, yang or jing. The term 'kidney' includes the pelvic organs, especially the reproductive organs.

Nowadays, fertility clinics in China utilise all the wisdom and observations made by TCM doctors over the last 2000 years and combine it with the knowledge of the reproductive system that modern Western medicine has uncovered over the last 100 years. It is a happy and exciting marriage wherein treatment protocols are refined and expanded according to advances in Western research, but still maintain two fundamental principles of Chinese medicine:

- Never damage the qi, the essential energy or life force, of the patient.
- Treat the unique and individual pattern of each patient.

Modern Chinese fertility doctors will only prescribe drugs or surgery if there is no other option. Instead Chinese herbs are prescribed; these are a potent form of medicine and include cultivated and wild plants that have been studied and analysed extensively over the last 2000 years. These herbs are rarely prescribed singly, rather they are made up in formulas consisting of up to eighteen or twenty different herbs. They will be boiled up in ceramic pots and drunk by the cupful once or twice a day. Some hospitals offer the convenient option of prescribed formulas made up with granulated herbs that eliminates the boiling step, an option that time strapped Westerners taking Chinese herbs are usually keen to take advantage of.

The prescribed herbs may have the effect of enhancing ova or sperm development, increasing the thickness and receptivity of the uterine lining, facilitating movement in the fallopian tubes or increasing secretion of progesterone after ovulation. In fact most aspects of reproduction can be influenced by treatment with Chinese medicine. Some aspects are harder to treat and most of these are situations that Chinese medicine diagnoses as severe kidney jing deficiency. Such a deficiency, often congenital, might manifest as complete lack of sperm production, primary ovarian failure or premature menopause. Also as women age, so do the eggs in their ovaries, and the kidney jing is said to decline. This is seen particularly in women in their late thirties and forties when pregnancy is much less common.

Modern IVF techniques can sometimes offer solutions for people who have kidney jing deficiency, although aged eggs are not easily made young and fertile again. Another cause of infertility that Chinese medicine does not treat well is absolute obstruction of the fallopian tubes. IVF was initially developed to help women with this problem, and it remains the most effective treatment.

However, in many cases of infertility or when there is no apparent reason for infertility, Chinese medicine has a lot to offer—but only to those who are prepared to accept a form of therapy that works gradually to correct imbalances and malfunctions. The nature of Chinese medicine that makes its action slow and subtle is precisely the nature that also makes it very safe. It is not an approach that appeals to everybody in these days of the quick fix. However it is clear from both my own experience with infertility and my experience working with Western women facing infertility that it strongly appeals to women who wish to retain some level of control over their infertility treatment. Working with Chinese medicine requires a large amount of input from the patient, and the plan of treatment is often worked out together with the doctor so it is relevant to the needs of each individual. The personal face of infertility treatment is never lost with Chinese medicine; rather, it is reinforced with every visit to the clinic.

Many different types of couples seek out Chinese medicine treatment for infertility. Following are some of their stories.

Some couples are philosophically opposed to using drugs or technological intervention and seek Chinese medicine and other 'natural medicines' for that reason.

*Annabel and Robert married when they were both almost forty and wasted no time in trying to conceive. Both of them were extremely healthy and led active lives. They both had a wholesome diet and had preferred to use herbal or dietary measures rather than pharmaceutical drugs if they were unwell. Annabel had a series of blood tests done to check her hormone levels and Robert had a sperm count done. Annabel's results were all textbook perfect but they were both shocked to discover that Robert's sperm count was low, the sperm he did have swam poorly and most of them were abnormal shapes. The specialists agreed that it was his experience as a farmer using sprays that may have caused the problem.*

*They decided to try Chinese medicine. When Robert consulted with me, I found a very robust and fit man. I relied on his pulse and tongue, diagnostic methods unique to Chinese medicine, to find the clues I needed. Robert's pulse had a steady, strong beat but his tongue was a bright, scarlet red—too bright, too scarlet. The tongue appearance indicated internal heat, and I prescribed herbs for the next three months that were designed to 'build the yin and clear the heat'. At the same time I advised he cut out the one cup of coffee he had each morning and cut down on the chilli he was fond of adding to his meals, since coffee and chilli are particularly heating. So is alcohol, and Robert agreed to keep his wine intake down to an occasional glass with meals. In three months, Annabel was still not pregnant but the sperm count had improved. The percentage of abnormal sperm was still too high, however.*

*Another three months and the sperm improved further, although still not reaching ideal parameters. Since Annabel was now forty, I asked how she would feel about using artificial reproductive technology to help things along. They were very opposed to using IVF and flatly refused to take any drugs but they did finally agree to a procedure whereby Robert's sperm were washed and sorted to select the best, and then several hundred were deposited by catheter in Annabel's fallopian tubes at the time she was ovulating. The procedure was successful the second month they tried it. Annabel produced a four-kilogram healthy baby boy.*

Other patients come to my clinic seeking treatment for infertility after they have done IVF procedures, once or many times, and have decided to try another approach. IVF may have been unsuccessful because the ovaries do not respond to the drugs, or the sperm cannot be persuaded to fertilise the eggs, or just fail for unknown reasons. In some cases the IVF program itself has proved to be too taxing psychologically or physiologically. Sometimes these are very difficult cases but the rewards are immense when pregnancies are achieved, sometimes against unbelievable odds.

*Maria's husband rang my clinic one morning from the IVF clinic where Maria had just been informed that this, her sixth attempt, would be cancelled like so many before because of inadequate response to the ovary-stimulating drugs. The specialist told a devastated Maria that there were no follicles left and that it was menopause that she would experience, not pregnancy. They both came to see me the very next day. Maria told me how three-quarters of her ovarian tissue had been removed because of dermoid cysts and the remaining quarter seemed to have great difficulty producing follicles and eggs. She experienced a lot of abdominal and lower back pain. After calming her mind by persuading her that even one-quarter of an ovary had the potential to produce enough follicles for another ten years of menstrual cycles we set about trying to see if it could be resurrected. Her symptoms and history indicated what Chinese medicine calls an obstruction of qi and blood. Fortunately, with repeated gentle persuasion from acupuncture needles, this quarter ovary proved very rapidly not only to produce follicles and release eggs, but produce good quality eggs at that. Maria's first successful (and pain-free) ovulation after the final failed IVF cycle came within a couple of weeks and to the great surprise of everyone she became pregnant and produced a healthy baby girl. Six months, eight acupuncture treatments and just two ovulations later she was pregnant again with her second daughter. Despite increasing fatigue and age Maria kept up the acupuncture and her attempts to keep the little bit of ovarian tissue alive. In the next two years she had two more pregnancies, one of which didn't survive, and one of which produced a much-wanted son. Because her main symptoms were pain and obstruction in the ovary, acupuncture rather than Chinese herbal medicine was the predominant therapy in this case.*

There are those who are willing to try everything from the outset. This can mean combining the best of all worlds— modern miracle technology for getting around obstacles in the reproductive tract or giving a leg up to sad and bedraggled sperm. Chinese medicine or nutritional programs can prepare the body and mind as much as possible to maximise chances of the procedures being successful. This type of approach throws traditional Chinese medicine smack bang into one of the most controversial modern medical arenas, but the beauty of this oldest of all existing medical systems is that it is universally applicable. Provided the object of its attentions is the human body, it doesn't matter if that human body is taking drugs that stop the pituitary dead in its tracks or having surgical procedures to remove eggs or sperm from their glandular homes, or is experiencing the most intense emotional stress in its history. The doctor of Chinese medicine can still make a diagnosis incorporating all those factors and their effect on the body and mind, and can prescribe treatment that not only focuses on the particular imbalance in that individual but may also enhance the effects of the drugs and lessen their side effects.

For some couples the problem is not in conceiving, but in staying pregnant. When a couple has had three miscarriages it is generally assumed that the problem may lie with the parents and not with chromosomal disorders in the embryo. Texts of Chinese medicine, as of Western medicine, often attribute recurrent miscarriages to a fault in the woman, although recent research indicates that pregnancies of the partners of men whose work exposes them to volatile fumes have a high risk of miscarriage.

The doctor of Chinese medicine will analyse the constitutional type of the woman and seek out the particular imbalance that is predisposing her to recurrent miscarriage. Often the doctor of Chinese medicine will diagnose a kidney yin or yang disorder, which is exerting its influence in the early stages of pregnancy. If the cause of the miscarriage is related to some factor in the uterine lining or the balance of hormones, Chinese medicine will remedy it quite quickly. If the problem lies in the production of less than healthy sperm or eggs, treatment of either the male or female partner may take some months before good results can be expected. Lifestyle and dietary changes will often be suggested, too. In either case the doctor will advise the couple to avoid pregnancy for at least the first three months of treatment. Miscarriage is understood by TCM to be very weakening to a woman's body and avoidance of pregnancy is very strongly advised until such time as the risk of another miscarriage is greatly reduced. Once the kidney qi is seen to be much stronger, and other factors that might contribute to miscarriage have been corrected, the next pregnancy can be expected to proceed without mishap.

*Noreen came to see me on the recommendation of her GP. She had a history of two miscarriages in the previous year, both at early stages. Western medical specialists had told her that there was no appropriate treatment they could offer her and recommended that she just try to fall pregnant again as soon as possible. But she realised that she was terrified of the possibility of a third miscarriage, and asked my opinion about using Chinese medicine to prevent this. Both Noreen and her husband were young and fit and had exemplary diets and lifestyles. Noreen's husband was a public servant and apparently had no exposure to environmental risk factors. However when we closely examined Noreen's menstrual cycle there was a small clue that was worth following up. She often got spotting before her period and her temperature charts showed an abnormal decline in temperature levels well before the arrival of her period. In addition she described lethargy, lower back pain during her period, poor circulation to her hands and feet and a general intolerance to cold. In TCM terms she suffered from kidney yang weakness, a diagnosis that is often associated with low progesterone levels. It is one of the easier hormonal balances to treat and after three months of taking herbs she noticed dramatic differences in her temperature charts and her energy levels. It was time for her to try to fall pregnant again, something she achieved in another three months. Noreen continued to take herbs throughout the first twelve weeks of pregnancy from which time everything went swimmingly.*

Sometimes acupuncture and Chinese medicine are used by patients in a support role. This support is as much psychological as physiological. While herbs may be prescribed to help the lining of the uterus, others are added to calm the mind and help sleep and sanity. Acupuncture has a wonderful calming and regulating effect and deals effectively with the anxieties felt by most women going through infertility treatment.

*Betty was referred to me by an IVF clinic after her baby died. The referral was made more for Betty's psychological and general well-being than for fertility. Betty had used IVF because her fallopian tubes were badly damaged and IVF offered her her only chance to conceive. She began doing IVF cycles when she was thirty-nine years old. In the following four-and-a-half years she did fourteen IVF procedures. One of these cycles produced a baby which died tragically young.*

*When Betty came to me, it was just a year since her baby had died and she still had much grieving to do. She agreed to take a break from the IVF clinic except to see the counsellor there, and to use acupuncture and Chinese medicine to try and help heal the wounds and regulate her body and its cycles. She was encouraged to give her body and mind a rest. We worked together for two months during which time Betty made visits to her baby's grave, and made a photo album of the baby's short life.*

*One eye was on the biological clock, though, and as soon as her mental state would allow, Betty was back at the IVF clinic. She used the support of Chinese herbs and acupuncture throughout the rest of her attempts. The second attempt resulted in a pregnancy, one that ended suddenly at twenty-five weeks, possibly due to infection. But this time Betty was soon back on her feet and the following year attempted three IVF cycles in quick succession. The last of these finally gave her the prize she had fought for so determinedly—she gave birth to a beautiful baby girl at the age of forty-four.*

As for my own story, what worked for me was a careful diagnosis of a subtle but complex imbalance in my reproductive system. Because I had all the symptoms of endometriosis I took quite strong herbs to try and reduce or remove any endometrial implants. At the same time I showed signs of kidney weakness which meant that this line of treatment had to be approached very cautiously or it would have weakened me and compromised my fertility further. It was a juggling game and it took more than a year to correct with constantly modified prescriptions. But by the time I did finally conceive, my kidney energy was strong and healthy. This was borne out by a mostly trouble-free and enjoyable pregnancy and above all a very strong, healthy baby. My daughter is now a delightful and bouncing twelve-year-old and a constant inspiration for my work with other couples experiencing difficulty conceiving.

Sadly, I didn't conceive again. This was partly because I couldn't face the monumental effort of daily boiling of Chinese herbs again when I was so exhausted by an infant who didn't seem to ever sleep!

But that's not the end of the story—there's Charlie. When Lara was three, we met and fell in love with a spirited and disturbed six-year-old, Charlie, whose single mum had just died. Charlie spent many weekends with us and we would have loved to adopt her, but unfortunately other plans had been made for her. I grieved her loss acutely for almost a year. Eventually, as the years went by and her official guardians moved out of Sydney, we almost lost touch altogether.

But you never know what's around the next corner. Charlie, at age thirteen, took matters into her own hands and ran away. She didn't know where she was going, she just took enough warm clothing and bedding to sleep in the park. We were living in Indonesia at the time and it was a most unexpected telephone request we got from the Department of Community Services to offer Charlie a home.

It took ten years but Lara finally had a sister, and a big one at that. Charlie brought to our family a wonderful sense of completion. As our wise old Javanese cook said to me, 'Sometimes you just have to be patient.'

# A NEW KIND OF FAMILY

## Alice and Jacqueline

### Trying: *Alice*

There's something fundamental about leaving your mark in the world, knowing that you're only here briefly. I think people hold that fairly dear, maybe subconsciously, and it doesn't become apparent to them until it's threatened in some way. Luckily in my case it didn't seem to be such a strong motivation. I'd always believed that social conditioning is more important than anything innate.

When I was a young girl I assumed having a child would be one of the normal transitions that you go through in life, and it would all fall into place in my mid-thirties. But that assumption was challenged when I met and started a relationship with Ned. Ned found out he was infertile when he was a teenager at uni. We got together when I was in my late twenties. Still, at that stage I thought, 'That's OK, we'll find a way around this. There are medical options that we can pursue'. There was a bit to deal with in terms of not being able to have the genetic baby of your partner, but for me that was never a huge concern.

At about thirty-two or thirty-three I thought 'OK, we need to start acting now. I'd better start making an appointment at a clinic.' At that stage we decided our only option was donor sperm. Ned was fine with that. We were both pretty pragmatic about it, given there were no other options available to us apart from adoption. The adoption process was a whole other kettle of fish with very difficult hoops to jump through to get anything happening at all. So the most doable option seemed to be anonymous donor insemination.

That involved signing up with a clinic and having a series of tests to ensure that you were OK physically, and going through a counselling process where they checked out whether you were a suitable candidate. We were then given a catalogue of anonymous donors from which you could select, with non-identifying information: height, weight, eye colour, profession, hobbies, etc. It was a pretty slim basis on which to choose the genetic father of your future offspring.

Then you start the cycle process which involves injecting lots of female hormones—estrogen-based drugs, which you have to inject on a daily basis. There are all sorts of potential complications and side-effects. To me it felt like having a huge case of PMT constantly, because you're taking massive doses of estrogen that cause you to super-ovulate. Whereas normally you would produce one egg a month, you produce multiple eggs per month, say ten to twenty, depending on the woman and the dosage of the drug administered. Physically it has a systemic impact on the whole body when you're producing that number of eggs. And hormones have very strong effects on the emotions and the psyche.

From the mid-1990s till 2000, I had fourteen cycles of ART, artificial reproductive technology. Nine were donor insemination, not full-scale IVF but still medicated, involving daily hormone injections and vaginal ultrasounds every couple of days. Then on top of that five cycles of full-scale IVF.

After nine cycles I was getting desperate, and I said to my doctor, 'Look, this is ridiculous. Will I try IVF now?' and she said, 'Yes, I think it's a good idea you do'. I switched to a clinic that required known donors; they didn't have a bank of anonymous donors. Thankfully, my best male friend agreed to be a donor. But I did four IVF cycles, and still no baby.

I didn't deal with repeated failure very well. I don't know how other people deal with it, I just found it devastating. Through the whole process you're aiming towards an outcome that you can't guarantee, and that in most cases doesn't work. Most IVF cycles don't work, so you're putting yourself through this enormously rigorous and often damaging and painful process, with no guaranteed outcome at

the end. That's apart from having depleted yourself emotionally, physically and financially.

I felt almost entirely isolated. I was desperate to make
connections and was always trying to find groups I could join.
But there's not a lot out there. Even though IVF has a certain
profile in the media and people are familiar with the process
to a certain extent, most of my friends and family didn't seem
to be able to deal with the process. There were a couple of
exceptions. A friend who has been through IVF successfully
was enormously supportive, and another who is just a great
listener and counsellor was there for me as much as possible.
But most people weren't able to provide the kind of support
that you need. A friend would perhaps inquire how my cycle
went, and I'd say, 'Well, it failed', and they wouldn't know what
to say. They haven't been through the process. Or I'd just been
to the loo and found what appeared to be an early miscarriage,
confide in someone, and they would say something like, 'Oh
gee, that's not like me at all. I just look at my husband and I'm
pregnant'. Often people would simply change the subject. I
understand why, but that itself added to the hurt and the
devastation.

Other kinds of family-related loss in society are acknowledged and there are rituals that you're able to share with other
people to enable you to resolve the grief. But the loss associated with failed IVF is not acknowledged by the general
community. There are no rituals to deal with this, so people
going through it are left entirely alone. And that for me was
one of the hardest parts of it. Plus, people have a limit to the
amount of support they can offer you. People get compassion
fatigue when it goes on for so long.

There were times I felt resentful about Ned's infertility. As it
got more and more difficult for me going through medical
intervention over the years, I couldn't help but think to myself
'Why can't we be like other people, just have sex and have a
baby? It's ridiculous that I've had to go through this incredible
trauma and how dare you be infertile?'

Of course it caused tension in our relationship. I don't think
many people who go through long periods of doing IVF don't

experience some tension, especially when it's not working and there's no end in sight. It's not like the more you try, the more likely you are to succeed. As the woman gets older, the chances of success diminish. So he was infertile and my fertility was diminishing. It was the double whammy of: 'If you were fertile when I was thirty-two there wouldn't have been a problem, and now I'm thirty-seven, all my good eggs are gone, and you're infertile'. So we had to deal with what appeared to be my increasing infertility on top of his infertility.

After nine donor inseminations and then four IVFs, it became obvious that not a lot was happening with my eggs. I have a very good friend who is extremely fertile and very supportive of my desire to be a mother, so we approached her. In fact my partner approached her, wrote her a note, not wanting to put her on the spot by asking such a big favour. It really is a big commitment to put someone through this process. So he wrote her a note, and she rang the moment she got it in the mail saying, 'Yes, yes, of course I'll do it'. So that was the absolute turning point in my IVF story, my chance to be a mother.

### Friends: Alice and Jacqueline

*So Alice underwent her fifth IVF cycle using donated eggs from her friend Jacqueline, and the donor sperm of her best male friend. This meant Jacqueline did an IVF cycle to produce a harvest of eggs for Alice. Jacqueline's eggs were fertilised by the male donor's sperm, and the resulting embryos transferred back into Alice's body.*

Jacqueline: Alice and I had been friends for five or six years, and I knew from very early on that she was trying to get pregnant, and at that stage the reasons for the infertility seemed to be on her partner's side; they knew he was infertile. I remember being very moved and very struck by her story. So was my partner. In fact, my partner had donated sperm for Alice and Ned several times in the past, but unfortunately that was unsuccessful.

I had some mad ideas about helping Alice. One of them was even offering to be a surrogate at one point, although I hadn't really thought that through. So the idea had been planted there a few months before I received this letter from Alice's partner. When the letter came I knew immediately what it was before I'd even opened it. I had already discussed it all with my partner, so I knew my response would be, 'Yes'.

*But the whole idea of donating eggs to another woman is still relatively new, isn't it, not to mention going through an IVF cycle for someone else?*

Jacqueline: I've been a mother for nine years now, and it's radically changed the person I am. So I could well understand Alice's desire, and the experience she was seeking to gain. I wanted to help her, give her some joy. There was no assurance that it would be successful, but I felt that it was an option that I was more than able to exercise, and I had full support from my family and my partner. As soon as the request came, I discussed it with all my close relatives. My mother and father and sister were all very supportive. I think perhaps they also had an understanding of that baby hunger.

*How did you feel, Alice, when Jacqueline gave such a quick and positive response?*

Alice: I was just delighted and overwhelmed. You don't approach this sort of thing lightly. It's a huge ask and had there been reservations on the donor's part I wouldn't have felt comfortable. But when Jacqueline responded so generously and so openly and so immediately, I felt my life was about to change. She had no reservations and was absolutely committed from the start. And so was the male donor, another dear friend who has been unbelievably supportive. So I remain absolutely, eternally grateful that both of them have made this possible.

*So has it redefined the relationship between you two?*

Alice: Yes, we went through a really rocky patch a while ago, where I think I was deeply traumatised by all the failed attempts at pregnancy. I was finding it hard to deal with anybody who had children. Jacqueline has always been very generous in including me in her family, but at certain points it felt really painful. Even though I know it came from generosity, for me it felt like the lack was even more apparent by comparison. And so I started to withdraw from a number of people, including Jacqueline. Luckily she's got the generosity and presence of mind to not let this type of thing happen without doing something about it. So she arranged that we get together and talk a few things through, and it was at that point that she told me that she had considered being a surrogate. I was absolutely overwhelmed, because I had had no idea, I was so caught up in my own trauma and loss. I was really touched by that and felt very positive about it. It reaffirmed our connection.

*Jacqueline, how did you interpret Alice's withdrawal at that time?*

Jacqueline: I tried to understand the procedure, but I was very hurt. I don't think people ultimately benefit from withdrawing into themselves and putting up barriers to intimacy. It took some thinking through, but I wasn't ready at that point to let go of our relationship, and I was quite angry as well. Part of the hurt manifested itself in some sort of anger. But I felt that there had been quite a history in our relationship. Alice was present at the birth of my daughter and is her godmother, and my children had always really enjoyed the company of Alice and Ned. So that family thing spurred me on to try to salvage things. It was difficult and painful to approach Alice, though, because I could sense that she was withdrawing.

*So how did you find doing the IVF cycle?*

Jacqueline: For me it was brief, and I knew that from the beginning, even though I did have reservations about some of the medical procedures. The first drug treatments I had were pills, followed by injections in the stomach which I'd self-administer or which were administered by my partner. The needles were uncomfortable but not too painful. It was mainly the logistics which I found intrusive and irritating. There was such a strict time schedule; things had to be done at a particular time, and I didn't really have any leeway. Then towards the end of the cycle, just before the egg pick-up, I felt quite a lot of discomfort in terms of being very swollen, very bloated, and feeling a bit vulnerable physically and emotionally.

*It must have given you some insight into what it would be like to do IVF repeatedly without success.*

Jacqueline: I still don't think I've got a really good grasp on what it'd be like to do that repeatedly without having a resolution. With my cycle there was a resolution, we picked up a good quantity of eggs that matured and then fertilised. So there was a sense of 'I've accomplished something; this has been good for something'. Then when Alice fell pregnant, I was just over the moon.

*So, Alice, did you ring Jacqueline immediately when you got the news that you were pregnant?*

Alice: Yes. I couldn't wait for the blood test, so that morning I did a pregnancy test and saw the blue line. I rang to let Jacqueline know that the test had been positive but it needed to be confirmed. Jacqueline came over that afternoon with her three children, and we took photos with the little stick with the blue line. Later that day it was confirmed by a blood test at the clinic. What had become increasingly impossible had now worked, and to bring all these people together—myself, Ned, Jacqueline and the sperm donor, into this process and have it work, seemed almost magical or extraordinary in some way. I mean it's a very unusual set of circumstances and to have it work the very first time we tried it was unbelievable. It was an incredible day in my life.

Jacqueline: Once the pregnancy was confirmed I was really

delighted. That evening we all had dinner together and popped some champagne.

*How do you see the relationship that will exist now between your family and this new child that's about to arrive?*

Jacqueline: I'm hoping it will be very close. My children all know about it, and the two elder ones who are six and nine understand what's actually happening. The younger one had a few difficulties. She said, 'Is it your baby or Alice's baby?' She was a bit perplexed.

As soon as we'd made up our minds to do it, we told them over dinner one night. And they were very excited. I had told them before that Alice had been trying to have a baby. And when they digested that there might be some kind of link between them and this new child, they were really thrilled. They love to count as many people within their family as possible. They feel a certain interest as well, a certain kind of kinship with that child.

Alice: It's one of the most delightful things about this arrangement, that wouldn't be the case if it hadn't happened this way. I don't really have much in the way of family cousins for the child, so I see it as the kids do—it's increasing the volume of family available to this child.

*In America, there have been situations where surrogacy has gone awry and the surrogate mother has ended up wanting the child. Did you feel a need to think through that issue at all?*

Jacqueline: A surrogacy situation would have been very different, but in terms of egg donation it's never really arisen as an issue that I might desire the baby and want to argue for my custody of him or her in any way. I do feel a certain sense of possession because my genetic material is being incarnated. I feel a strong link, and therefore a more intense interest in the child. I don't think there's any negative implications of that, I'm hoping they're all positive.

*Does that genetic link that Jacqueline's talking about sit comfortably with you?*

**Alice:** Yes, it does. This child is so lucky to have somebody else so invested in his welfare. From where I sit now that's a wonderful thing, I see it very positively, as Jacqueline does. Genetically speaking, I've got no problem at all. Strangely enough my genes aren't that great healthwise, and I know Jacqueline's genes are great and she's a wonderful person and all those things you want your child to come from, to be a product of.

*Do you envisage your child having two mothers in any sense?*

**Alice:** Family is fluid, it's being redefined. What motherhood is is being redefined, and I'm comfortable with redefining it in such a way that this child has extra people around it that will be a network, a loving, genetically linked network. That it involves mothers and children and cousins and half brothers and half sisters is fine by me. If a mother is someone who loves and has the best interests of the child at heart, then this child has two mothers.

Some people think, 'Oh my God it must be a terrible sense of loss not to be able to reproduce yourself and your partner'. But paradoxically, I feel really privileged because this expands the circle of family and love around the baby. And I am the birth mother. This child is being nourished by my blood, it's a part of my body, so he's intimately mine in that biological sense. That helps also resolve any dilemma around the idea of it not being my genetic material, because it's so much a part of me and it feels a part of me. I see on the ultrasound that it is a part of me.

*So you're forming new sorts of family relationships here?*

**Alice:** Yes, Jacqueline's children are the half siblings of my child genetically, so on that level there's a kind of new definition, a new kind of family that we're building, emotionally, and genetically. There's a lovely closeness and intimacy there. But there's a very clear line in terms of who the mother of the child is. And Jacqueline of course made that possible, that she has her own family and so do I. We're now related in a very unique way.

*What about the male donor, your good friend? What degree of involvement does he want?*

Alice: It seems to me what he'll offer is a really loving additional presence in this child's life that most children don't have the opportunity to have. He's an incredibly giving and intelligent and warm person and I'm sure that he'll be there in certain ways for the child. Maybe you'd get that from a fantastic godfather or a wonderful uncle, adding an extra dimension to the child's life, enriching it without being the parent. Obviously he's the genetic donor, but there's a clear distinction between him as the donor and my partner as the father. We're very fortunate to have this special link with him.

*What about your mother, Jacqueline? How did she respond when you told her you were going to donate your eggs?*

Jacqueline: She was very excited and positive. Both my parents were supportive, but particularly my mother felt that it was great for Alice. She was also happy that it would help repair a relationship, because she was aware of the rough patch that we'd been through. She's also thrilled because she feels a certain link to this child as well.

I don't think it's any sort of possessiveness that's going to demand great rights to this child or anything like that. I think she just feels delighted that she has another kind of incarnation for her own genetic line in the world. A new sort of grandchild.

*Have you encountered any negative attitudes towards the fact that you're having a donor baby?*

*Alice*: Not really. What we're doing is experimental in a sense. We're essentially adopting an embryo, an embryo produced by the love of our best friends. So we've had mixed reactions from the people that we've told. Most are fairly open to it and think it's unusual but wonderful in a weird kind of way. Some people find it altogether too strange and too difficult to wrap their heads around.

There is one person in Ned's family who is finding it difficult to deal with the origins of this child. It's just so far outside their frame of experience, in terms of traditional family, what family means. People like that are not particularly open about their reservations. They're rather guarded, understandably. But time will tell how this evolves. When there's a little baby, an actual, concrete little human being, things may change radically.

*Jacqueline, have you been very involved in the pregnancy?*

*Jacqueline*: Yes and no. My experience of pregnancy was so different that I've found it sometimes difficult to connect with Alice's experience. Because of the trauma that has preceded this, she was initally extremely cautious and afraid of committing to the child, which is totally understandable. My initial thing was to respond with immense joy, and I guess I wanted Alice to feel that joy, and I was disappointed when she didn't feel the joy because she felt the fear as well. I've kept away a bit, and have wanted her to come to terms with that herself.

Things have changed radically in the last few weeks, now that the baby is very much a real thing and is very much a growing concern! And I think now I feel more at ease in relation to Alice about it.

### The pregnancy: Alice

Unfortunately it hasn't been an easy pregnancy. They transferred two embryos, but I lost one twin around six or seven weeks. When I miscarried, it looked as if I was losing a lot, and it was unclear whether the pregnancy was going to continue, whether I could maintain even one baby...I had continual threatened miscarriage up until ten weeks of pregnancy.

I've had miscarriages in the past, so I found it very difficult to deal with another imminent loss. This one was even more profound, because there were other people involved and because the pregnancy continued a lot longer than earlier pregnancies I had. I could see the matter that I was losing, and I could see that it was a potential baby.

Every day was filled with panic. 'When I go to the loo this time, will there be more matter? Is this the first baby or the second baby that I'm losing?' Every time you stand up and you feel some fluid, 'Is this my baby?' Trying to manage the normal things of life around that, like work, was difficult. People wondering what you're doing, why the hell aren't you at work today? Not wanting to tell people it's because I have to lie flat on my back to try to preserve the life of my baby. I dealt with that for several weeks, without a resolution in sight. Not knowing if the baby was dead or alive.

*That's one of the legacies, isn't it, of repeated failed treatment and miscarriages—that the innocent joy of pregnancy is not available to you?*

Yes, your experience in the past has been seeing that blue line with the positive result, only to have it followed by the devastation of losing the baby each time. That's the only experience that you've had. I wanted to be able to respond with more joy, but I was extremely cautious and uncertain. I couldn't believe I could be so lucky, how could I? How could my fortunes change so radically? So I had to steel myself against what I felt was the strong possibility of failure, despite the initial success. On the other hand I clung desperately to the hope that this time it was different, the circumstances were so different because Jacqueline had donated the egg. But until that period was over, I couldn't feel the confidence you need to feel joy.

Jacqueline was fantastic when I was going through that protracted miscarriage phase, she was so supportive. It's only really now that I'm twenty weeks pregnant that things are looking a lot better. I'm now able to believe that there may be a positive outcome, that there is a viable baby who will be here next year. Now I can feel the baby kicking and it's concrete in a way that it never has been before in my life.

*How has your partner Ned responded to the pregnancy?*

He's thrilled. Originally he assumed he would never be able to have children at all, and now he has the opportunity, he's just delighted. And that delight overwhelms any difficulties he might have with the idea of not being able to reproduce himself. Plus he's much more of the nurture than the nature school as well. I don't think he has a very strong desire to see a little Ned running around. If there's a little person running around that's his child, that is what's fantastic. Whether it carries his genes or not is not the primary concern for him.

*When you look back on the IVF experience, what was the most damaging aspect?*

I think you get very cavalier about the physical toll that IVF takes. Because you so desperately want this goal you almost drag yourself over shards of broken glass to get there, and bugger the pain, the physical difficulties, they're marginal because your commitment is so strong. Over time, though, the emotional toll, the trauma does build and is crippling. Throughout the whole process you never know if there's going to be an end to the pain. The loss is not something that you can recoup somehow, unless you do have a baby at the end.

You lose your sense of self, because who you are contracts around this intractable problem. Who I was used to be a person that could make things happen, but who I was in IVF was someone that was completely immobilised, powerless, at the mercy of medical intervention, drugs, fate, and isolated to boot.

You become obsessed. It's inevitable, because you're inject-ing yourself several times a day, having blood taken for blood tests several times a week, at the clinic all the time, having vaginal ultrasounds every couple of days. Your life is reduced to a set of procedures that's supposed to produce some kind of goal for you, and you need to be focused on that. It also impacts on your ability to do your work, to pursue your profession. You can't go away for example when you're in a cycle, on a work trip, you have to physically be there to be fiddled with and jabbed. But the fact that you and your life is contracting is very difficult to communicate to other people.

*Did you ever come to grips with the fact that you may have ended up childless?*

No, never. Ned once said to me, 'Well, maybe you'll just have to face the fact you're never going to be a mother', and that was devastating, I didn't want to hear those words spoken, I didn't want to acknowledge that. I refused to let go of the desire of wanting to be a mother. I didn't know of a way that I could resolve that desire and live happily. Maybe that would have come with time, but certainly at the point where we arranged the double donor situation, I was not prepared to say I'm going to die without children, I'm going to live a life without children, I was not prepared to say that.

*Did you ever worry about being permanently damaged by IVF, on an emotional or even psychic level?*

I was really at the end of my tether with so much failed IVF. I still wonder what the long-term impact is. I wonder what happens to people who never succeed. I wonder if there are suicides that have come out of this process. I don't know if there's any research about that. Personally I don't know how or if I would have coped if it had never worked. To people who've not been in it, it might seem self-indulgent and frivolous to say that this kind of desire for a child was so strong that it could ruin your life if it didn't work out. Maybe it is. But until you're in it, you don't know. If you end up dying childless, having spent ten years of your life going to a clinic at six o'clock in the morning to be jabbed with needles and have repeated pelvic examinations each month, and end up bleeding on the toilet, I don't know if you ever get over that.

I used to worry about being permanently damaged. I worried that it may be a wound that would never close. But now the pregnancy seems to be going OK, what you try and do is focus on the future. I don't know if you ever get over the IVF process entirely. But something fundamentally changes when it works, and you need to be emotionally present and well for the baby, and I think you start to focus on that, and I think that's really important.

*What story will you tell your child about his or her creation?*

Luckily having been a member of the very wonderful Donor Insemination Group for many years, we've got the good oil on how to explain all this to the child. There's quite a few donor children out there now who are growing up. The best way to approach it is to answer the child's questions as they come up. When the child starts to want to know something about where it came from, you start to introduce in a very loving way, the truth of where it came from. I guess our story will be something about how Mummy and Daddy really wanted you but we couldn't do it ourselves so we had to ask Jacqueline and our male friend and because they loved us and they wanted us to have you, they helped us, and they gave us an egg and some sperm and that's where you come from.

*It's a very contemporary story, isn't it, this story? It very much hinges on where we're at with technology, and yet it also seems to involve very old tenets of friendship.*

And family. I don't have any reservations about the technology, because in this instance it's being used in a totally beneficial way. Technology pervades and has pervaded for centuries, every aspect of our lives. But I think, for us, this is a totally appropriate way to use technology, and I don't think it detracts from the fundamentals of parenting and child rearing. I'm grateful that I live in a time where the technology has advanced to this level, because I'm pretty sure that I wouldn't have had the chance to bear a child if that wasn't the case.

*Yet some would say that IVF conception isn't an act of love, that it's cold and clinical.*

That's not my experience of the situation. My experience is that not only my partner and I, but two of our dearest friends were involved in this act of conception, so the critical mass of love involved in this is just enormous. To me the whole thing has been imbued with love and couldn't have existed without love. A sexual act can exist without love: this could not have.

*Postscript: Alice finally gave birth to a healthy baby boy in April 2001.*

# 'ODAHALLO' MEANS 'I LOVE YOU' IN ETHIOPIAN

## Anne and Sam Storey

*Anne:* Hoping I'd be pregnant each month started to drive me a bit nutty and the thought of going through the IVF business was pretty awful, especially knowing that it has such a low success rate. I had a strong feeling our relationship wouldn't make it through if we did that, but I had a strong feeling that our relationship would make it if we adopted a child. At the time I seemed actually to be able to let go of the fantasy of being pregnant and carrying a baby and breastfeeding and doing all that sort of stuff that you think about. I mean it comes back here and there but the main thing was just having a family. I didn't really need to have a child that was our blood. In fact I sort of wish that we'd decided on adoption to begin with and that we hadn't pushed ourselves so much because in the end the decision did come very easily.

*Did you at any stage feel the need to know why it was that you couldn't conceive?*

*Anne:* Maybe I'm just a great big avoider. I could have gone and had counselling about why it was that it didn't happen but I was getting a bit sick of wondering why I couldn't do things. It wasn't happening, it didn't happen and something else was growing out of that that was far more important. It's been so alive, the whole thought of adopting this beautiful little boy. I know that it is the right thing to do. Maybe one day I'll look into it but I don't think so, it doesn't seem important really.

Sam, Bereket and Anne

*I know in the past we've talked about your discomfort physically, sometimes about sex, and I wondered whether that discomfort had any part in the decision not to go down the IVF path?*

**Anne:** I don't know. Maybe if I went and had my head shrunk for a few years I might be able to work that one out. Maybe it is something to do with being poked and prodded and having my body messed around with in a way that I don't want it to be. Maybe it's a lot of stuff lurking from other things that have happened.

Maybe I'm taking the easy option of not having to open myself up by giving birth or going through fertility treatments where you're out of control of your body and your life. You're also out of control when you go through an adoption process too, in a huge way, but it's a totally different thing.

*How did you come to terms with the idea that you couldn't conceive naturally? Did you have to get rid of negative thoughts about your body not working for you?*

**Anne:** I always used to feel like an empty shell and that negativity didn't go until we consciously decided we were going to adopt a baby. We went to a seminar and we met the most amazing people there. It was incredible meeting someone else who actually knew what it was like.

At that first seminar we got into the lift with the other people going and they looked a bit embarrassed about being there, didn't they? They wouldn't give us any eye contact or anything. People were obviously still battling with being on fertility treatment. They were getting older and they looked exhausted 'cause God knows what they'd been through. We were so excited about what we were going to do but it felt like so many of those people were doing this because there was nothing else to do. Then there was this other couple who were the only ones with a bit of life and colour in their faces. We ended up talking to them and that changed it completely for me. I went from feeling like I was the only person in the world who'd been through it, which is extremely selfish but that's the way it feels at the time, to feeling like there were other people you could talk to about it. This pair had such great spirit and they were just going to go for it. We're very close friends now.

*Were there certain painful things during that time that made you uncomfortable?*

**Anne:** It was always pretty hard going, listening to a friend tell you that they were going to have a baby—oh God, it was horrible. I was endlessly in tears about it and I wasn't very good at being happy for someone else. I couldn't separate from it at all and I always came back to why we weren't doing it. I don't know if anyone else really asked us that much, did they? I think they knew not to after awhile.

**Sam:** It was a very difficult time because we have a lot of friends in their mid-thirties and it seemed like one after the other people got pregnant and started their family. I went through periods of great anxiety. I felt like the world's moving on and I'm treading water. Every evening there'd be yet another friend ringing up with the good news. That was really hard. I was always thinking, 'Oh, shit here we go, and now Annie's going to be off her trolley for the next couple of hours grieving' and that'd get me really emotional and I'd be freaking out as well.

*And how did you cope with that?*

**Anne:** Built this house in record time apparently!

**Sam:** Yeah, we became demon owner-builders...

**Anne:** There were situations where everyone in the room was either pregnant, had had a child or was pregnant again. One time the blokes were outside—I don't know what they were doing out there but I was inside with all the women and I just didn't fit in. I didn't fit into anything really. I was on the outside all the time. But the worst thing was actually avoiding people with kids. I regret that but at times you just had to do it because you felt like you were the one constantly watching people do it but never doing it yourself.

*Why do you think it is that people do have trouble with the idea of adoption?*

Sam: I think it's like we're hardwired to produce our own offspring. We're conditioned to think family only happens in one way. Everyone's used to all that stuff about characteristics that you share. People say 'Isn't he just like Uncle Joe Blow' or 'He's got just the same features as his grandmother'. It's very hard for people to pull back from that and consider an alternative way for it to happen.

Something else that you have to deal with all the time is well-meaning relatives who say, 'You know you'll probably find once you've adopted Bereket you'll fall pregnant and you'll have your own baby'. You get really angry. You feel like you are constantly fighting this battle, having to say, 'Why are you always contrasting it with a natural-born child coming? What's wrong with this being it? This is the primary thing and being absolutely fantastic and we don't need to go any further than that'.

*When you did decide to adopt did you feel yourself opening up to a whole new set of possibilities in life and how did you then start to visualise yourselves?*

Anne: I thought about it as an amazing adventure. It's weird. You get this catalogue of countries you can adopt from and we decided to go with Ethiopia 'cause we met a couple of people we'd really liked from there. Plus we wanted it to be a country that we'd like to go back to. We went to a circus-type thing in Canberra and there were lots of people with adopted kids and also lots of Ethiopian people there with kids and that was great. Everyone was really into adoption and explaining all about it. It was rich and inspiring and exciting. These people have a really good support group. They go away a lot so we went away with them for a few days and it grew out of all that. We became close to a lot of those people now, they're almost like family members. So we decided to travel over there for six weeks last year and that was really exciting.

It was so important to wander around the place and see parts of the country and meet the guy who was running the whole adoption program. I had this thing about smelling Ethiopia. I wanted to smell it before we went again. It was very exhausting and we got sick a lot but it was the most fantastic thing we've ever done.

*You did have doubts, though, didn't you, about it, because there was certain criticism from people who believe by adopting from a culture that's so different from our own that you are negating that culture?*

**Anne:** There were major doubts and they're still there. They'll always be there. We don't have any doubts that we want to adopt Bereket at all, but it's a very selfish act. We want babies, we want kids and some people challenge us about it and say that they don't think it's right and others think we're heroes which is absolute rubbish and I don't know where we sit in amongst all that.

**Sam:** The reason we're going ahead is that on a very fundamental level we know if Bereket isn't adopted he grows up in an orphanage without love, despite the best intentions of the staff. But if he is adopted he'll have an extraordinary amount of love and warmth in his life.

In an ideal world you wouldn't adopt from another country, that country would be able to look after its own tragedies and the results of those tragedies or at least the children, but that's not the sort of world that we live in. But that's all you can say that's black and white about the whole thing because every other aspect of it is grey. There's all these opposing views about whether it's good or bad, there's all the politics about the third world and the first world and us taking advantage of the misery of the third world and white versus black and white being the colour of power.

*The actual process of adopting has not been easy, has it? It's taken three years and it's been painful in lots of ways, despite knowing you are going to have a child at the end of it. What have been some of the biggest difficulties you've faced throughout that?*

*Sam:* I think growing up in middle-class Australia, you have the power to sort your life out, it's just a matter of putting some effort and work into it. It's not the same for everyone of course but with adoption all of a sudden you don't have any power. You're dependent on a government process and it needs to be there, but nevertheless a government process in a third world country that's not nearly as efficient as what we're used to in Australia. So it's slow, it's very difficult to find out any information about exactly where you're at in terms of the process, how far you are through, how long things are going to take.

*Anne:* Last year when all our paperwork had finally gone through we were told it would be a three-year wait till we could be allocated a baby. That was hell for me. It was after two years of getting through the bureaucratic stuff of social worker visits, etc. I had to keep pulling myself back. The process starts off with getting fingerprinted at the police station and then you go to the doctor and have health checks done. There's four social worker visits to your home, which depend on the time frame of the social worker allocated to you. Ours took ages. We had to write a ten-page life story and be interviewed separately and together. The social worker writes your file up and sends it off and it sits on someone's desk for a while, then it gets processed in Australia and eventually goes to the country that you're adopting from.

That sounds pretty straightforward but we had a lot of hold ups. Like it can sit on someone's desk for three months and nothing will happen. Then the whole adoption program shut down in Ethiopia because there was an epidemic of measles and a lot of the babies died and the people that were running it were exhausted and had to stop for six months. There's lots and lots of little hiccups along the way that you've got to be prepared for.

*Sam:* Once you're actually allocated a child you get the smallest bit of information and if you're lucky a photo of the child. As soon as you see that photo you start bonding straight away even though he's just a picture. You're on tenterhooks because you don't even know whether they're going to make it to the end of the process. There's people around, we've met them, who've been waiting for a child and halfway through the child has died. Sometimes there's an epidemic of something or other and it just wipes out whole wards in orphanages and stuff in countries like Ethiopia and you have to start again. So you've bonded to this child who you've got no contact with. You have no control over their welfare and they may die in the next six months. And that's on top of all the bureaucratic stuff.

It's a fantastic lesson in waiting and patience. You try to stay busy and distracted and ultimately you fail, but you try all the same 'cause you've got no choice.

*Have you got an image in your head now of what it's going to be like when you have got him? Do you think it's going to be very different for you?*

**Anne:** It's weird getting images because at this point what I'm having trouble with, we both are, is the overwhelming sense of love that you have for this person that you are endlessly having to push back inside of you. It's like literally forcing it back down your mouth into your stomach because you can't put it anywhere. I don't spend a lot of time thinking about what it's going to be like because we just don't know how long it will be and it puts you away in the head. I bawl my eyes out most days but I've also gone numb just to get through the last little bit.

**Sam:** I know that we can only be naïve at this stage because it's all just concepts and theory, and once the reality of it happens that's when we'll start to work our way through it all. But my head's constantly full trying to imagine possibilities of how it's going to be. Particularly because this adoption comes with the fact that Bereket has an older brother who's five-and-a-half-years old. They were separated when they went into the adoption program because his brother failed the medical test and is HIV positive and now lives in a Mother Teresa orphanage in Ethiopia. I mean that's part of all our self-doubt. The two brothers, the only surviving members of their family are going to be split by however many thousands of kilometres of distance and culture and we had to make the decision that we're adopting Bereket, but unofficially we are going to adopt his brother Dawit as well.

Which of course brings us back to Australian history, stolen generation stuff and people who were pushed into orphanages, and what their childhood experiences were like with no contact with any surviving family, no knowledge of who they were, the hopelessness of that. We've had to think about that from Bereket's brother's point of view and the ways we're going to try and meld our lives with his to some extent and keep the relationship between the two brothers alive.

*Do you think this will answer your need to parent?*

Sam: It already has in small ways. Despite all the waiting and the anxiety it's growing in us. Even though some days you wonder when the hell it's going to happen, underneath you know it's rolling on and it's going to happen and it's fantastic. Because of Bereket's brother being left behind it's also this big unwieldy thing and you don't quite know what shape it's going to take. I suppose that's just being a parent, you never know what you're in for really with your children.

Anne: I remember people saying you don't have to have children. There's other things in life, and I said 'No. I do have to have them'. But I don't want to think that this is going to be the peak of everything we've worked towards. I'm already planning which things to do that don't involve Bereket as well because I think that's a bit obsessive. I would hate to put on him that he's the answer to everything because there's so many other things in our lives that are really strong.

*Why did you feel you had to have children?*

Anne: I know it sounds corny and pathetic but it's that nurturing thing, a continuation of the love you had from your family. It's a very selfish life without kids, isn't it? You'd have to find new friends that weren't into it if you didn't have children or maybe you could just enjoy other people's children. That's always an option but then you're the endless observer. That I couldn't stand.

Sam: I grew up in a big family, a very extended motley bunch of related and unrelated people and I think you've got to know who your clan is and have your clan around you to help you through life. It's a fundamental thing. I don't think not having kids is just selfishness. Obviously people can make that choice and not necessarily be selfish but it's what's important for you and your experience of family. If it's been positive and in my case large, you just want to keep that going.

*Anne and Sam were told they had the all clear only a couple of days after our first interview, and collected Bereket a few weeks later. They agreed to a second interview when they'd had their little boy for about two months.*

Anne: The beginning was quite strange because we knew about him but he had no idea about us, so that was really difficult for him. We went to pick him up with the agent, Lakew, who was two hours late, so we were pretty anxious by the time we got there. He took us into the living room and a little girl, Lakew's niece, brought him in and shut the door and left. He was very upset and started crying and wanted to get away, and we didn't quite know what to do. He was sick as well, so he spent a lot of time sleeping and avoiding eye contact with us, and we spent the first week looking after him and trying to make sure he got better. I don't know how we felt really, we just sort of did it. Yes, he was beautiful and everything, but it was all so strange and having your child sick, who you don't know, in a country like Ethiopia is pretty weird.

Sam was afraid he was going to die. I was too, especially the first night I was really quite frightened, because he couldn't breathe properly and he was panting all the time, he was vomiting and he had diarrhoea. He could have died if we hadn't had him looked at straight away, and hadn't got the right medication for him. So it was a pretty major responsibility and his illness killed so many kids over there.

Sam really felt like he just wanted to have him close to his skin all the time, and when he did, Bereket was much happier. So Sam spent most of the first few nights sitting up with him against his chest, stroking him and cuddling him and telling him that he was special and that he'd be OK, because he was extremely sick. That created a bond with those two particularly, quite quickly I think. Sam found it all a bit overwhelming, so his way of coping was to take over, and I took a bit of a back seat in that way.

When we picked Bereket up we found out about his half-sister Helen for the first time. That was a real shock, because she's twenty-five and she's at an age where she could have actually looked after him if she was able to, so the first thing we wanted to do was find out where she lived and meet her, which we did. But everyone who goes to Ethiopia who chooses to seek family out will find more family than they first thought. We were walking down the road to meet her, and we had no idea what she looked like, but we could see this young woman standing in front of the hotel. She just walked up to Bereket and put her arms out to him, and spent the whole interview holding him, and he was really contented. She hadn't seen him for maybe nine or ten months, so he'd changed a lot. She just spent the whole time crying.

The lady who translated for us was fantastic. We talked with Helen about her brothers, and we had to explain to her that her other brother had HIV which she didn't realise, and we explained to her that Bereket was coming with us to Australia, which she didn't realise, so it was all a huge shock for her. She'd lost contact with them. I don't really know why that happened but she certainly wanted to keep in contact with them. It was difficult to see her with him because they're so similar to look at, they've both got the same eyes and the same-shaped face.

It was really painful for her to hold him and then to have to hand him back at the end. We asked her if she'd like to come with us to visit Dawit because she hadn't seen him for so long. She was really surprised at how ill Dawit was, he looked so different to when she'd last seen him. He found it really distressing to see her and to see Bereket and us, and having to watch us go as well. Having to get on with his life, basically in a prison, he can't even leave the compound where he lives. So it was absolutely horrible seeing him. I still don't know whether it was a good idea or not, I hope it doesn't make him sicker, having us come and then go again. But we had to do it for Bereket's sake and for ours, I don't think we could have gone there and known he was alive and not met him. Now Helen has regular contact with him and takes him gifts which is really nice. But pretty cold comfort really, considering he's lost his whole family. We kept seeing them over and over, and every day you'd leave the house with this big ball of emotion in your tummy because you were going to be facing them again, and feeling so guilty about taking Bereket away from them.

I don't know whether it would have been better for him to stay there, but if he was to stay with Helen and we supported her in looking after him, he would still only have her. She was living on her own in a little room in the back of someone's house, so he wouldn't have as many opportunities as with us. But there's something about your blood family that always comes back, no matter what, it's so strong. I hope when he gets older he'll understand what we've done. There's no way we could have handed him over to her, because our life would have fallen into a million pieces, so in the end it was a selfish act to take him.

We'll live with this for the rest of our lives. Because we didn't know about Helen we weren't prepared for the possibility of an alternative to adopting Bereket. That's the imperfect nature of intercountry adoption. We've now decided we have to go back for visits every year. Helen said she felt it was good that Bereket would have a second chance in Australia, but in the last few days in Ethiopia we couldn't stop asking ourselves whether she could look after Bereket and Dawit alone, and whether she would want to. We weren't really in any state to take on all the responsibility for the situation. But what's important is that it's up to us to allow the survivors in this family to maintain a relationship with each other. We have to try everything in our power.

We talk to Helen on the Internet constantly. We're trying to support her, and we're trying to get her interested in studying at the moment so she can get qualifications for decent employment and we're sending gifts and photos and everything we can, as often as we can. We want to go back as soon as we can, but it's an expensive place to travel to, Africa, so it's unclear. Bereket seems really happy with us, and we're really happy with him, and he's settled down very quickly into a really lovely life with us. When we see him happy like that, we think, well, maybe it is OK. Helen asked us to promise her to never forget her and Dawit, so we don't want to forget them, can't forget them.

Being a parent feels like I expected it to feel like. Which is really bizarre because most things don't when you imagine them. But he's such a beautiful little happy boy and he certainly tells us when he's not. Everything stimulates him and excites him, and that's what I was wanting, and he loves sleeping, and he's into everything. He loves being cuddled and nursed and he loves his mum and he loves his dad just as much and he's really happy with both of us. I don't think we could have asked for much more than that.

I've been taking over more and more from Sam, putting him to bed and cuddling him and reading to him, and giving him his bottle because it's really important for me to do that with him, more than I think it is for Sam. He's missed out on a lot of nurturing, I suppose his mother died about nine, ten months ago, so for all that time he hasn't had any of that, and he loves to be cuddled, he loves to be held close to our bodies and to my body and rocked and nurtured, and it's a beautiful thing to be able to do with him, it's so simple.

I need to feed him and cuddle him more for my own sake than his. I mean Sam enjoys it too, but for most dads their babies come along and they're tiny and mum looks after them for such a long time, whereas we've got an instant little fun thing, and Sam just loves playing with him. But when I put him to bed I rock him in my arms, whereas Sam puts him in the cot and strokes him and it's a different way of doing it altogether, and I don't know whether it's a boy thing but he doesn't feel the need to nurture him so much, and nurse him.

Maybe the difference is that Sam didn't have the huge longing to have kids that I had from early on. Though over the last year he did, particularly in the last six months, and in the last two months it hit him in a big way, that he needed to be with him and have him, and it just got stronger and stronger. It came up on him much slower. In the three years that we waited it didn't upset him that it was taking so long, he did a whole lot of other stuff. But when Bereket was real and he was on the other side of the world sitting in an overcrowded foster home, Sam just had to get over there, no matter what. Which is good, because if we'd both been nuts at the same time it would have been a nightmare.

Having Bereket feels like it's filled the void I felt before. I always felt like a bit of an empty shell, whereas now I feel full and it feels complete. I still feel sad that we didn't know him from when he was a little baby. He's nearly two now, so he's getting more independent. He's talking now, and he runs around, so I miss not having him as a little baby but it doesn't matter, it's been fantastic. I've still got no desire to go on any fertility program which is probably what I would do if I wanted to have a biological child. I suppose if it happened it would be good, but even though adoption is so complex and difficult and there's so much sadness for the people left behind, I think for his sake if I had the choice of the two I would adopt again, definitely. I think we need for him to have a sibling, and I think it would be easier for him to have another adopted sibling than a biological one. Especially if we could get another child from Ethiopia, it makes sense to me to do that. I realise now from when I put him to bed and give him a bottle, that sometimes I really miss the idea of breast feeding and stuff like that. It comes out quite strongly sometimes but not enough to want to go through a fertility program.

I think I'm kidding myself if I imagine I'm going to fix things up a bit for Bereket's brother Dawit. We've got so many resources and I feel like it's presenting itself as, 'Well, what are you going to do about it?' But there's something that's going to grow out of it. I need to sit with it for a while and work out where to go next. It's not enough to just come home and think, 'That's very sad but there's nothing we can do,' because I'm sure there are things we can do.

# STRIKING GOLD

## Geraldine Cox

I was always a bit gaga as a teenager. When I started having sex at sixteen I didn't have much knowledge about things like condoms or taking precautions. But I knew I wanted a baby. In fact I never used a condom until I got divorced in my forties, which is a pretty unusual thing.

At about twenty-two I had an intense love affair with a Greek guy. He thought he'd struck gold when he got a girlfriend who wasn't panicking about the pill or condoms or anything like that. But after a couple of years of normal regular sex I hadn't gotten pregnant so he suggested there might be a problem. He put me into hospital and I had all the tests and it turned out I had blocked tubes. That was when I knew that it was going to be very, very difficult for me to conceive a child.

We wanted to get married. He was very maternal. In those days the only thing you could do for blocked tubes was to have water or gas pumped into your tubes until your eyes were going to bug out. There weren't any surgical miracles or other fabulous medical interventions as there might be now. The procedure itself was very painful. They kept on pumping you full until sooner or later you felt like you'd burst open. I've never experienced childbirth but I can't imagine it being more painful than this. I underwent agonising days on the top of the table.

That relationship broke down partly because he couldn't imagine life without children and so any plans we had to get married were shelved. We were in love but for him, as a Greek man culturally and personally, it was pretty important to have children. So I got the shove.

It was especially difficult to know for sure at twenty-two that

I couldn't have children, because I felt duty bound to tell anyone I had a romantic relationship with. Most women who find out they are infertile are already in a marriage and have something fairly binding going with their partner and it's something that they usually face together. I had to disclose it to lovers like it was something to be ashamed of. I would have felt terribly deceitful if I'd married somebody and hidden it from them.

I was more than ashamed. I felt a freak. I was brought up believing that women had children. Because I knew I couldn't I felt distant and separate and not as good as, I felt inadequate. I was also a lot more promiscuous than I think I would have normally been. I had to prove I was just as feminine as other women, if not more so. I was obsessed with sex. I thought that was what would make me attractive to men. Even the word 'infertile' is negative. It's something you can't do.

I decided if I wasn't going to settle down in the suburbs and have children like every other woman I needed an alternative. I contemplated going into a convent briefly but it didn't feel right. I went into Foreign Affairs instead and in many ways my life has become very much richer for not having children. I've had a life of glamour and travel that many other women I knew would have killed for. A lot of my friends who were in the suburbs hanging the nappies out on the line doing all the things that I longed to do, were gnashing their teeth because I was travelling and working in embassies. I wasn't tied down by children and I must admit I did enjoy it. But it wasn't the life I was looking for.

*Geraldine eventually adopted a baby from Cambodia. Lisa Devi turned out to have multiple disabilities. She had cerebral palsy as well as being deaf, autistic, epileptic and diabetic. After seven years Geraldine relinquished her into care. This was one of the hardest decisions of her life. All subsequent attempts at adoption were unsuccessful though Geraldine has unofficially fostered several children.*

My desire to be with children is totally out of proportion in comparison with other women's. I remember when I was

having my water and gas treatment I'd walk down the street
and I'd see a little pothead with a kid in a pusher with no
shoes on and with a snotty nose and all dirty and I'd want to
rush up and thump them and say, 'How can you have a child
when I can't?' I still feel that when I see people in the street not
taking care of their children. I want to go up and give them a
swift kick. There was a time when I'd see babies who'd been
left outside a supermarket while their mother ducked in for
something and I'd have to fight the urge to steal them. Twice I
actually had my hand on the stroller, leaning over it and was
inches away from just picking up the child and running off
with it.

But I know if I'd been able to have kids I'd have had a
normal life as a wife and a mother and I don't think I would
have been doing what I'm doing now. I'm convinced, regardless of ideology, that running this orphanage in Cambodia is
what I was put on this planet for.

When I started working with the children in 1993, I was
forty-eight and I understood finally that I should have been
doing it fifteen, even twenty, years earlier. I just hadn't got the
plot. I was so consumed with trying to make my destiny
conform to an idea of what I wanted it to be that I couldn't see
the forest for the trees. I wanted a child, I wanted my child.
When really the work I'm doing now is more rewarding than
giving birth to and rearing my own child would've been. It
took a long time for me to grasp that I could make alternative
arrangements, that the excessive love I have for children is
what you need to do the work I'm doing. You have to be
consumed with the desire to be with children, to live with
them and to be part of their lives otherwise you wouldn't be
any good at it. I don't think a woman who just sort of liked
kids could manage it.

The orphanage I run doesn't only take children who are
affected by the war, though they were the original group. I also
have children whose parents have died from AIDS. I have kids
who have escaped from the army. I have children who would
normally be sold into prostitution, or slavery. Simply put, we
take children from Third World conditions. Living there is just

like being in a large home, I eat with them, I sleep with them, I have showers with the older girls, we go on field trips together. I look at their homework, I smack them from time to time, I do everything that happens in a home, only it's multi-plied by seventy. Of course I have help. I have volunteers and ten paid Cambodian staff who earn a local salary to help with the day-to-day running like cooking and cleaning.

I do have favourite kids but I try not to let that show. What these children need is just so overpowering. A kid will actually go and cut a finger and then come to me all bloody to get my attention. Their need to be loved and held is so great and you know, have their little cuts kissed better—it's really, really quite overwhelming. When I come back from being away on long trips it's like a head of state coming home, I can't even get out of the car without being swamped. I don't doubt for a moment their love for me because of my love for them.

It's absolutely a love thing. It's no sacrifice, it's not a religious conviction, I'm also massaging my own needs here. I'd hate to be described as a woman who sacrificed all to go and live in a Third World country. It makes me chuckle because I can't seem to get across to people that I'm doing the only thing that I ever wanted to do, in the only place that allowed me to do it. If that happened to be Cambodia well then, lucky them.

What I feel now is even better than the feeling I was looking for all those years I was trying to have my own child. These children need me so much more than any baby I could have given birth to. In Australia and other developed countries there are government agencies that will step in and provide for a child who is orphaned or whose parents really can't look after it, but in Cambodia if I wasn't there, there wouldn't be anybody for these kids. I know I'm filling a hole for them that no one else will or can. That's very satisfying.

When I'm with the children I can't imagine not being with them. I'm not capital 'S' sorry any more about not having my own kids. When I was forty-five if somebody had said, 'Here, take this pill and you can have a baby today', I'd have taken it, but I wouldn't have done it at forty-eight. By then I'd met the kids. What I know is that if they'd had the technology they have now when I was young I would definitely have put my hand up for it.

I also know I no longer feel like a failure in my own body. I do feel a sense of regret that always stays with you. I see my friends look with pride and satisfaction at their children. Knowing they've got their eyes, or they walk like their mother or they've got mannerisms like her or their hair is the same colour. Their kids have physical things that stamp them as part of their mother. I know nobody is ever going to look at a child after I'm dead and say, 'Oh, doesn't he look like Geraldine', or, 'Doesn't she laugh like Geraldine'. After I go there won't be anybody that I've left my mark on in that way. That's something I think about from time to time. I would've liked to leave a little bit of Geraldine somewhere in the world.

I'm fifty-five now and I've finished menopause, but I still have times of the month, which I presume are hormonal, where I'll have this enormous wave of loss, absence and I'll have a little weep. It doesn't happen every month, maybe only three or four times a year. It's a reminder of the pain I suffered when I was a lot younger. How my period made me feel useless, regardless of whatever else I was doing.

Infertility is a hard thing for a woman to accept because society demands fecundity of us in the same way it demands we be a size ten or a size twelve. You can't get on a bus or go to a department store without seeing women with children, in the same way you can't go out into the street without seeing women in a size that you would like to be. I don't think you can ever escape it. It's shoved up your nose every day. You have to learn to live with it, and for it not to hurt you. It doesn't hurt me anymore.

I think if I'd let go even a little bit of my determination to have a child of my own I might have seen other alternatives earlier. But I didn't allow that to happen, I just kept on banging my head against that brick wall. For women in Australia, there are opportunities to investigate. Maybe fostering, maybe taking children with special needs into your home for a weekend, respite care for families in need. It's important to look at other ways to expend motherly urges. That was something I was never prepared to do. Stupidly. There's a real need for infertile women's desire to parent to be given to those kids who are unwanted or who have problems.

People make distinctions between childless and childfree. I don't see myself as either. I'm certainly not childless, I've got seventy and I don't want to be free. I look at my seven-year-old and I'm fifty-five now and I'm thinking, 'Yep I'm going to be around for when she gets married'. And the wonderful thing about what I'm doing is that I have always got babies, I've always got two-year-olds, I've got six-year-olds, I've got ten-year-olds, I've got them when they turn fourteen and start causing problems. For me, the journey of being a mother is never going to be over.

# A NOTE FROM A COUNSELLOR: DEALING WITH REPRODUCTIVE LOSS

Kathryn McPherson

### The impact of reproductive loss

Few of us are prepared for significant loss. Formal education is geared to teaching the general foundations of knowledge within traditional subject areas. Children often leave school after eleven or twelve years of education having received little information about human relationships and loss. Western society tends to deny death—it isn't talked about and children often hear confusing accounts of what happens to someone when they die. Young children are often fascinated and at the same time anxious about death—by what happens to one's body and one's inner self when one dies. Questions about death tend not to be answered openly and honestly and opportunities for learning are lost. I have worked with many people experiencing intense grief who have commented that they didn't understand that what they were experiencing was part of a normal, albeit painful, process of grieving. Many presented to counselling expressing the fear that they were losing their minds.

### Death of a baby

The death of a loved one is a loss that results in intense emotional pain and distress. When the death of a loved one is a child, the loss is so terrible that it elicits feelings of distress at a community level and indescribable emotional pain for most parents. Many people who have become parents acknowledge how terrible it would be to lose their child or children, many say they do not like to even think about the possibility that their child might die as it creates high anxiety and feelings of vulnerability.

When the family member who has died is a baby, the death is also appropriately acknowledged as the terrible loss that it is. When a baby dies the life that was so short is taken away. The hopes and dreams of the parents for their baby are lost— this beloved member of the family is dead. Memories and mementos of a short but often intensely experienced relationship are cherished and often recounted over and over again. Friends and family often rally around and offer support—some are able to listen to the bereaved talk about their baby and the pain they are experiencing. Others find this difficult.

When a baby dies unexpectedly and the cause is unclear the parents face the additional distress of their baby's body undergoing an autopsy to determine the cause of death. When a loss like this occurs without warning, there is no chance to prepare emotionally, to deal with anything that has been unfinished in the relationship or to say goodbye. Shock, rage and anxiety occur along with the numbness and disbelief. The loss may feel unreal in the early days and weeks, like a nightmare from which one will soon wake and everything will be all right and the loved one will be fine.

When parents lose a baby, they face many months of intense yearning, regret, despair, hopelessness and sadness. The support of others over the first year is very important and it provides something of a buffer. Many parents I have worked with have commented that the support shown by others, the concern and caring shown in response to their suffering had been of great comfort to them. No one can lessen the intensity of the separation pain and the longing for the deceased but such acts of caring do help. Studies have shown that the perception of social support can assist the bereaved in their recovery and those without support can take longer to recover.

Relapses into intense grief are common and the bereaved may say that the pain of separation feels unbearable and they cannot envisage it dropping away. Some relapses are triggered by anticipated events such as the first birthday without the baby, the anniversary of the death, the first Christmas, the first holiday away.

### Loss in pregnancy

The loss of a pregnancy is also a significant loss for the prospective parents and sometimes for other family members such as grandparents.

Following a miscarriage there may be attempts to make sense of the loss. Why did it happen? What was the cause? Was it something I did? When a miscarriage occurs in the first pregnancy, there are often fears that the couple will never be able to conceive again. For parents with one or more children, the loss is still felt deeply, no less so because there are other children in the family.

Many women experience dreams and nightmares following a miscarriage. Some dream that they have given birth to their baby and everything is all right. Others experience nightmares in which they are faced with terrible threats to their safety or the safety of family members. The nightmares often have an extremely vivid quality, where fear and terror are experienced and escape seems impossible. Upon waking, some women say it can take many seconds to realise it was only a nightmare.

Some women report that for a period of time after their miscarriage, they sometimes found themselves wondering whether they were still pregnant. Some begin to think that perhaps the doctor was wrong and that somehow the baby was still there and perhaps everything would still be fine.

### Loss after twenty weeks

For many prospective parents who reach the halfway mark in pregnancy, confidence grows about the remainder of the pregnancy. Most pregnancy loss occurs in the first trimester and so it is understandable that parents feel confident about the pregnancy and the baby that is obviously growing and making her/his presence felt.

When a baby dies after twenty weeks the loss is recognised by society as the death of a baby, and often the accompanying rituals are observed. It can be agonising for parents to suffer such a loss. Time and care are taken to assist parents in acknowledging this loss. Parents are often given the opportunity to hold their baby, to have footprints and handprints taken. The loss is usually acknowledged by the professional caregivers who are involved at this time and by the wider community. While this is the case in many instances of loss, not everyone is well supported after the loss of their baby. In addition to the grief experienced, these particular couples are often left feeling bewildered, isolated and angry about the medical treatment they receive.

### Loss between twelve and twenty weeks

For couples who miscarry after twelve weeks there can be a sense of bewilderment and shock. Many have breathed a sigh of relief that the first trimester is behind them and they can now focus on the remainder of the pregnancy. The woman's physical shape changes over this period and she becomes obviously pregnant. When a loss occurs after the mother has felt the first flickers of movement the separation pain can be very intense. To suffer a loss during this period is very difficult to tolerate—the baby stands no chance of survival—nothing can be done if the miscarriage is imminent.

The grief experienced by prospective parents is about their baby-to-be. The attachment and emotional investment with the baby is real and grief is the inevitable response to the loss of such a relationship. Slowly the bereaved parents will recover and plans will be made, often tentatively at first, to start trying again. Many parents need months to recover before they can contemplate such action. Others feel a need to become pregnant quickly, as not starting a family is part of a wider loss for them. It is impossible for them to avoid reminders of pregnancy. Bereaved prospective parents see pregnant women or newborn babies every time they go out. Many have commented that it is as though they have radar for detecting them—they just jump out before them. Some women say they cannot help but focus on the women who appear to be as pregnant as they would have been, if they had not had the miscarriage. Others say that it is not as painful seeing a newborn baby, because it is not their baby. Rather it is the appearance of the pregnant woman that triggers the grief—she would look like that woman—if the loss had not occurred.

### Loss under twelve weeks

When a loss occurs during early pregnancy, the grief experienced by the prospective parents can also be intense and painful. The loss is as real for these prospective parents as it is for parents who lose a baby. A prospective mother in particular is often likely to form an attachment to her 'baby-to-be' from very early in the pregnancy. When the pregnancy has occurred after a struggle with infertility, the attachment can be felt deeply.

There is a tendency for the significance of the loss associated with early miscarriage to be minimised, and this is particularly hurtful when the loss is felt deeply by the parents. Recovery can take many months. Couples endure the excitement and joy experienced by others who conceived at around the same time and who will therefore give birth near the time their baby would have been born. I have worked with women who have said how painful it was for them to go to the maternity ward of the hospital, sometimes the same one they had booked into, to congratulate and meet their friend's/sister's/cousin's new baby. Some of these women have been told by friends or family members that they must be happy for this person and share in their joy—a most unrealistic request for many of these bereaved couples who are still suffering their own grief. While some women may be able to feel pleased for their friend/sister/cousin who has just given birth, for others it is a powerful trigger for an intensification of their grief. Many women will actively avoid seeing the newborn babies of friends or family until they consider that they can face it.

### Recurrent miscarriage

Women and their partners who suffer recurrent miscarriage carry a very heavy burden. These people have endured the distress of one pregnancy loss only to have it happen again with a subsequent pregnancy. For some it happens again and again. Fear, distress and anxiety mount as they consider the possibility that perhaps they will never be able to have a baby together.

Women who become pregnant after two or more miscarriages are understandably more likely to report distress and fearfulness about the prospect of another loss. The distress resulting from each miscarriage makes it difficult to be optimistic about a possible future pregnancy. While some couples are well supported by family and friends, others are not. They report feeling isolated, and perceiving that those around them are trivialising their losses. Some comments that women have reported they received included:

'Well, at least you know you can get pregnant—you were only six weeks, lots of women have miscarriages early in pregnancy and they don't react like you.'

'Well, you think your situation is bad! A friend of mine has had four miscarriages and those pregnancies were far more advanced than yours—you should try to think positively about it rather than feeling sorry for yourself.'

'You seem to be in a real mess about these miscarriages—isn't it possible that your distress is causing the problem. You are going to stand no chance of getting pregnant again either if you remain this negative and upset.'

Some women report that the losses are viewed competitively. Indeed, I have talked to women who have not considered the miscarriage they have experienced to be significant and who feel little distress. While this type of response may occur for some, it does not invalidate the grief experienced by another who is suffering deeply as a result.

Women who have had miscarriages know that it is possible for another miscarriage to occur. When pregnant again, some mark off every day in their diaries until they pass the point of the previous miscarriage/s. From this point, many report that their anxiety and concern diminish in intensity, but this is not always the case. Attempts by others to reassure often do little to comfort these women and denial is often an inadequate strategy. To be told, 'It won't happen again' is unlikely to bring comfort because in reality these losses have happened before and could happen again.

### Recovery from miscarriage

Prospective parents vary in the time involved in their recovery from miscarriage. It is not uncommon to find that there are differences within the couple in recovery from this loss. It often takes women longer to recover from such a loss, but not always. Slowly couples will begin to look to the future and consider when they might start to try again. As part of the recovery process couples often recount their experiences of trying to conceive, their feelings when they learned of the pregnancy, the changes experienced by the mother and the fantasies and hopes held by both parents about their future together as a family. Many couples mark the loss of their 'baby-to-be' by engaging in a ceremony of some sort that allows them to speak to their baby, to express their sadness over the loss and to say goodbye. Some couples will buy something to represent their memories of their baby and to have something to remember their baby by.

The arrival of the due date is a period of higher distress for most couples and they often think about what their lives would now be like if only they hadn't lost their baby. It is important for many bereaved people to be able to talk about their loss, to think about these 'what ifs', as this is part of the normal grieving process.

## When a pregnancy is terminated

Another form of reproductive loss can result from having an abortion. Some couples are told during pregnancy that there is a fetal abnormality. The decision to terminate such a pregnancy can be an agonising one, as many prospective parents bond to their pregnancies from early on. While some couples will choose to continue the pregnancy, others will decide they do not believe they could cope, that the impact of the disability would be too great for them and their family to manage. For many, it is not just about the impact of the disability in a year's time but also in five, ten and fifty years' time. Many people experience intense grief prior to and following a termination for such reasons. The grief can be complicated by intense feelings of guilt and anger, on top of feelings of sadness. Some people express relief as well as sadness and some feel guilty because they feel relieved.

For others, pregnancy occurs by accident and while the pregnancy is normal, they are not in a position emotionally or financially to adequately care for any child born. Making the decision to terminate a pregnancy because of the belief that one could not cope can be very difficult. Some women express feelings of guilt about the decision to terminate their pregnancy. The grief experienced in relation to abortion is often hidden away from others and many do not disclose what has happened, because they fear not being understood, or being judged.

## Infertility and loss

Many women have grown up with hopes and dreams of becoming mothers, having a number of children and raising them to adulthood. It is a rite of passage many of us take for granted. Many couples hold hopes, expectations and fantasies about their 'family-to-be', and about themselves as parents, even before they start thinking about pregnancy. Decisions about where to live, how many rooms to have in the house are made and are all part of preparing the nest. When infertility occurs against this backdrop, couples can feel very isolated.

They can only watch others parent while they grieve for the offspring they assumed they would have by now, and try to maintain hope.

The grief linked to infertility is recurrent, intense and sometimes chronic in nature. After many months of unsuccessful trying, most couples seek medical advice and in so doing open the door to an often stressful and invasive process required to become pregnant with medical help. Those initial tests mark the beginning of a difficult and often traumatic journey. While it is true that many couples have success with early attempts using Assisted Reproductive Technology (ART) others experience a very different reality. Some couples try to conceive over a number of years and undergo numerous attempts at in vitro fertilisation (IVF). While some of these couples will ultimately succeed, others will not. They will be faced with finishing treatment after a substantial emotional, physical and financial investment, and still have no baby.

It is these couples whose grief is often unseen by others. Their grief in relation to their ongoing childlessness may be unknown to members of their family, to their friends and colleagues. The grief is real, however, and many of these people feel isolated in a world where everyone around them seems to either have children or be pregnant.

For couples who are given reason to be hopeful about ART or IVF treatment, because of their youth or the nature of their fertility problem, it can be particularly difficult to walk away from repeated failed treatment without their hoped-for baby. Some couples are told from the outset that their chances of ultimately achieving treatment success are slim. At one level, these couples are spared the anguish of repeated treatment failure. However at another level, they are then faced with other reproductive options such as adoption, donor gamete or embryo treatment, if they wish to create a family in some other way. I have worked with couples who have said they have become 'too worn down by the recurrent treatment failures and infertility' to face another set of hurdles and possible losses.

## Loss of control

The losses associated with all forms of pregnancy loss—whether neonatal death, stillbirth, miscarriage or infertility—range in significance for each individual. These losses may include:

- The loss of control over an area of one's life as important as having a baby.
- The loss of the dream of having a baby with one's partner—a child born from that union.
- The loss of 'the hoped-for' conception occurring as a result of lovemaking with their partner in the privacy of their home.
- The loss of having a baby at a particular stage of life—when it was planned, and at around a similar stage of life as close friends or siblings who are close in age.
- The loss of privacy, which relates to having to discuss details of one's sexual life with medical professionals as well as undertaking invasive medical procedures.
- The loss of one's sense of womanhood or manhood, if this is tied with perceptions of having a baby and being fertile.
- The loss of sexual intimacy and sexual spontaneity in one's relationship with one's partner.
- The loss of self-confidence and/or self-esteem.
- The financial losses associated with ART—the treatment is costly, particularly for those who do not experience early treatment success, and there are no guarantees. Some couples spend thousands of dollars and do not experience treatment success.
- The losses associated with interruptions to one's career for those who try repeatedly and unsuccessfully to become pregnant using ART. While some women are able to juggle a career and repeated IVF treatment, many find it is just not possible. Some move to part-time work while others have no option but take extended leave or leave the job. For some the treatment may take place over many months or years, and it can be difficult to return to some careers after a lengthy absence.

Studies have shown that there is an increased likelihood of clinical depression for those women who undergo repeated treatment failures over a long timeframe. It is understandable that couples who experience chronic infertility, invasive and intrusive testing, multiple treatment failures and ongoing childlessness are more likely to become depressed. Some develop symptoms of anxiety and panic attacks in addition to grief symptoms.

Rage and anger can be directed at the self, self-destructive behaviour and even incidents of self-harm can result. For some the anger is directed at those who are emotionally the closest.

Some women begin to experience anticipatory grieving when they have suffered a number of pregnancy losses. For some the grief is triggered by the recurrent negative thoughts about treatment (understandable given the history of treatment failure for some), while for others it relates to experiencing what are believed to be pre-menstrual symptoms. For others still, who have been pregnant in the past, the current physical state is not seen to correspond with early pregnancy so treatment is perceived to have failed. Despite the fact that the hormones taken during treatment can make it very difficult to determine what any physical changes might indicate, this is often of little comfort to those who believe the loss is coming as they count down the days to the pregnancy test.

### Impact on self-esteem and self-confidence

For many it is difficult to separate treatment failure from a belief that one has failed. Chronic infertility cuts across their lives and has an undermining effect on their confidence, on their view of themselves, their relationships with others and their work lives. It can be difficult to remain positive in the face of repeated treatment loss. Many people I have worked with have expressed fear that they will never recover completely.

For some couples who struggle with infertility, the subtle and sometimes not-so-subtle judgments of others can make it harder to maintain a positive self-image. The advice given by others to 'relax and you will get pregnant' carries a message that somehow the couple's anxiety is the cause of the infertility. Other couples have been told that perhaps they are really ambivalent about pregnancy and the ambivalence is undermining fertility is some way. For couples who want to create a family, these statements add to the burden they carry and do little to bolster them in a time of need.

It is very difficult to maintain one's normal level of self-esteem in the face of chronic, repeated treatment failure. Added to this burden is the fact that social support can wane over time. Some couples are told by others that they do not know when enough is enough—when to accept that they will not be able to have a baby together. For some couples, however, pursuing treatment repeatedly over time is what they need to do—they need to exhaust every treatment option before being able to resign themselves to the finality of their loss. No one can really know what the depth of meaning of the loss is for these couples. It is easy for others, many of whom are parents, to judge, and to advise the couple that they 'should just accept it—it wasn't supposed to be'. Such comments can add to the woman's/man's/couple's sense of isolation.

### Paternal loss

Many men suffer as a result of reproductive loss just as women do, but may express their grief differently. Some men I have counselled have remarked that they felt they had to push their emotions into the background and focus on moving on and looking at what could be done in the future. Some said that this thinking was an important coping strategy for them—it gave them some structure when they felt overwhelmed with distress.

Others still expressed their distress very directly and emotionally, they were tearful often and would want to talk about the loss over and over again. Others said they put 'their distress away' and closed it off while they 'threw themselves into their work' or 'getting fit' or other interests in an attempt to experience some respite from their distress. Some noted they had no choice about focusing on work, as there was the mortgage and ongoing living expenses to consider. The bills weren't going to stop and focusing on an area where they felt they had some control helped reduce the pain.

*John and his partner Louise had tried to have a baby for three years and on their second IVF treatment attempt they were successful. John said the pregnancy had been such a long time in coming that they couldn't believe it. On Father's Day Louise gave John a present from their 'baby-to-be' and he was delighted. He said he could picture their child—he felt certain they were having a boy—they began to think of their lives as a family. When Louise miscarried at eleven weeks they were shocked and intensely distressed. John said he just couldn't believe it and he experienced periods when he felt angry, helpless and hopeless. Despite these feelings he attempted to comfort Louise and he said he couldn't help thinking he had to be strong, he had to provide the comfort and hope. John said he didn't often talk about how he felt—he didn't talk to his friends—only to Louise really. He said that sometimes he felt even closer to her as a result. At other times, he felt estranged from her and from the world in general. He said that it took months before he felt he was recovering. When Louise became pregnant again they were relieved but also cautious and somewhat anxious. John commented at the time of the eighteen-week ultrasound that he wouldn't allow himself to feel really elated until he held their baby in his arms in the delivery suite.*

Some men report feeling peripheral when a loss occurs—particularly when it occurs in relation to infertility or miscarriage early in pregnancy. The focus of infertility treatment is on the woman for the most part and despite some men's attempts to accompany their partners to all blood test and procedures, there can be a sense of being on the outside of the experience, yet deeply affected by it. To put it in the words of one man, 'I felt bloody redundant most of the time except on the day of the egg collection procedure when all of the sudden I had to produce the sperm. You wouldn't want to suffer from jitters in that department because the pressure is really on ... those eggs have been collected and now it is your turn'.

## Recovery from loss

There are marked individual differences in the way people respond to loss. There is no right way to respond.

Recovery from loss can be affected by a number of factors, including history of previous losses, personality style and support system. Good social support provides people with opportunities to express their distress and receive some care and comfort. Personality traits like the tendency to optimism or to pessimism for example, have a role to play in how each individual interprets and evaluates what happens to him or her over time. For some their personality style will be such that the recovery process will be shorter and less complicated.

People who have been affected by loss express their grief in their own very personal ways.

### Crying
Crying functions for many as a way of expressing and ventilating feelings of distress, frustration, despair and sadness. Crying has nothing to do with 'not coping'—it is about the emotion related to the loss. Some people do not cry very much in their grief, and they worry about what this could mean. It is important to remember that each individual needs to find his or her own way of expressing the distress and slowly coming to terms with the loss.

### Talking about the loss with supportive others
Having a need to talk about the loss over and over again can assist people in acknowledging the loss. Talking about the relationship, about its history, about the circumstances of the loss and how one felt or reacted can assist the bereaved in their grief. Talking can also address the implications of the loss—the fears and concerns held for the future.

### Writing
Many people write about their loss, their thoughts and concerns about it. Recording these thoughts in writing can help some people to see evidence over time that the intensity of their emotional pain is changing—slowly becoming less

intense. I have worked with women who have looked back over such writing six to twelve months later and have said they were comforted to see the changes. It can be hard in the middle of acute grief to feel that there will be a recovery, and writing sometimes helps to reassure that a change in the distress is taking place over time.

### Distracting oneself

Some people have said that following the early days of their grief that they found it was helpful to find some activities that took their mind off their loss. Others found it useful to try to do things they used to enjoy. For some these activities served to provide some structure for themselves over the day. Doing things that provide a sense of satisfaction or achievement was also mentioned by some bereaved people as useful beyond the early period of their grief.

### Being kind to oneself and making allowances for one's grief

People who accept that they have suffered a significant loss are less likely to become distressed about the fact they are distressed. Grieving can be exhausting—particularly during periods when it is very intense. As a result there is less energy for other things—other people and other responsibilities. For some people it can be difficult to give themselves permission to grieve. There may be a belief held that she/he should somehow be over this by now—that the feelings are in some way self-indulgent or inappropriately intense. In my view, however, the meaning of the loss cannot be changed by willing oneself to care less or to have it matter less, because attachment within relationships does not work this way.

### Supporting the bereaved

The bereaved need time to come to terms with the reality of their loss.

The response of family and friends is important. When those who care are able to communicate this caring to the bereaved, they provide an important source of support and comfort. Not everyone knows what to say or how to respond, particularly when the loss is less tangible, as with miscarriage and infertility. It is far better to say 'I heard about your loss—I don't know what to say except that I was really sorry to hear about your miscarriage/failed treatment, etc' than to say nothing. It is better to approach the person one to one and not mention the loss in a social situation. Shortly after a loss, it is better to 'stay in the present' with the bereaved than attempt to focus on the future.

What are the most effective ways of supporting the bereaved following a reproductive loss? Some common elements to caring and comforting are set out below and reflect the comments made by many bereaved people as to what was comforting for them:

1. Others being prepared to listen and acknowledge what was being said by the bereaved.
2. Just 'staying with' the distress and not having to hear or talk about the experience of other people.
3. Being encouraged to talk further if this was desired and not change the subject.

    It is important to stay with the focus of what is being said and let the bereaved say what she/he needs to say. It may not feel as though you are doing much but for many bereaved this is a very important support and source of comfort. Accept their need to talk about the loss over and over again, as this aspect of grieving is part of slowly coming to terms with the loss.

4. Acknowledging the significance of the loss. To say 'It must be so difficult not being able to get pregnant when you want to have a baby so much' communicates how hard it is to the person affected by the loss.
5. Being offered support—to hear someone say, 'If there is anything I can do please let me know'; 'I'll call again on Monday to see how you are if that is OK' and then having them call.
6. Having someone subsequently raise the subject of the loss and ask the bereaved about it.

    Don't assume because a month or so has passed by that the

loss is no longer having an impact. Asking the bereaved lets them know that you appreciate that grief takes time and that it is natural to still be grieving some time later. Some of the people I have worked with have commented that after the first month or so it was like the loss had not happened, or that it had just been forgotten by others and that can be hurtful. Many people affected by reproductive losses have told me they really appreciated the efforts of others to comfort them. Some said that sometimes the person trying to comfort occasionally missed the mark, but what was important was that their loss was acknowledged, they were not judged, and the caring for them was communicated.

## Seeking counselling

Seeking counselling is not a reflection on you in some negative way, it is a reflection of what has happened to you. Counselling can be useful for individuals and couples in providing another source of support and understanding, and can provide specific services, like grief counselling and relaxation training. It is your right to ask the counsellor about her/his qualifications and experience and what to expect of counselling if this has not been outlined to you. If you are not comfortable with the counsellor consider changing counsellors.

I hope this book will raise people's awareness of this often unrecognised, insidious and chronic type of loss and grief. There are times when I am affected by the grief of the people I have worked with, but I have chosen to remain in this area for more than ten years now because it is rewarding and satisfying for me personally. I feel humbled at times that people trust in the process of therapy and in me as a psychologist when they are feeling vulnerable and often fearful. Like everyone else, I sometimes miss the mark, but hopefully people think I am doing my best.

What I do know is that most people I have worked with have recovered from reproductive loss despite being so deeply affected by it at the time. Some of these people went on to have children—others did not.

# CONTACTS

## Miscarriage, stillbirth and neonatal death

*Stillbirth and Neonatal Death Support (SANDS)*
PO Box 379
Guildford NSW 2161
02 9681 4500
Fax: 02 9681 5954
Email: general@sida.asn.au

*Bonnie Babes Foundation*
PO Box 2220
Rowville VIC 3178
03 9800 0322
Fax: 03 9800 0311
Email: enquiry@bbf.org.au
Website: www.bbf.org.au

*National Association for Loss and Grief (NALAG)*
NALAG NSW
PO Box 379
Dubbo NSW 2830
02 9976 2803
Also branches in ACT, Vic, SA
Email: nalag@hwy.com.au
Website: www.nalag.org.au

SIDS Australia (Sudden Infant Death Association)
(offices in all states/territories)
GPO Box 9914 in your capital city
1800 651 186 (24-hour support)
Fax: 02 9681 5954
Email: general@sida.asn.au
Website: www.sidsaustralia.org.au

Bereavement CARE Centre (Counselling Advice Referral Education)
Ph/fax: 1300 654 556
Website: www.bereavementcare.com.au

# Infertility

ACCESS Australia Infertility Network
PO Box 959
Parramatta 2124
02 9670 2380
Outside NSW 1800 888 896
Fax: 02 9670 2608 (fax)
Email: info@access.org.au
Website: www.access.org.au

OASIS Infertility Support Inc.
GPO Box 2420
Adelaide SA 5001
08 8223 7434
Email: oasissupport@geocities.com
Website: http://www.chariot.net.au/~oasissupport/

Australian Infertility Support Group
D Thompson
PO Box 6117
South Lismore NSW 2480
Email: aisg@nor.com.au
Website: http:www.nor.com.au/community/aisg/infertilitylink

Donor Conception Support Group
PO Box 53
Georges Hall NSW 2198
Leonie & Warren Hewitt
Email: warrenh@ozemail.com.au
Website: http://www.ozemail.com.au/~warrenh/

*Infertility Resource Page*
Website: http://www.cundle.com.au/gen/infert/infres

# Counselling

Some ART clinics also offer a general counselling service to infertile couples and fertile couples who have experienced reproductive losses. The Australian and New Zealand Infertility Counsellors Association (ANZICA) has a list of members available on request. The Australian Psychological Society (APS) has a data base of registered psychologists which outlines their areas of clinical expertise.

# Adoption

Each state has a welfare department like Family and Community Services, who offer adoption resources for people wishing to adopt, adoptees and relinquishing parents.

NSW and Victoria also have private adoption agencies.

*Australian Adoption Network*
*Australian Families for Children*
National Coordinator
Ricky Brisson
PO Box 7420
Bondi Beach NSW 2026
02 9371 9244
Fax: 02 9371 9544
E-mail: affc@ihug.com.au
Website: http://www.topend.com.au/~aican/

*Adoptions International of Western Australia*
Principal Officer Trudy Roswald
A/principal Officer Stephanie Wilson
St Brigid's Centre
60 John Street
Northbridge WA 6003
08 9328 2555
Fax: 08 9328 2544
Website: http://www.multiline.com.au/~aiwa/

*Post-Adoption Resource Centre*
Scarba House, 24a Ocean Street
PO Box 239
Bondi NSW 2026
02 9365 3444

*Link Up (NSW) Aboriginal Corporation*
PO Box 93
Lawson NSW 2783
02 4759 1911

*AIATSIS-Adoption Service*
Australian Institute of Aboriginal and Torres Strait Islander
Studies
GPO Box 553 Canberra ACT 2601
02 6246 1111
Fax: 02 6261 4285
Website: http://www.aiatsis.gov.au/lbry/fmly_hstry/fmly_hstry

*Australian Adoption Information and Resources Webpage*
Email: Jenni.Rice.@vu.edu.au
Website: http://www.staff.vu.edu.au/Jenni/ausadopt.htm

## Indigenous Services

All major Australian cities and many larger towns have
Indigenous-controlled health services. Wherever possible

these organisations have specific services for women. Many large hospitals also have specific support services available for Indigenous clients.

*Australian Indigenous HealthInfoNet*
School of Nursing and Public Health
Edith Cowan University
100 Joondalup Drive
Joondalup, WA 6027
08 9400 5104
Fax: 08 9400 5449
Email: healthinfonet@ecu.edu.au

Professor Neil Thomson, Director
08 9400 5053
Email: n.thomson@ecu.edu.au

Ms Bronwyn Gee, Manager
08 9400 5104
Email: b.gee@ecu.edu.au

NACCHO
*National Aboriginal Community Controlled Health Organisation*
02 6282 7513
Email: webmaster@cowan.edu.au
Website: http://www.ecu.edu.au/chs/nh/clearinghouse/naccho/aboutus.html

*Central Australian Aboriginal Congress Inc*
25 Gap Road
PO Box 1604
Alice Springs NT 0871
08 8951 4444
Fax: 08 8953 0350
Website: http://caac.mtx.net/

*Congress Alukura by the Grandmother's Law*
The Alukura (Arlwekere) is an Aboriginal women's community-controlled health and birthing centre
08 8953 2727
Email: alukura@gov.net.au

*Danila Dilba Health Service*
GPO Box 2125
Darwin NT 0801
8936 1700
Website: http://www.daniladilba.org.au/welcome.html

*Gumileybirra Women's Clinic* is also located at Danila Dilba and provides services for the Aboriginal and Torres Strait Islander women.

# GLOSSARY

**amniocentesis** A technique where a sample of amniotic fluid is taken from the uterus using a needle and ultrasound control. Foetal cells are cultured from the fluid and the chromosome makeup of the baby can then be studied. The process increases the risk of miscarriage by .05 per cent. The technique is generally offered to women over thirty-six or who have an increased risk of having a baby with chromosome malformation.

**Assisted Reproductive Technologies (ART)** The term used to describe the range of medical treatments available for the infertile. It encompasses techniques like IVF and GIFT that are used to bring sperm and eggs together to help people become pregnant.

**assisted hatching** As women age, their eggs tend to have a harder outer 'shell'. It is thought that after fertilisation the growing embryo may have difficulty 'breaking through' this shell. A tiny hole is drilled in the shell using acid or laser. Antibiotics and steroids are given to the patient as part of this treatment.

**cholestasis** Cholestasis is an uncommon condition usually presenting in late pregnancy with severe itching all over, but especially on the hands and feet, without any sign of a rash. It is caused by a build-up of bile acids in the blood. The cause is unknown but is occasionally genetic. It can occur on the combined oral contraceptive pill and in subsequent pregnancies; oestrogen has been argued as the common etiological factor.

Its significance is that it is a nuisance for the mother and appears to increase the risk of unexplained and unpredictable foetal distress and stillbirth in the foetus. It is hard to work out how often it could affect the baby because the last study to address the natural history was published in 1976. Since then all publications have discussed their experience with intervention for this condition with excellent results.

**chorionic villus sampling** Another test to check the chromosomal makeup of the foetus. A small amount of placenta is obtained at about week eleven using a needle and ultrasound guidance or a catheter through the cervix to the edge of the placenta. This technique increases the risk of miscarriage by around .05 per cent.

**curette** A surgical instrument shaped like a scoop or spoon used to remove tissue or growths from a body cavity. Used colloquially to mean the procedure where tissue or growth is removed from the womb by scraping it.

**donor insemination (DI)** Semen is placed into a woman's vagina or intrauterinally with a syringe to enable her to become pregnant. The sperm comes from a donor who may be anonymous or known, and may or may not be the woman's partner. DI takes place both formally in fertility clinics and privately. If the woman is using a clinic, frozen sperm is obtained from a well established sperm bank where the donor will have been extensively medically screened.

**down regulation** The 'shutting off' of messages from the pituitary gland to the ovary, enabling control over the events in a cycle. The ovaries are suppressed in order to prevent eggs from releasing prematurely.

**ectopic pregnancy** A pregnancy outside the uterus. Ectopics can occur in the abdomen, ovary or cervix but 95 per cent happen in the fallopian tube. Consequently they're often called tubal pregnancies.

**egg pickup (EPU) or egg retrieval** A procedure, done under sedation or general anaesthetic, to collect the eggs contained within the ovarian follicles. A needle is inserted into the follicle and the fluid containing the egg is withdrawn.

**embryo** A fertilised ovum until it is ten weeks old. After ten weeks the embryo becomes a foetus.

**embryo transfer (ET)** The placing of embryos into the uterus (or less commonly the fallopian tube) using a fine catheter.

**endometriosis** A condition caused by pieces of endo-metrium growing in areas other than the normal location within the uterus.

**endometrium** The lining of the uterus that grows and is shed each month, where the fertilised egg implants and grows.

**falloposcopy** A tiny camera is guided into the fallopian tubes to view the inside of the tubes during a laparoscopy.

**foetus** After ten weeks, i.e., during the later stages of develop-ment and until birth, the embryo is known as the foetus.

**follicles** The cell surrounding a developing egg in the ovary.

**GIFT (gamete intra-fallopian transfer)** Instead of being fertilised in the laboratory, the eggs are placed directly into the fallopian tube with the previously collected and prepared sperm. More closely mimics natural conception and is carried out via laparoscopy under general anaesthetic. This technique was developed to try and avoid the religious objections to in vitro fertilisation.

**HCG (human chorionic gonadotrophin)** Initiates the action of the luteinising hormone which is necessary to mature the egg/s and release them from the ovary/ies. It is expected that the egg/s will be released 36–38 hours after this injection is given.

**HMG (human menopausal gonadotrophin)** Provides the hormones FSH (follicle stimulating hormone) and LH (luteinis-ing hormone) to artificially stimulate the ovaries to produce extra eggs. Given by intramuscular injection. Now not often used.

**hyperstimulation** Correctly known as ovarian hyperstimula-tion syndrome (OHSS). A certain level of hyperstimulation is necessary in an IVF cycle so that more eggs are produced than in a normal cycle. However, hyperstimulation generally refers to a potentially dangerous condition characterised by ovarian enlargement, abdominal distension, shortness of breath, nausea and pain. It may require hospitalisation.

**ICSI (intracytoplasmic sperm injection)** One carefully selected sperm is injected into the centre of the egg to achieve fertilisation. Originally used when the sperm was of reduced quality, it is now more widely used when there has been failed or unreliable fertilisation using the usual in vitro techniques.

**infertility** The inability to achieve conception after a year of unprotected intercourse or DI (six months if the woman is over 35) or the inability to carry a pregnancy to a live birth.

**intramuscular** An injection into the muscle, usually the buttock or thigh.

**intra-uterine insemination (IUI)** A process where sperm are transferred by catheter into the uterus to overcome cervical problems in women and low sperm count, impotence or retrograde ejaculation into the bladder in men.

**IVF (in vitro fertilisation)** Procedure where the egg and sperm are mixed in the laboratory. The resulting normally developing embryos are transferred to the uterus via a catheter. IVF is also used in a more general sense to mean all techniques employed by ART (assisted reproductive technology). The technique was first developed for women with blocked tubes. The term 'test tube babies' is a response to the fertilisation occurring in a laboratory.

**laparoscopy** A surgical investigation using a telescope-like instrument to look at the female pelvic organs. Incisions are made at the navel and at the top of the pubic hairline. Nearly always carried out under general anaesthetic.

**minimal stimulation** Treatment protocol using minimal drug stimulation of the ovaries, so usually only one or two eggs are produced. There is a risk they may be ovulated prior to egg pickup. The second half of the treatment, after egg pickup, is usually the same as in any other treatment cycle.

**miscarriage** This occurs when the baby dies and the pregnancy ends prior to the twentieth week of gestation.

**neonatal death** The birth of a child who has breathed after delivery on the day of birth or within twenty-eight days of the birth.

**oestrogen** Hormone produced by the ovaries that stimulates the lining of the uterus to grow and thicken.

**progesterone** Hormone produced after ovulation that prepares the lining of the uterus for implantation of the fertilised egg.

**retrograde TEST/GIFT** Same as TEST or GIFT but the fallopian tube is approached via the vagina and uterine cavity, guided by ultrasound. A laparoscopy and general anaesthetic are therefore avoided.

**SMET (sperm motility enhancement test)** A procedure to improve the motility (movement) of the sperm.

**split ejaculate** The first half of the ejaculate is caught in one container and the rest in a second container. The first half usually contains the vast majority of sperm.

**stillbirth** A stillborn child is one weighing at least 400 grams at delivery, or if weight is not known, is of at least twenty weeks gestation; who has not breathed since delivery, and whose heart has not beaten since delivery.

**subcutaneous** An injection under the skin—usually on the arm or abdomen.

**TEST (tubal embryo stage transfer)** Transfer of embryo/s after IVF to the fallopian tube using laparoscopy. No longer routinely used.

**yin and yang** The concept of yin and yang is crucial to the development of traditional Chinese medical thought. It is a system of binary classification where everything falls under one or two symbolic categories that represent Heaven and Earth, or yin and yang. The relationship between yin and yang is antagonistic yet interdependent and in this schema this relationship is the universal law of the material world. Examples of yin phenomena are the earth, the moon, night, woman, what is cold, heavy or solid, the body, winter, rest. Yang phenomena include heaven, the sun, daytime, man, what is warm, light or gaseous, the mind, summer and activity. Yin and yang are at once opposite and complimentary.

# THE AUTHORS

**Geraldine Doogue** presents Radio National's *Life Matters* and ABC TV's *Compass*.

**Professor Robert Jansen** is Clinical Professor at the University of Sydney and Medical Director of the Sydney IVF service. He is also a director of Access, the national group representing consumers of infertility services, and principal author of more than 100 papers or textbook chapters on infertility problems.

**Petria Wallace** works as a television journalist in the ABC's news department. She and her partner Andrew and their son Thomas spend a lot of time at Clovelly beach in Sydney, swimming with the gropers.

**Penny O'Donnell** is an educator, journalist and mother. She teaches media studies at the University of Technology, Sydney.

**Vanessa Gorman** is a documentary filmmaker and television producer. She has worked for ABC TV and spent five years travelling the world filming for the science and technology program *Beyond 2000*.

**Michael Shaw** has lived in Melbourne, Sydney and most recently Byron Bay on the NSW north coast, where he runs a giftware sales agency. He enjoys music, travelling, sport and spiritual exploration.

**Sue Daniel** works as a journalist for ABC Radio in Sydney, and as a freelance photographer. She's a mum, swimmer and voracious reader, and owns two cats.

**Ian Walker** is a documentary filmmaker, broadcaster and writer. He's currently surfing the highs and lows of new fatherhood, and enjoying the ride.

**Rachel** is a twenty-eight-year-old Indigenous mother from the Northern Territory. She works in an Aboriginal health organisation.

**Dina Panozzo** is a freelance actor/writer currently playing mother at home. These pieces are extracts from a performance in progress called *Monster Mouth Baby*.

**Sahara Herald Shepherd** has worked for a number of years as the national event coordinator for the international music festival The Big Day Out. She likes house-hunting and fantasises about being a good gardener.

**Lea Batalha Trindale** works at SBS Television as a news editor. She and her husband Miguel are originally from the Portuguese-speaking community of Macau. In late 1999, they lost their baby son Juju at birth.

**Amanda Collinge** works as a TV journalist in Sydney. She has worked as a radio presenter and foreign correspondent for Australian and overseas media.

**Jo** grew up in Canberra, left when she could, met John in Alice Springs and didn't aspire to babies or a family until one day she did. She now lives in Canberra with her partner and her two children.

**John** was born in Sydney. He is a failed actor, a failed accountant, a failed bureaucrat and a failed community adviser. He now works as a consultant. He was committed to non-fathering until Jo's hormones demanded that change. He now claims to love being a dad.

**Heather Grace Jones** is a journalist, community worker and writer. She likes expensive politics, cheap gags and can go either way with her women.

**Elisabeth** is an environmental biologist. She has a fondness for crosswords, barbecues and running amok.

**Leesa Meldrum**, denied access to IVF clinics in Melbourne, took her case to court and won on the grounds that she had been discriminated against as a single woman. The decision caused an uproar in Federal politics and a national debate that still rages. Prime minister John Howard publicly condemned fertility treatment for single and lesbian women, and the Catholic Church challenged Leesa's case in the High Court. Leesa works at the RSPCA and has two dogs.

**Tom Morton** is a journalist, writer, broadcaster and part-time triceratops.

**Joanna** is a midwife who lives at home with her husband and three children.

**Sophia** is Joanna's sister, the youngest child of Italian parents. After thirty years in Melbourne, she now lives in Sydney and works in the western suburbs as a secondary schoolteacher.

**Graham Burge** trained as a mechanical engineer and now runs his own business in the heavy transport industry.

**Dee Burge** worked as a kindergarten teacher for seventeen years and now runs two small businesses in editing and publishing. She and Graham live in outer Melbourne and have two black labradors.

**Barry Dickens** works as a journalist and playwright. He teaches English part-time and has the world's largest collection of wheelbarrows.

**Dr Maggie Kirkman** is a psychologist whose research interests include infertility and assisted reproductive technology. She is currently National Health and Medical Research Council Post-Doctoral Research Fellow at the Key Centre for Women's Health in Society, University of Melbourne.

**Jane Lyttleton** opened her first Chinese medicine clinic in the early 1980s. She attempts to combine the 2000-year-old experience of Chinese medicine with the latest advances made by modern medical science. She lives in Sydney with her husband and two daughters.

**Alice** is a university lecturer who works in the area of Technology Studies, especially new digital technologies and their impacts on definitions of life.

**Jacqueline Milner** lectures in Art History and Design Theory and is the mother of three children.

**Anne and Sam Storey** live with their son Bereket in a property outside Braidwood, New South Wales, in a self-sufficient mud brick house they built themselves. They love camping and have two dogs, Slim and Oi.

**Geraldine Cox** has had a life of adventure. She has travelled widely, living in Cambodia, the Philippines, Iran, Thailand and Australia. She has been sacked from jobs, confronted the Khmer Rouge, enjoyed men and raised money from recalcitrant governments. She is a woman of passion, which these days is concentrated in the orphanage she runs in Cambodia.

**Kathryn McPherson** is a clinical psychologist who has worked in the area of reproductive loss for almost fifteen years, as well as in palliative care and with people suffering from chronic pain. She works as a counsellor in private practice. She lives in Sydney with her husband and two children.